MW01146302

Augusts

in Africa

6/17

Augusts
in Africa

Safaris into the Twilight:
Forty Years of Essays and Stories

Thomas McIntyre

Foreword by Craig Boddington
Illustrations by Andrew Warrington

Skyhorse Publishing

Skyhorse Publishing books may be purchased in bulk at special discounts for sales promotion, corporate gifts, fund-raising, or educational purposes. Special editions can also be created to specifications. For details, contact the Special Sales Department, Skyhorse Publishing, 307 West 36th Street, 11th Floor, New York, NY 10018 or info@skyhorsepublishing.com.

Skyhorse® and Skyhorse Publishing® are registered trademarks of Skyhorse Publishing, Inc.®, a Delaware corporation.

Visit our website at www.skyhorsepublishing.com.

10 9 8 7 6 5 4 3 2 1

Library of Congress Cataloging-in-Publication Data is available on file.

Cover design by Chuck Cole
Cover photo by Thomas McIntyre

Print ISBN: 978-1-5107-1397-0
Ebook ISBN: 978-1-5107-1401-4

Printed in the United States of America

"Did you ever think about going to British East Africa to shoot?"

"No, I wouldn't like that."

"I'd go there with you."

"No; that doesn't interest me."

"That's because you never read a book about it."

—*The Sun Also Rises*

My opinion of traveling is brief: When traveling, do not go too far, or you will see something that later on will be impossible to forget.

—Daniil Kharms

Contents

Foreword

I suppose a great writer might approach every piece with the thought that it's the most important thing he or she has ever written. I suspect that's the way Thomas McIntyre approached this book, but I cannot know for sure, because I am not and have never been a great writer and thus, now 60-something, am somewhat unlikely to become one. One might describe me kindly as a decent reporter and perhaps not a bad storyteller, but a gifted writer I am not. So I tend to approach writing assignments pragmatically, somewhat like planning and conducting a military operation, something I was once considered fairly adept at. The steps are simple: assess, plan, proceed, with the first, at least theoretically, ongoing.

My assessment: This is an important book by a gifted writer. My plan: To relate why, and, along the way, explain why I am significantly honored to pen this foreword for my old friend, colleague, and occasional competitor, Tom McIntyre. So let's proceed.

The body of literature we call Africana has yielded the richest treasure trove in the entire world of sporting literature. At one time it was rivaled by the wonderful stuff written about the great game of the Indian subcontinent,

but the days of the Raj are long over. Partition of India and Pakistan separated the mountains and deserts from the forests and jungles, and modern India's burgeoning human population has left little room for wildlife and none for hunting. Pursuit of India's great game—tiger, leopard, gaur, sloth bear, sambar, and so much more—has faded into dimming memory. A full generation has passed since a significant sporting book has come from that region, and there will be no more.

One might argue that, today, Africa's wildlife is similarly slipping away. In one sense this is true: Overpopulation, meaning encroachment by agriculture and livestock and resultant habitat loss, is pushing Africa's wildlife into ever-shrinking protected enclaves. Sadly, today there are huge expanses of Africa holding virtually no wildlife, and the concept of "wild Africa" is increasingly elusive. That said, Africa is a very big place. Much wild game remains, in some cases more than what Tom and I first saw more than 40 years ago.

You see, "protection" can and does take at least two distinct forms in Africa. Let's understand that in Africa's developing economies there is little room and no money for altruism. Wildlife must somehow pay its own way, or must give way to villages, herdsmen, and plows. Some of those protected enclaves are national parks, the most famous and scenic of which are well-funded by an active photo safari ("ecotourism") industry. Regrettably, the total acreage of Africa's parks reflects just a tiny percentage of a mighty land mass. Most of the rest of Africa that actually retains viable wildlife, though larger, is also not a major percentage of the whole. However, surprising though it might be to non-hunters and infuriating to anti-hunters, outside of the national parks, most areas that still hold significant wildlife reserves are protected by hunting and hunters.

This takes at least two paths in modern Africa. On the southern tip of the continent much wildlife is privatized, brought to market as a cash crop monetized in breeding stock, venison, and harvesting by (mostly foreign) sport hunters. The success of the game ranching industry is such that wildlife in South Africa alone has burgeoned from a few hundred thousand head in 1970 to an estimated 17 million today. Namibia is a similar success story.

Elsewhere on the continent the road is bumpier, but large areas ranging from designated game reserves to government and tribal concessions are purely looked after by hunters' dollars. Let's accept that much of this is marginal land, lacking the beauty and species diversity of Africa's great parks. As such, ecotourism in significant volume is not viable—but hunting is, because we crazy hunters willingly place ourselves in marginal lands, working hard, sweating much, and paying dearly for the possibility—never the certainty—of harvesting a handful of Africa's legendary beasts. Our currency funds the game departments, such as they are, but, more importantly, at the local level, creates employment, distributes legally taken meat, sinks wells, builds clinics and schools, and funds anti-poaching efforts, much of which today are conducted not by governments, but by safari operators who probably have the most to lose.

There is much to be optimistic about regarding African wildlife and African hunting. The hunting safari industry is bigger than ever. At this writing, fully 20 African nations use some form of regulated sport hunting both as a management tool and to generate revenue—placing value on wildlife. This is many more potential destinations than when Tom and I first hunted Africa in the 1970s. The African continent hosts nearly 20,000 hunting safaris annually, a far greater number than ever before. A majority of these are the modern short-duration "plains game safari," an option that didn't even exist when Tom and I were young. These affordable safaris have opened African hunting to people from all walks of life. Thousands of new hunters realize their dreams of Africa every year. Since planning an African safari is a bit more complex than applying for an elk tag, it means that many thousands more are dreaming of that life-changing first safari. And, I can assure you, any hunter who has visited Africa once is ruined forever, and will spend the rest of his or her life dreaming, planning, and hoping to return.

Most do. When Tom and I first hunted Africa, I think our motivation was similar. Having read about it and dreamed about it since grade school, we went once so as to get it out of our systems once and for all. This plan didn't work particularly well for either of us!

All these facts combine to make good writing about Africa a most viable business, even in our 21st century. Even so, I must concede that Africa has changed, and continues to change. The Africa that Tom and I saw in the 1970s is not gone, but is no longer the same. Although there are many more countries available and many more safari operators, today's game country is smaller, the safaris shorter and more "packaged." This is not exactly the same as "canned," although, regrettably, that option is also out there.

Even in these days of internet and outdoor TV there remains a hungry market for good reading about Africa, so I am sure many more books will be added to the body of Africana. But this may be the last truly important hunting book in this genre.

The reason for this is twofold. First, Thomas McIntyre and I began our African careers in Kenya. This was purely an accident of timing, and I would never suggest that Kenya was, even in its halcyon days, the "best" safari country. But it was the birthplace of African hunting as we know it, the genesis of our safari traditions, and the inspiration for so much of the great writing in the English language that has come out of Africa. Tom and I were fortunate (perhaps "driven" is a better term) to start at very early ages. Kenya closed big-game hunting now 40 years ago, so Tom and I are among the few left standing who had that experience, and we are the last journalist-hunters who shared the Kenya experience. We met some of the great old hunters and heard first-hand accounts. It gives us a different perspective, certainly not "better," but more completely balanced. Since then we have continued our African odysseys, journeying widely across the continent . . . but always with first-hand knowledge of where it all came from.

My own African obsession has been at least as strong as Tom's. After that first safari to get it out of my system once and for all I have spent too much of my adult life scheming and planning and returning, now well over 100 African ventures in 18 different countries, a collective of many years of tramping Africa. So, one might reasonably ask, why is this book from Thomas McIntyre more important to the body of Africana than one I might write myself? The answer is both simple and complex.

The simple: I have squandered my African experience in a series of "ten-year books," each a decade-long snapshot in time. The fourth and perhaps final is in the works, and I don't see myself going back to the beginning in a single volume. The complex: Thomas McIntyre is a far better writer! This is a fact I acknowledged before we were out of our twenties, so I have long since managed to accept it and deal with it. As all good writers must be, Tom is a keen observer and voracious reader. He brings to this volume the full weight of more than 40 years of not just hunting in Africa, but dreaming about Africa, reading about Africa, and studying Africa.

It would be a stretch to say that Tom and I are close friends, but we go back a long, long way, with careers that have been sometimes parallel, sometimes diverging, and occasionally colliding. Tom and I are pretty much the same age, and we started our writing careers at about the same time.

Not in desire but in actual timeline, Tom beat me to Africa by a couple of years. I was off with the Marines, still dreaming and saving my pennies, when Tom "got 'er done." We probably sold our first stories at about the same time; his was about Africa (mine was not), and, appropriately, you'll find his first story as part of this volume, and be bemused, as I was, at the potential shown by a then twentysomething writer.

Tom and I met in the early 1980s at the old and long-defunct Southern California Safari Club. Although in the company of many older and more experienced safari hands, we were looked upon as oddities, two very young men who had used our own money to mount our own safaris. By then, I was working as an editor for Petersen Publishing Company, and most of those safari club meetings were held at Scandia, Bob Petersen's restaurant, just down Sunset Boulevard from corporate headquarters. Tom was writing successfully in what, I suppose, is a classic example of something my friend and mentor, and at that time our star gunwriter, John Wootters used to love to tell me: "Them's as can writes; them's as can't edits."

I stayed in the office for 15 years, hunting and writing a bit and editing a lot, and then, finally, I made good my escape to the writing side. Today I consider myself first and foremost a journalist, but I've diverged into related activities: outdoor television, internet, public speaking. Tom is as he was, and as he should be, an amazingly talented writer, constantly striving to improve his craft. I have always enjoyed his work!

A couple of times we've crossed swords, once childish, another more philosophical. Those two years that Tom beat me to Kenya were in fact critical. Although none of us recognized it at the time, and certainly didn't predict the abrupt closure in May 1977, Kenya was on its last legs as a hunting country, with government-sponsored poaching gangs roaming the countryside. My Kenyan safari wasn't nearly as successful as Tom's. Did I feel a bit of jealousy? You bet!

Tom and I share our addiction to buffalo from our initial African hunts, but it would take more safaris before I took my first lion, in 1983; and my first elephant and leopard, in 1985. In 1986, in for a penny, in for a pound, I choked it up and took a southern white rhino, a major stretch for me then, but a small pittance compared to what such a hunt costs today. It was a delightful hunt, conducted by my Kenya PH, Willem van Dyk, returned to the South Africa of his ancestry. Hunting a free-range area, still possible then, it took us most of two weeks to find the correct bull that was causing mayhem. Tom declared emphatically that it didn't count for the "Big Five" because it was a white rhino, not a black, a position I note he maintains in this volume! From a historical perspective, he is correct—but I'm sure the rhino don't care one way or the other, and today's primary arbiter in such things, SCI, doesn't make the distinction. As I said, childish, with no winner and no loser.

The other time we butted heads was a subject of more substance, with geopolitical implications. Tom took a position that, in hunting Zimbabwe, we were supporting and prolonging Robert Mugabe's despotic regime. Once again, honestly, he may be correct. However, over the years, I've hunted that country both as Rhodesia and Zimbabwe, some 20 times and many months in total. My ties are too close, and I took the position that by going on safari there we are supporting Zimbabwe's wildlife and honest people trying to survive in a ridiculously crumbling economy. It's impossible to say who was right and who was wrong, and, more than a decade after that collision, improbable as it seems, that regime remains in power and continues to dismantle what once was a great little country.

Hey, two writers of the same age and similar experience in a very specialized field, just two disagreements over the course of 40 years? That's not too bad a record! Especially since I have long stated, both publicly and to Tom personally, that I consider him the better writer. To his credit, he has never acknowledged this one way or the other, but I trust that, in his heart of hearts, he knows it's true, and I think you will see the difference in this volume.

Although often alluded to herein, I do not believe this will be Thomas McIntyre's final word on Africa. The saying that "he who has drunk from the waters of the Nile will always return" is only partially true. It applies equally to the waters of the Limpopo, the Zambezi, the Luangwa, the Rufiji, the Congo, the Aouk, and all of Africa's watercourses great and small. Tom and I are not just "no longer young"; at our years it's an overstatement to call ourselves "middle-aged." But Lord willing and health allowing, we will return to Africa, not just because we are compelled to, but because we love it so much.

So I don't believe this to be Tom's last writing on Africa (and I hope it is not), but it may well be his last African book; and it is his one and only compilation of the totality of his African experience, written in keeping with the greatest traditions of Africana. As a writer, albeit not as good a one as Tom, let me state that this business of doing forewords is tricky. In the long term, far beyond my lifetime and that of the author, a foreword joins our names; in the short term, a foreword for a competitive book may well do me out of sales and royalties! It isn't an assignment to be entered into lightly, so I have accepted some requests and demurred on others. In this case I am honored, in part because of my deep respect for the author's talents, in part because of our long (but occasionally stormy) history, and certainly in part because of the deep and abiding love we share for Africa and African hunting.

Herein, from a master's hands, you will find a healthy and eclectic mix of a bit of fiction, some well-researched history, and a whole lot of personal experience spanning a wide swath of Africa. As I said, Tom's experience and mine have sometimes paralleled and sometimes diverged. We start here in Kenya, and continue to other countries we have shared: Cameroon, C. A. R., South Africa, Zimbabwe. I especially enjoyed his chapter on driven boar in Tunisia, an off-beat and excellent destination we've shared—but few Americans have visited. (Tom, hunting farther south, saw a lot more pigs than I did!) And I enjoyed his account of Senegal, not just off the beaten track—I suspect more Americans have walked on the moon than have hunted in Senegal!

There are other great hunting countries that Tom has not visited, but Africa is a very big place and no one can see it all. We who love Africa are compelled to see as much of it as we can, so I hope this is not Thomas McIntyre's final writing on Africa. But it is, far more than a snapshot in time, a master work from a great writer on a much beloved subject, taking us not just across the miles and miles of bloody Africa, but across the centuries, to the beginning of African hunting, to the present, and on to the future, whatever it might hold. Take time with this book, and savor every morsel.

Craig Boddington
Bella Forest, Liberia
March 2016

Prologue

I SPEAK OF AFRICA at the twilight.

This is a book 40 years and more in the making: the span of over 500 full moons, the light of many falling on me on the world's second largest continent. And the time was passed not within the confines of national parks or on the verandas of tourist lodges. I passed it, in short, as a safari tramp.

It is of no special note to suggest that few other books of this kind are likely to be written from here forward, merely a reflection that the world discovered in them has passed on, or more to the point, retreated to a place of August days now lying in greater abundance in the past than are likely to be seen in the future. The Africa of four decades ago has receded, or been confined, to where it is of hardly any import to the "real" world of this early-yet-somehow-already-superannuated 21st century.

There is a misconception about the wildness of Africa, by the way. Wilderness makes up a smaller percentage of its landmass than that of the earth as a whole. The greater part of Africa, outside megacities such as Lagos, Cairo, and Kinshasa, is a rural landscape of thin soils, inhabited by subsistence agriculturalists and pastoralists. If it were not for hunting areas, which in sub-Saharan Africa amount to some 540,000 square miles, two Texases, 120 percent of the land contained within African national parks, and not for the contentious practice of trophy hunting, wild animals would, for the most part, lack critical habitat and essential value, beyond the short term of bushmeat and illegal products, such as ivory. No amount of parks alone can halt the extinguishing of wildlife in Africa.

Without hunting there is no other incentive but to turn the land over to livestock or hardscrabble farming, while killing or harassing any predators or herbivores who are drawn out of parks by the prospect of easy meals. By halting big-game hunting, wildlife is not only turned, perforce, into "problem" animals once it crosses park boundaries, subject to summary execution at indiscriminate numbers beyond all that are taken on license, but it is virtually impossible to maintain natural population dynamics within the artificial borders of those parks. If you believe Africa would be a better place with ever-dwindling numbers of big game within the limited confines of national parks, by all means lend your support to the prohibition of trophy hunting.

Writing about Africa when you are not African, even ethnically, is fraught with imperiousness, bidding outrage. (Africa is Africans', and the lions are now acquiring their historians.) When asked if that's all you got, though, you have to say, that's *what* I got.

The once far wilder Africa known to hunters was a continent that could be written about with genuine passion only by an American, acknowledging how bumptious that sounds, and likely is. By the 1880s, for the vast majority of English, French, Germans, Portuguese, Belgians, even Italians, Spanish, and Arabs on the continent, Africa was no longer a land for the actual adventure of exploration or the frontierless wanderings of freebooters. From then till the time of *uhuru* and the "wind of change," it was where third and fourth sons sought rewards, and many, though not all, of the daughters of traders and overseers sought out those sons in the hope of sharing in the rewards, which rather seldom materialized as robustly as might be desired. Even for the tribe of renegade white Africans of the nation of South Africa, the greater southern part of the continent was not about venturing but about lowering the bar of aristocracy to make "every man a king," no matter the class in which he originated—as long as he could afford enough *kaffirs* to do the laundry, cook the meals, nappy the babies, and keep the num-num hedge trimmed neatly. And this made true adventure in Africa implausible, if not impossible, for them all.

Americans, lacking the colonizer's contemptuous familiarity, never shared such jaundiced—or simply unsentimental?—views of Africa. They stayed free of the scramble and mandates, establishing no colonies there as they concentrated on slaughtering the bison, persecuting the Indian, plowing under the decamillennial topsoil of their own plains and prairies, and annexing the ragged tatters of Spain's insular empire. Not for us in Africa, at least, the provincial staples of, in the words of Graham Greene, broken contracts, resort to arms, gradual encroachment, or the wedding of martyrdom and absurdity. If for no other reason, we left Africa to the Old World because Americans make such atrocious colonists; the first time we tried we had the poor taste to become insurgents. In our foolhardy attempts at colonialism, typically on some far-flung archipelago, we strove to present a *Quiet American* façade to the rest of the world, as opposed to the impenitent cart-whip and *Schutztruppe* governance of the Great Powers (all right, there was the Philippines, to our disrepute, perhaps Vietnam, to our dismay, and some might argue about our motives in southwestern Asia; but we have certainly never demonstrated quite the same crude relish for subjugation as did the more enthusiastic colonizers of the 19th century, at least not firsthand, leaving it to surrogates often in the employ of fruit companies), inspiring in Africans in imperial yokes in the mid-20th century a longing for the day the good and just United States would appear with waves of fighter bombers in the sky and boots on the ground to liberate them, even though it was a promise only vaguely alluded to and certainly never to be kept. (The "bookish" Woodrow Wilson, it is suggested, offered in the wake of the First World War a rhetoric of self-determination that was the spark for the anti-colonial nationalism, and tribalism, that would enflame the 20th century, misguiding millions and enriching the ruthless few, as it turned out.)

The Africa that Americans have always known most concretely existed in what we wrote about it in our works of hunting and exploration. Since the days of the nominal American Henry Morton Stanley and for every generation thereafter, Americans from Roosevelt to Hemingway to Ruark to Capstick to Boddington (who has been gracious enough to write a much appreciated foreword to this book, but who over and above that represents this era's single most knowledgeable and significant authority on the African safari—there could hardly be anyone living, and few dead, who has ever had or will have more extensive experience on the continent, to which I can never possibly hope to hold even the smallest candle) defined Africa in ways that no European colonist ever would or could. The African adventures Americans sought most enthusiastically would have at best seemed frivolous to European colonials who viewed wild animals as, for the most part, impediments to commerce, such as farming and ranching, or as commerce themselves—commodities to be brought directly to market or to be sold to sportsmen who were largely Americans.

Expatriates from Europe saw their Africa unromantically and dispassionately (and not a little imperiously) with what they took to be frosty logic in a tropic zone—recognizing it as a refuge from a checkered past, a place where the natives could do with uplifting (while doing the heavy lifting, unpoetically) a land in which one could get the most out of one's remittance, or in homage to Leopold's ghost, as a bottomless pit of resources ripe for the exploiting, even if hands needed lopping off now and then. And so it fell to a Dane (Denmark's involvement in Africa never exceeding the odd trading post or two, and the sale and barter of Dane guns) to write "I had a farm in Africa...." And a Chicago-born resident of Ernest Hemingway's hometown of Oak Park to write *Tarzan of the Apes* when he had never seen Africa. (All the great English safari memoirs seem to have been written about times before the colonial era, and the best of the adventure tales, such as *King Solomon's Mines* by the Norfolkman H. Rider Haggard, came out of experiences of an Africa prior to a Kenya Protectorate, Northern and Southern Rhodesia, the Royal Niger Company, or German East Africa.) Americans had the advantage of being able to come to Africa unencumbered by the accepted empiricisms of colonials.

All of Africa was to Americans, even throughout most of the 20th century, uncharted, at least in their perception. The physical maps they drafted were, again according to Greene, "dashing," demonstrating "a vigorous imagination" in which no European cartographer, not after the 19th century and the whimsy of features like the Mountains of Kong, dared to indulge. The "many blank spaces" that were the passion of Conrad were ones which Old World mapmakers prudently left as such, while they were inked in by New World cartographers according to frolics of their own. So terms such as "Cannibals" and "Dense Forest," as well as dotted lines eschewed in favor of resolutely solid ones, to avoid any suggestion of uncertainty, were the creatively confident aspects Americans brought to the terra incognita on their maps of the "dark continent," and even more so to the terra incognita of Africa contained in their minds.

Peter Hathaway Capstick

AUTHOR OF:
Death in the Long Grass
Death in the Silent Places
Death in the Dark Continent
Maneaters
Safari: The Last Adventure
Peter Capstick's Africa
The Last Ivory Hunter
Last Horizons
Death in a Lonely Land
Sands of Silence
VIDEOS:
The Peter Capstick African Series
The Television Movie Awards Winner, 1986, 1987

CLASSIC REPRINTS:
The Peter Capstick Library
LIMITED EDITIONS:
Capstick Collector's Library

Master Bryan Ruark McIntyre   14 July, 1991

Dear Bryan,

Welcome to our world! I have been a friend of your father
through admiration of his work as well as his personality for
many years now. His joy of you exceeds, <u>probably</u>, my own, but I
welcome your second generation which I hope will have the
influence and honor that your father has achieved.

You are gifted with a grand middle name, but never think that it
is in any way superior to that of your surname. Robert Chester
Ruark was a great and grand writer, but you have more genetic
accumulated ability than he ever dreamed of. You are Bryan Ruark
McIntyre and you will do well to keep your names in the order
they were given. You are a McIntyre which far, far exceeds a
Ruark....

Bryan, your world will not be mine or that of 1991. Probably the
earth will be quite a bit more populated by the time you decide
to inflict your opinions on it. Yet, if you choose this dross of
tears that is accumulated in writing, perhaps you will show that
blood tells.

I wish you warm campfires, empty creels because you have
released what you have caught, and the joy of outdoor writing
that your father and I have shared. If there is a better life I
know it not.

Go well and straight, Bryan, and may you have the joys that your
names indicate.

Warmly,

(uncle) Peter

Peter Hathaway Capstick

Forty years ago, the Africa I knew, and witnessed the changing of, was clearly at the beginning of the end of this impudence: of—in the southern Kenya country of the northern Serengeti, the Rift, escarpments, baobab, and fever trees—roaming at will across vast safari concessions with a lorry and a Land Cruiser; the insolence of tented camps, raised in hours and struck in less to set up in another place to test the hunting there; of the assumptive sense of an inalienable right to be in this land with its exceptionally strange and antipodal suggestions of the past wild America that for us of that 20th century had only been rumored. The raw arrogance of a young enthusiasm in the taking of animal life.

Forty years ago I could still tap into the continuum of the experience of Africa known to other Americans from Stanley onward, in the same lands in which they had known them. Then it began to end, or, at the very least, to undergo irreversible alteration.

Start with the closure of hunting in Kenya and consequent statistically tragic fate of its wildlife and system of conservation. For the safari, where not outlawed outright, the trend became one of crowding onto private lands with enclosed private stocks of wildlife, not to mention howls of execration toward aspects of the safari such as the killing of named, as well as maned, lions. Not that what I first experienced in Africa does not still survive in pockets here and there, but in those days that was the way "safari" was nearly everywhere it was carried out.

The extreme unlikelihood of my ever repeating this kind of safari was never enough, though, to dissuade me from returning to assorted parts of Africa in the hope of finding something like "golden joys" once more. Even if what I did find might be something less or quite different from what I was expecting, it was always Africa. And like much of hunting and fishing, the most freedom to be enjoyed while being licensed.

I have now come far enough to see that what stems from that quest are stories of a type not always likely to be taken seriously, at least not as seriously as they once might have been. The times in their wisdom will mark them as adrift in a limbo between travelogue and the dispatches of a *flâneur*, with serious writing on Africa today expected to be about issues of wildlife destruction, child soldiers, Islamic fanaticism, famine, transmissible diseases, and genocide. The stories in this book will be taken by some as silly or peripheral, or branded through an abundance of political correctness as unspeakable in this so enlightened day and age. Then you remember that what people do not consider a serious occupation is as important and has always been as important as all the things that are in fashion, as has been said.

Therefore, here are stories I have from four decades of safari-ing in Africa, from among the most transforming days, weeks, and months of my life. There may even be readers, and things more curious have happened, who will peruse them with interest. For those who know it well, I hope these tales may be accurate reflections of their own experiences on the continent. For others, who have journeyed to Africa briefly, or even not at all, I would like to believe there is nonetheless a transporting insight or two to be found in them. And if there is more than one account on the hunting of the Cape buffalo, that is only because it, the buffalo, may simply represent the ideal combination (the "perfect game") of size, strength, intelligence, potential hazard, and availability (you always want to hunt them again) to be found in any large wild animal, and indicative of what draws us back to Africa, in search of, if I may, existential experience and stories that are too good not to tell.

I may say this is the last time I speak of Africa; but that is, of course, patently absurd. I am some remove, God willing, from being done with safari-ing there. Nobody quits Africa that readily. After all, I have not yet found what I am really looking for there, even if I am incapable of explaining, perhaps most acutely to myself, what it is that I am, like that leopard whose dried and frozen carcass was found close to the western summit of Kilimanjaro, seeking. I continue to search for the sources of my own Niles, the map to Ophir, to the heart very much not of darkness. I have no rationale, therefore, for not returning; quite the opposite. Regarding Africa, this is a case in which for me, an American, ignorance must assuredly be bliss.

Africa Passing Relentlessly Beneath the Sun

To Begin . . .

*T*he first story I ever published—when I was young and showed promise—
with a hero with an unpronounceable name, is a text rife with overwrought,
often personally distressing prose, the jejune insights of an insufferably callow
youth with a magpie mind, besotted with Africa after one safari, and owing
more than minor debts and revealing slavish devotion to better writers (a trait
perhaps not restricted to this story). Whenever I am tempted to revise it, though,
I remember that it is a snapshot, a schizzo, of when, returning from a week of
hunting mule deer in Colorado, I was told I had a piece, after so many rejections,
accepted for publication; and that night I lay in bed, staring at the tenebrous
ceiling lit by reflected moonlight, dreaming that I might now be a writer, and
dreaming all the other stories there would be to write. I could hardly know then
that so many of them would be about something as arcane as hunting in Africa.
If perhaps my first story had been about collecting Eurasian ghost orchids, you
might now be reading an entirely other book.

PROINSEAS PADRAIG O'CADLA, long used to having things his way, was surrounded by such an uncontrollable dynamism as to make him long for the abiding acedia of his adopted and distant Dublin. A hard man to please, he condescendingly found the fatalism of the Irish Republic to be the perfect counterpoint to his own adrenal disposition. Thus, armed with his bespoke English firearms and enough preconceptions to qualify as excess baggage, he had come here to find something no less than an off-the-rack brand of satori. Instead, under this high, East African, bright morning sky in sight of white-capped Kilimanjaro, he had not found a single placid person he could feel easily superior toward. It was not, to be sure, what he had bargained for.

Mketi and Mmaku, for example, who were hunkered under the wait-a-bit bush, were laughing excitedly at the bwana as he missed too many convenient wingshots to be conscionable. They had, of course, seen him consecrating the previous day's windfall kill with glass after glass of French brandy and phonetic interpretations of Turkana war chants long into the night. Had they asked, and had he understood, he would have explained carefully the near impossibility of hitting sandgrouse while a hangover (the precise size, shape, and texture of a tennis ball) burrowed into your skull.

"*Ndio, ndio,*" they told him, pointing to the flock of sandgrouse as the birds drew in their wings and began to fall precipitously toward the steel-colored river like a shower of arrowheads.

"Very well, gentlemen," he expressed in his high-priced English. "I have borne your mockery sufficiently long." Bringing the double purposefully to his shoulder, he took the first bird with the right-hand barrel and swung fluidly back to take the second with the left. Pleased no end with himself, he watched them make their feathered falls to the ground, like leaves drifting.

Mmaku was up at once and running with a natural grace any number of years of professional dance training could not impart. He collected the two birds and brought them to O'Cadla who handled them gently and approvingly, savoring their fading warmth. Here then, for a life deficient in very real moments, was one. And if that was a fiction, it did sustain him.

He noticed that the African was also smiling, and he wondered if it was for the same reason. For O'Cadla, the sudden deaths of animals were (he told himself) tragedies of a perfection no dramatist ever approximated; and to be the author of such a production invariably brought about in him emotions whose only outlet was a form of rictus. To wit: He just couldn't keep from grinning.

"We will go," he said, motioning with his thumb to the hunting car. Mmaku waved to Mketi who brought the other birds and shell boxes. The Land Cruiser for O'Cadla, as he climbed in, had that unmistakable odor of a car long used to the cartage of dead game animals: canvas and amino acids.

The camp by the river (dismissed as being too small for crocodiles until an old bull almost made off with the teenaged cookboy as he drew water) was nearly down by the time they returned. O'Cadla found Fisher on the big shortwave radio to Nairobi, making arrangements for the next hunting block. O'Cadla nodded to him as he passed, another destination in mind.

A hundred yards beyond the parked lorry the vultures were congregating like conventioneers, while the marabou maintained a Hudibrastic disdain. As O'Cadla drew up on them they began to back away suspiciously and finally were forced to lift ponderously off the ground to roost with hunched shoulders in the surrounding acacias. In their wake they left a dusty, gray, skinned, boned carcass that at first might have been taken for that of a large and muscular headless man. Who had a tail.

O'Cadla had been unprepared for it. They had found the spoor by chance and had trailed it a very short distance to a small grove of trees. He was waiting for them there, his head massive and sleepy and his coat tinted pale green by the shade. He stood, and O'Cadla took him down with a single 375 bullet, only to have him stand again. He was looking O'Cadla in the eye as he took the second bullet through his heart. It was not, somehow, how O'Cadla would have wanted or imagined it, and it only emphasized his growing sense of circumstances going beyond his usual ability to control them. As for the lion (even though, more than any single thing on the planet, he had succeeded in humbling this man, his killer), he had deserved better than he got.

O'Cadla turned and walked back to the diminishing camp, his self-image and worldview changing in ways unknown to him. The vultures returned warily to lavish their attentions once again upon the lion.

They drove north that day through the dodgy splendor of Nairobi and spent the night at Lake Naivasha. The next day they crossed the Rift Valley.

The road took them through the Mara Game Reserve, the plains peppered with wildebeest. A cloudburst hit as they climbed the Soit Olol Escarpment into Block 60. On top the brush was thick, and Fisher said it would be right good and sporty for buffalo. They rounded a bend and had the bonus of finding a lone elephant bull lumbering monumentally across the road. The fissured soles of his feet turned back as he lifted them, his tusks thick and curved inward at the tips, his hide oily black from the rain. He took no notice of them whatsoever.

"Pity, that," Fisher said. "I had hoped the season would be reopened by your arrival.

"There is nothing really quite like walking up to one of those old brutes with malice aforethought," he continued, coming down himself with an attack of excitement. "As you get closer, he gets bigger and your gun gets smaller. Finally, you are absolutely certain that you are facing a 40-foot, ironclad monster with only a 22 short in your hands. It is one sensation the theater does not offer. And I should imagine that it is a sensation which has changed only slightly from when the first bloody hunter went up against his first bloody mammoth. Once you've done it, nothing is quite the same again either—except doing it again. Odd thing, that.

"Christ! but I sometimes do think you are the finest creatures on the planet," he shouted out the window, snapping off the wheezing windshield wipers for punctuation, the rain having ceased.

During all of this, O'Cadla unaccountably experienced a tingling in the back of his neck that was something very new to him. He would have been at a loss to explain.

The sunlight was falling between the clouds as they pulled up in front of the whitewashed game department office. The young scout who handled the registration book was enthusiastically official. He, personally, had seen a 50-inch buffalo just yesterday and would be most happy to take them directly to it. Fisher thanked him and promised without fail to look him up at the very first opportunity.

As they stepped out onto the covered porch, an old man stood there. His white hair and beard and black skin gave him the disembodied appearance of a photographic negative. He wore an army sweater and tattered shorts and kept his feet in tire-tread sandals. He was leaning motionlessly against the wall with his hands in his pockets, watching the rainwater as it steamed off the grass. Fisher halted and with genuine feeling greeted him as "*Mzee.*" The old man turned his head slowly and shook the white's hand politely; but it was obviously a thing of no importance to him, as they had been of no importance to the elephant. Fisher spoke to him and the old man nodded vaguely, wanting to get back to his watching. As they left, O'Cadla shook his hand also (trying to affect the old man's nonchalance) and was shocked by the weight of the serenity he felt. Its atomic number would have been something in excess of gold's.

"That chap," said Fisher as they got back into the car, "was one of the first game scouts out here. When they found he could shoot and knew a bit about elephant, they put him on control work. For 40 years he lived with the tembos, slept with them, moved when they moved, knew them by name. And when they would wander into some poor bugger's shamba and raise a ruckus, or some old boy would get stroppy and start chasing people about the bush, he would kill them. He has killed more elephant than any man living. He loved them and he killed them well. Paradoxical, that. But, to be able to kill them as they deserve, you must love them. He hasn't held a gun for 10 years. He's become very much like an old bull himself, standing there in the shade all day, staring off at something none of us can see."

O'Cadla, whose eyes had not left the old African who saw only sunlight and wet grass and no necessity of a smile, knew then that he was undone. He would be doomed to come again to this place that offered such a peace at a cost so far beyond the present means of his heart. He would have to make himself worthy. The land, that he had had every confidence of escaping from uncharmed, had charmed him—in a way that was by no means benign. There remained only one last question.

"But he must do something else?"

"I doubt," Fisher said, clashing the gears, "that there is anything else nearly so pressing."

Running Scared

The 1970s . . .

I WAS AFRAID it would be gone if I waited. I was certain that if I did not go at once, it would in some not-so-very-mysterious fashion disappear, or be confiscated. Obsessed, I have never been so absolutely certain of anything else.

So at 22, with no evident prospects and against the better judgment of just about everyone, I invested a minor inheritance in a post office box I had located in a Nairobi phone book and asked to be shown the sights.

The reply arrived in an envelope with lions on it. They would be looking forward to seeing me.

For the next year I trained. I went into the desert and shot jackrabbits, rolling tires, and rocks. I ran and sweated and did not consume alcoholic beverages (no small feat for a twentysomething). Damn, but I was proud of myself. And while I plotted, they closed, then opened, then closed elephant hunting on me. But I decided not to be dissuaded by even that and pressed on. Finally, one morning I stepped off a plane under an overcast, high-altitude equatorial sky and knew I was a long way from home.

The airport worker on the tarmac who held the stairs wore a black turtleneck fisherman's sweater and had a face carved from ebony wood— so startling, and yes, exotic, were his features—and the uniformed customs agent had tribal scars and stretched earlobes. There was talk of leopards killing family pets in the suburbs. And what I was experiencing was not the allure of far-away places with strange-sounding names. It was dread.

Later that day I sat in the lounge of the New Stanley Hotel with John and his friend Liam while they toasted a fellow professional. Who had recently been eaten by a lion (they said). In his camp bed while he slept (they also said). And though he had been a fine hunter, it was a most comical way to go, didn't I agree? It was a prank at the expense of a greenhorn—me—but I agreed.

The first dawn there was the trumpeting of elephant as they tore down trees to feed. It chilled me—knowing there was something even bigger out there when we were already tracking lion or buffalo. And God, how it terrified me to hunt buffalo.

We followed them into brush so thick that the longest shot possible would be at 20 feet. And it could not be a miss. Jumping a large breeding herd sent them off at a tear, trampling every obstacle ahead of them with a sound described in the words of a Yoruba hunter poem as thunder without rain. Other times, we could sense in the silence a small herd of bulls creeping away on the tips of their hooves, looking back for any sign of us—hoping, perhaps, to come up behind and have a spot of fun. And if buffalo weren't dread enough in those dark thickets, then it was the bushbuck barking suddenly and invisibly beside me, or the ominous thumping and John saying to be careful, bit of a rhino just over there—somewhere—or forest hogs big as heifers or the platter-sized hoofprints of secret elephant, swelling with water.

I could not help but be impressed, and at last I understood from what shadows might have arisen a harrowing mythology of dragons and demons and beasts of all manner of crimson-stained tooth and claw. But what really scared the bejesus out of me was that after two weeks of crawling on my hands and knees through that kind of stuff, I was acquiring a taste for it. Was this, then, why I had come so far and spent so much money, to end up viewing life—my life—as decidedly cheap? I had no easy answer.

In camp at night was a hot shower and a clean change of clothes. Then we could fix a drink and sit down with the plate of "toasties" and talk, though never, it seems, of what happened that day if it had gotten notably horripilant. And there was the fire. I don't think I was ever so infatuated with fires before. One night, after a week of hunting buffalo without firing a shot, I was wearing my woven-paper Hong Kong 98¢ beach sandals to which John had taken an immediate and obviously unwarranted dislike—a prejudiced offense to his aesthetics he never bothered concealing from me. Then, somehow, one of them was missing. It took me a moment to locate it.

"John," I inquired politely, "correct me if I am mistaken, but by any chance is that my flip-flop roasting on an open fire?"

John admitted with an enchanting smile that it did, indeed, seem to be. "And did you cast it there?"

That would be a fair estimate, he reckoned. Leaving me with no alternative, of course, but to feed in the other one. Rising with what dignity I could muster, I proceeded to walk unshod to my tent, without wondering too much where cobras went at night.

Since I couldn't hunt elephant, I settled for the photographing of a herd of cows and calves at an exceedingly close range. Now an elephant cow with a calf is probably the most intractable animal on earth, and I bore this in mind as we stalked to within a few yards of them, a tricky wind coming at us for the moment. John presented a brief tutorial on where to shoot to kill an elephant, and after I exposed several frames we backed out furtively.

When I was a score of yards from the herd I stood and began to walk upright to the car. Then John said five of the most riveting words I believe I've ever heard.

"Oh oh," he said. "You should run."

No need to ask why. I ran. But as I did, I looked back.

She was a large cow; and as she loomed above John, he took his William G. Evans 500 Nitro Express and two 578-grain solids from his gunbearer. She was coming on implacably, slate against the sun, her ears back and her head down. And John stood there, steadfast, fully prepared to kill her if she crossed a deadline he visualized ahead of him. And she as prepared to kill him if she made it across that line. Ah, but he looked brave. And she magnificent.

And as I ran, looking back, I wanted to yell at her to stop, lose our scent, change her mind. I wanted to yell, "Go back! Don't die! Because when I finish this run, I am going to run back here. And I want to find you."

And that is Africa: Just when I thought I was out . . .

Buff!

The 1970s . . .

*T*hey saw the buffalo after killing the elephant. The PH switched off the engine and eased out of the battered olive Land Rover, carrying his binocular. His hunter slipped out on the other side, and one of the trackers in the back, without needing to be told, handed his 300 down to him. The hunter pushed the 220-grain solids into the magazine and fed the 200-grain Nosler into the chamber, locking the bolt and setting the safety as the PH glassed the buff.

It was nearly sunset; and already in the back of the Land Rover lay heavy curves of ivory, darkened and checked by decades of life, the roots bloodied. They had found the old bull elephant under a bright acacia late in the afternoon, having tracked him all day on foot. He was being guarded by two younger bulls, his askaris; and when the hunter made the brainshot, red dust puffing off the side of the elephant's head, and the old bull dropped, the young ones got between and tried to push him back onto his feet, blocking the insurance rounds. The bullet had just missed the bull's brain, lodging in the honeycomb of bone in the top of his skull, and he came to and regained his feet, and they had to chase him almost a mile, firing on the run, until he went down for good. By then it was too late to butcher out the dark red flesh;

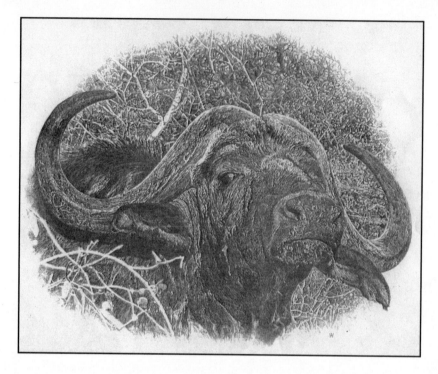

they left that task until the morning when they would return with a band of local villagers and carry out everything edible, down to the marrow in the giant bones. They took only the tusks that afternoon; yet when they finally reached the Land Rover again they were very tired, pleased with themselves, and ready only for a long drink back in camp.

So when on the way to that drink the PH spotted a bachelor herd of Cape buffalo (with two exceptionally fine bulls in it), it was all a bit much, actually. He motioned his hunter to come around behind the Land Rover to his side, and crouching they worked behind some low cover toward the bulls, the mbogos.

The first rule they give you about dangerous game is to get as close as you possibly can—then get 100 yards closer. When the PH felt they had complied with this stricture, to the extent that they could clearly see yellow-billed oxpeckers hanging beneath the bulls' flicking ears, feeding on ticks, he got his hunter into a kneeling position and told him to take that one bull turned sideways to them: Put the Nosler behind the shoulder, then pour on the solids. It was then that the hunter noticed that the PH was backing him up on this bull buffalo with an

8X German binocular instead of his customary 470 Nitro Express double rifle. The PH just shrugged and said, "You should be able to handle this all right by yourself."

Taking a breath, the hunter hit the buffalo in the shoulder with the Nosler and staggered him. The bull turned to face them and the client put two deep-penetrating solids into the heaving chest, aiming right below the chin, and the buffalo collapsed. As the hunter pushed more cartridges down into the magazine, the second fine bull remained where he was, confused and belligerent, and the PH urged the hunter to take him, too: "Oh my yes, him, too."

This bull turned also after the first Nosler slammed into his shoulder, and lifted his head toward them, his scenting nose held high. Looking into a wounded Cape buffalo's discomfortingly intelligent eyes takes you to depths few other animals seem to possess, depths made more profound by the knowledge that this animal is one very much capable of ending your life. That is a time when you have to be particularly mindful of what you are doing out there in Africa and make your shots count—especially when your PH, already suspect because of the way he talks English and the fact he wears short pants, who is backing you up now on dangerous game with an 8X German binocular, especially when he leans over and whispers, "Look: He's going to come for us."

Another careful breath and the hunter placed two more bullets into the bull's chest beneath his raised chin, just the way he had on the first one, except this bull did not go down. That left the hunter with one round in his rifle, and as he was about to squeeze it off he mused about whether there would be any time left afterward for him either to reload or make a run for it. Now, though, there was this enraged buffalo who had to be gotten onto the ground somehow, and all the hunter could be concerned about was holding his rifle steady until the sear broke and the cartridge fired and the bullet sped toward the bull—but just before the rifle fired its last round the buffalo lurched forward and fell with a bellow, stretching his black muzzle out in the dirt. Then he went silent.

Standing slowly, the hunter and the PH moved toward the two downed buffalo (the rest of the small herd now galloping off), to find them both dead. Only then in the dwindling light did they see that one of the first bull's horns, the horn that had been turned away from them when the client first shot, had been broken off in recent combat and a splintered stump was all that remained. He had been a majestic bull at one time, but at least the second bull's horns were perfect, matched sweeps of polished black horn, almost 50 inches across the spread. And there, both men stooping to squint at it, glittered a burnished half-inch steel ball bearing buried in the horn boss covering the bull's head like a conquistador's casco.

The ball bearing had served as a musketball fired from an ancient muzzleloader. Whoever the native hunter was who fired it, he must have had an overpowering lust for buffalo meat, and for buffalo hunting. What became of him after he shot and failed to kill with his quixotic weapon at much-too-close range was probably best not speculated upon.

WHEN I FIRST heard that story I was a boy of 10. It was told by a gentleman of my acquaintance (a man who taught me how to hunt then, and with whom I hunted until he grew too old), who had experienced it on a safari to then-still-Tanganyika half a century ago. Like the best hunting tales, it was twice told after that. Unlike other tales, though, it never grew tedious in the tellings, at least for me, only aging gracefully. Every time I heard the gentleman's excitement in telling it, as if it were the first time and he had been transported back to those Tanganyikan plains, and saw the massive head on the wall with the steel ball shining in the horn, it explained something to me of why a person could get daffy about hunting Cape buffalo. Its power as a legend was such that it sent me off to East Africa to hunt buffalo myself when I was of an age to.

Black, sparsely haired, 1,500, perhaps 1,800 pounds in weight, some five foot at the shoulder, smart and mean as the lash, and with a set of immense but elegant ebony horns that sweep down, then up and a little back, like something drawn in three-dimensions with a French curve, to points sharp enough to kill a black-maned lion with one hooked blow—horns known to span 60 inches across the outside spread—the African Cape buffalo is, along with the Indian gaur and the wild Asian water buffalo, one of the three great wild cattle of the world. Of these, the water buffalo has largely disappeared into domestication—with a few animals transplanted to Australia and South America having gone feral—and the gaur is confined to a significant extent to subcontinental national parks and preserves. The Cape buffalo alone among these has little or no truck with men, other than of the most existential kind. Making it the last native wild cattle that can truly be hunted.

With his ferocious temper, treacherous intellect, and stern indifference to the shocking power of all but the most outlandishly large-caliber rifles, the

Cape buffalo is routinely touted as the most dangerous member of the African Big Five (which also includes the lion, leopard, black rhino, and elephant). Whether or not he is all that depends, as does almost everything under the sun, on what you mean. He is certainly not as sure to charge as a rhino, or as swift as the predatory cats; and in the words of a late well-known sporting journalist to me, "nobody ever got wounded by an elephant." But the buff is fleet enough; and when he makes up his mind to charge, especially when injured, there is no animal more obdurately bent on finishing a fight. In open flat country he may present no serious threat to a hunter adequately armed, but you so seldom encounter him on baseball-diamond-like surroundings— rather more often he'll be in some swampy thicket or dense forest where he is a clever enough lad to go to cover, and fierce enough to come out of it when it is to his advantage.

The best measure of the Cape buffalo's rank as a big-game animal may simply be the kind of esteem professional hunters hold him in. It is a curious fact of the sporting life that big, tall, strapping red-faced chaps who earn their livelihoods trailing dangerous game, all come in time to be downright maudlin about which animals they feel right about hunting. Most, therefore, first lose their taste for hunting the big cats, so that while they will usually do their best to get a client his one and only lion, their hearts will not entirely be in it: The predacious cats in their appetites for meat and sleep and sex are simply too close to us for absolute comfort. Then there is the rhino, the hulking, agile, dumb, blind, sad, funny, savage, magnificent Pleistocene rhino, that was run to the brink of the Big Jump we term extinction, only to be pulled back all too near to plummeting over. To hunt a black rhino lawfully today is a quarter-million-dollar proposition, involving diplomatic negotiations and something like an Act of Congress, and it seems questionable how truly wild and fair such a hunt might be, though none of that makes the black rhino any less unpredictable or hazardous.

Of the Big Five, then, that leaves only the elephant and the Cape buffalo to feel at all right, in the long run, about hunting; and to my knowledge, hardly any real professional hunter, unless he has lost interest in hunting altogether, ever totally loses his taste for giving chase to these two.

There is no easy way to hunt elephant or Cape buffalo. For either of them you must be able to walk for miles on end, know how to read animal sign well, and be prepared to kill an animal who can just as readily kill you without batting a stereoptic eye (it only adds to the disquieting mien of the Cape buffalo that its eyes look mostly forward, so much like a predator's)— and this makes elephant and buffalo the two greatest challenges for taking good trophy animals, and the two most satisfying. Something about hunting them will get into a hunter's blood and stay. To offer one further bit of testimony on behalf of the buff, consider the widely known piece of jungle lore that the favorite sport of elephant is chasing herds of Cape buffalo round and round the bush, and the buff's position as one of the world's great big-game animals seems secure.

Which is why I wanted to hunt buff, and went to do so in the southwestern corner of Kenya, north of the Maasai Mara and east of Lake Victoria, in the Chepalungu Forest on top of the Soit Ololol Escarpment above the Great Rift Valley on the northern outskirts of the Serengeti, to arguably the loveliest green spot in all green Maasailand, and one which I dearly hated—to begin with, anyway.

To find buffalo there we put on cheap canvas tennis shoes (because they were the only things that dried overnight) and slogged every day into the dim wet forest (filled with butterflies and spitting cobras; birdsong and barking bushbucks; gray waterbucks and giant forest hogs; rhino, elephant, and to be sure, buffalo), parting a wall of limbs and vines and deep-green leaves woven as tight as a Panama hat, through which one could see no more than 10 feet in any direction. On going in, the advice given me by my professional hunter, John Fletcher (who stayed on in Kenya when it all ended), was that in the event of my stumbling onto a sleeping buffalo (as well one might) I should try to shoot the animal dead on the spot and ask questions later. It took only a momentary lack of resolve at such a juncture, he assured me, to give a buffalo ample opportunity to spring up and winnow you down. And that was the root cause of my hating this exquisite African land: It scared the hell out of me, and I hated nothing more than having my imagination overextended by fear.

As we hunted the buffalo, though, a change began to come over me. We had unheard-of luck on cats at the outset of the safari, so that at dawn on my fifth morning of hunting in Africa, while concealed in a blind, I had taken a very fine leopard as he came to feed on hanging bait. And then, the evening of the same day, we had incredibly gotten up on an extremely large lion, *Simba mkubwa sana* in the eager words of the trackers, and I had killed him with my 375, establishing what may very well have been some sort of one-day East African record for cats, with the only two of my life, which we duly celebrated that night. When our hangovers subsided two days later, we moved off from that more southern country near Kilimanjaro to the Block 60 hunting area above the Rift, assuming we would take quickly from the forest there a good buffalo (a bull with a spread over 40 inches wide—ideally 45 or better, with 50 inches a life's ambition—along with a full, tightly fitted, wide boss), then move on again to the greater-kudu country we had, until the luck with cats, not hoped to have time to reach.

Instead of a good buffalo in short order, though, we had to go into that forest every day for two weeks, first glassing the open country futilely at daybreak, then following tracks back into the cover, trailing the buffalo who had returned to the forest before dawn, their night's grazing done. In that forest where lambent light shafted down as if into deep water, we picked our way for two weeks over rotting timber and through mud wallows, unseen animals leaping away from us on all sides, we creeping our way forward until we heard low grunts, then the sudden flutter of oxpeckers (more euphoniously known as tickbirds) flaring up from the backs of the buffalo they were preening, and then the flutter of alarmed Cape buffalo flaring up as well, snorting, crashing so wildly away (yet also unseen) through the dark forest that the soggy ground quivered and the trees were tossed about as if in a windstorm, the report of wood splintered by horns able to be heard for hundreds of yards through the timber.

That was the sound a breeding herd of cows, calves, and young bulls made as they fled; but other times there would be the flutter of oxpeckers and no crashing afterward, only a silence the booming of my heart seemed to fill; and we knew we were onto a herd of bulls, wise old animals who were at that moment slipping carefully away from us, moving off with inbred stealth, or maybe stealthily circling back to trample us into the dirt. For much of those two weeks, then, I saw things in that forest through a glaze of fear as ornate as the rose window in a medieval French cathedral.

I discovered, however, that you can tolerate fear roaring like a freight train through your head and clamping like a limpet to your heart for just so long; and sometime during those two weeks I ceased to be utterly terrified by the black forms in the bush, and instead grew to be excited by them, by the chance of encountering them, by the possibility that my life was actually on the line in there. My heart still boomed, but for a far different reason.

What was going on in that forest, I saw, was a highly charged game of skill: You played it wrong, you might be killed; you played it just right, you got to do it again. Nothing more than that. But when something like that gets into your blood, the rest of life comes to lack an ingredient you never before knew it was supposed to have. I believe it got into mine one evening when we chased a breeding herd in and out of the forest for hours, jumping it and driving it ahead of us, trying to get a good look at one of the bulls in it. Finally, we circled ahead of the buffalo into a clearing of chest-high grass where they had to cross in front of us. We hunkered down and watched them as they came out. The bull appeared at last, but he was only a young seed bull, big-bodied but not good in the horns yet. As we watched him pass by, a tremendous cow buffalo, the herd matriarch, walked out, maybe 60 yards from us, and halted. Then she turned and stared directly our way.

If she feels her calf or her herd is threatened, the cow buffalo is probably as deadly an animal as there is; and at that moment I found myself thinking that was just the most wonderful piece of knowledge in the world to have. It meant she might charge, and, may God forgive me, I wanted her to. Very much.

"All right," John Fletcher whispered, his William G. Evans 500 Nitro Express—with two 578-grain bullets in it and two more cartridges, like a pair of Montecristos, held not like cigars, between his finger, but together in his left palm under the fore-end so they would not separate if he had to jam them in an instant into the broken breech of his double rifle—carried it across his body like a laborer's shovel, "we'll stand now, and she'll run off. Or she'll charge us." Nothing more than that.

We stood, John Fletcher, I, and the trackers behind us, and the buffalo cow did not twitch. We saw her thinking, or at least watching with care, weighing the odds, her nostrils flaring. John Fletcher and I brought our rifles up at the same instant without a word and took aim; as soon as she started forward, I knew I was going to put a 375 into the center of her chest, exactly where my crosshairs were, and if she kept coming, as a charging buffalo always had the intention of doing, I would put in another; but I would not run. As the seconds passed, I felt more and more that, for perhaps one of the few times in my life (a life flawed and warped in so many ways, from when the wood was green), I was behaving correctly, naturally, no fear clouding my vision. To know absolutely that you are capable of standing your ground is a sparkling sensation (but then, I was young). Then the cow snorted and spun away from us, following the herd, her calculations having come up on the debit side. I took my finger off the trigger, then, and carefully reset the safety. And all the trackers came up and clapped me on the back, smiling their nervous African smiles, as if to say, "You did well." I was glad we hadn't had to kill the cow after all.

When, at first light on our 14th day of buffalo hunting, we reached the edge of a small dewy field, though, and spotted three good bulls feeding 100 yards away and I got my first chance to kill a Cape buffalo, I did not kill him at all well. Though he was the smallest-bodied buffalo of the three, old and almost hairless, his horns swept out nearly 45 inches, much farther than the other two's, and when I fired—low, near his heart, but not near enough—he began to trot in a slow circle as the two younger bulls came past us at an oblique angle, just visible in the edge of my scope. I shot him again and again, anywhere, and again, and Fletcher fired the right barrel of his 500, and at last the buffalo went down and I had to finish him on the ground. There was still, I had to admit, after the bull lay dead and all my ammunition was gone, enough fear left in me to prevent my behaving completely correctly.

We went on hunting Cape buffalo after that right up to my last day on safari, John Fletcher looking for an even better trophy for me, and me looking to make up for the first kill, hoping there was still time. On the last morning of hunting we flushed a bushbuck, and I had only the briefest second to make the fastest running shot I have ever tried and took the sturdy little antelope through the heart as he stretched into full flight. Suddenly I was very anxious about having another try at buffalo before leaving Africa.

We found the herd that evening when John and I and my photographer friend Bill Cullen were out alone, the trackers back helping break camp. The buffalo had been drifting in and out of the forest all that gray, highlands afternoon with us behind them, following their tracks—a bull's cloven print, sizable as a relish tray, standing out from all the others in the herd. It seemed that we had lost the buffalo for good, though, until a small boy, no older than four or five, wearing a rough cotton toga and carrying a smooth stick, appeared startlingly out of the bush before us and asked in the Maasai language if we would like to kill a *mbogo*.

A little child led us along a forest trail to the edge of the trees, where he pointed across an open glade to the bull. The Cape buffalo bull, his tight boss doming high above his head, stood in the herd of 10 or 15 other animals in the nearing dark, only a few yards from heavy cover, in which in no more than half-a-dozen running steps he could be completely concealed. John Fletcher, for one, was something more than uncomfortably aware of this. He remembered too well how I had killed my first bull, and though he'd said nothing, he knew how much the buffalo had spooked me. If I wounded this bull, now, and he made it into the forest with the light going, and the second rule they give you for dangerous game being that you follow all wounded animals in . . . well. . . .

Fletcher looked at me sharply. There was no denying it was a good bull, and the trackers and camp staff wanted more meat to take home, and there was still a little light, and—and oh, bloody hell!

We knelt at the edge of the trees, and Fletcher whispered to me, "Relax, now. Keep cool. Take your time. Are you ready? Are you all right?"

I cut my eyes toward him, then back to the buffalo. I was, at that moment, as all right as I was ever going to get. This was where it counted; this was what it was all about; this was exactly what I'd come here for. It was in my blood now, only Fletcher might not know that. So, I told him.

"Where," I whispered, easing the 375's safety off so it didn't make a click, "do you, want me to shoot him?"

John Fletcher stared at me even harder then, but this time he whispered only, "In the shoulder."

You can see where a Cape buffalo's shoulder socket bulges under his hide, and a bullet entering his body there will travel through into his spine where it dips down from his humped back to become his neck. That was where I laid my crosshairs, and when the 270-grain Nosler hit him there it broke his shoulder, then shattered his spine. And the bull was down, his muzzle stretched out along the short grass, bellowing his death song (what the professionals call "music" when they hear it coming from a wounded bull laid up in cover). The rest of the herd wheeled on us then, their eyes clear and wide and most uncattlelike, the smell of the bull's blood in their nostrils. I finished the bull with one more round to the neck; and the herd was gone, vanishing as quickly as that bull could have vanished had my nerve not held and I had not behaved correctly.

That last night in camp, while the African staff jerked long strips of buffalo meat over the campfire to carry back to their wives and children, John Fletcher, Bill Cullen, and I sat in the dining tent and ate hot oxtail soup and slices of steaming boiled buffalo tongue and drank too much champagne and brandy, and laughed too much, too. We finished breaking camp at dawn the next morning and returned to Nairobi.

Perhaps I have gone on with this story at too great a length already, but I wish I could go on even further to tell you all the other Cape buffalo stories I know (maybe I'll put them in a book someday; perhaps I have), such as how when you awoke in the middle of the night and stepped outside your canvas tent, you might make out, just there on that little rise at the edge of camp, the silhouettes of feeding buffalo against the cold stars as your urine steamed into the grass. Or the two bulls who came out of the timber with their horns locked, fighting with the crashing force of the crazed brutes that they were at that instant. Or how one of the many herds we chased out of the forest and across the green country led us into a majestic cloudburst, and the storm wind swirled around so that our scent was swept in front of the 50 or 60 funeral-black animals and turned them back on us, and as they started forward I asked John what we did now, and he said lightly, "Actually, we might try shooting down the lead buffalo and climbing onto its back."

There are other stories without buffalo: How a she-leopard in a tall tree battled a fish eagle over a dead impala. Or how when you killed an animal the sky was a clean delft bowl tipped over you and empty of birds out to the farthest horizon, but how in one minute a dozen naked-headed vultures were circling lazily overhead, sprung from nowhere, waiting to come down to create bare white bones in the tall grass. Or how we could be crossing country in the hunting car at 30 miles an hour and one of the trackers in the back drummed on the cab roof, and when we stopped he leapt down and unerringly wove his way 200 yards out into the scrub, and when we caught up to him he would be pointing placidly at a bush where only then did we see the still-wet newborn gazelle curled underneath it in its nest, staring unblinking at us, the tracker seeming to have sensed its burgeoning life waiting out there.

But the story I wish for most is the one in which I am back in those African highlands I grew to love, hunting the Cape buffalo I grew to love too, probably still scared, but only enough to make me sense my true heart nesting inside the cage of my ribs, beating, telling me, over and over, of what I am capable.

August in Africa

The 1990s . . .

"IT'S AFRICA."

That was Ant Baber's verbal shrug as he downshifted the open Land Cruiser through the mud of the yard of his cousin's pig and cattle ranch, on the way to shoot helmeted guinea fowl. It was a cold August winter's morning; and the cousin was standing ankle deep, surveying the cement rubble of the main water tank demolished by his parked lorry's slipping capriciously out of gear at dawn and rolling backward into the tank.

Ant gave his cousin a sympathetic wave as we passed. Half a smile was hoisted on the cousin's face and his palms turned outward, his way of saying, "It is Africa." South Africa, where Charles Anthony "Ant" Baber, licensed professional hunter, retired rugger player, early 30s, and his young, blonde, Kenya-born wife, Tessa, owned a private wildlife reserve, Ant's Nest, outside Vaalwater, Northern Province (now Limpopo Province). This was where I was beginning two weeks of trying to do a little of everything, or at least a good deal of much, that can be done in South Africa.

Think of Africa as a vast, three-star restaurant, to which some come solely for the entree (the usual big-game suspects—buffalo, sable, nyala, and so on). They forget that there is a complete menu, including appetizers, fish, dessert, even cheese board, that should not be overlooked. I had "done" Africa with alacrity (gemsbok on Sunday, eland by Tuesday) enough. So this time I wanted to indulge assorted flavors of sport: guinea fowl on the wing at Ant's large family ranch, the Triple 13; big game from horseback at Ant's Nest; and later, trout on the fly in the Drakensbergs. In short, the complete bill of fare.

Now we drove past herds of copper-hided impala on our way to the first course. We had only three "guns" this morning—two Germans winding up a safari with Ant, and me starting mine—and could have done with eight or more. We tried to walkup guineas, nonetheless, and tried some extemporaneous beats. Driving to the end of a narrow valley, Ant gave the beaters yellow vests and white flags, and we trekked off into the thorn bush.

It was more than good to be walking in Africa again after seven years; but I soon saw that trying to drive helmeted guinea fowl can look a great deal like an episode of the popular BBC herding-dog show, *One Man and His Dog*, with the blackface sheep on acid. Spotting a bustling flock of guineas (maybe 100; for all I knew, 200) in the distance to the south, we spread out in our ragged line of guns, deploying the beaters in the classic "horns of the bull" encircling maneuver of the Zulu *impis,* and then watched the birds run deliriously off to the north, out of range of even 50-caliber rounds.

So we walked on, hoping to put guineas up—which is a little like hoping to make a brick float. I was also carrying a borrowed Sauer-AYA, stocked (pistol grip, cheekpiece, and all) exactly like a Nitro Express, and choked about the same. So I was doubly surprised when a band of guineas flushed from a field of rocks and passed to my right, and I swung the awkward gun on one, saw it fall, then on another, and watched it drop, too.

Ant's black lab, Rufus, quickly fetched my entirely unexpected right-and-left. Definitely an eye-of-the-beholder bird, the guinea: stooped and agitated on the ground, its head naked blue and red, topped by headgear presumably filched from the pope's Swiss Guards, its grey feathers spangled with pointillist white dots. A big bird, and fine eating, particularly in curries, it is deceptively hard to hit, especially when truly driven. As I learnt that evening.

At sunset, Ant put out more flags and organized a proper drive on a huge flock in a field of winter wheat. He sent me out along a line of scrub at the edge of a stubble field, the green wheat just beyond it. The sun was starting to drop, like something ripened from a tree. Beaters began moving through the wheat, and the guineas began flying. When guineas fly they come *en bloc,* like one dark, solid wave of birds. So getting off two shots before the wave crests is good, four outstanding, six memorial. I managed four shots at the high birds, killing one on the third. Then they were gone, landed in the scrub behind, back to running on the ground where they were most comfortable, as night fell like the *mouton* of *Les Bois de Justice*.

The second dish came the next day when Ant, his hired hand, Tracy, and I mounted up and rode off from the whitewashed, thatched ranch house at Ant's Nest, I on Ant's tall bushveld horse Saladin. Along with giraffes, eland, kudu, gemsbok, blesbok, steenbok, bushbuck, wildebeest, hartebeest, impala, zebra, warthog, bushpig, duiker, the odd leopard, et al., Ant also had a pair of white rhino on the place, their scent on the wind making Saladin skittish. Still, he was fine to ride into a giraffe herd, carrying me much closer than I could ever get on foot, let alone by vehicle. As we rode on in the cool breezy morning, I could see the merit of Orwell's dictum of four legs good. The animals we rode among saw only hooves on the ground; and we saw Africa in a way, and at a pace, better known to animals than men.

We sighted a herd of wildebeest and followed, hidden in the protective coloration of horses, trying to get a look at a blesbok bull traveling with it. In a while the wildebeest with blesbok in tow moved into thorn too thick for us to penetrate, so we circled away, pulling up for a moment near a dry wash to plot our next gambit. Fresh rhino spoor was upon the ground, and I noticed the way Saladin carried his head—craning and nervous. This was my first occasion on this horse, and I did not quite know what to make of his cues.

There was no telling what initiated it—a gust of wind, a breaking branch, a fragment of underdone potato, but most likely a warthog, scenting only horse, poking its snout out of a nearby hole—but as I sat with wrists crossed on the domed saddle horn, Saladin erupted, 1,100 pounds of equine muscle translating 10 feet laterally, leaving me twixt heaven and earth without warning, some 17 hands high, time dilating to allow me to consider the approaching impact. I hit with an overfed thud on dirt rather than rocks and on that portion of the anatomy best constructed by the Creator for such a collision.

Ant was off his horse at once, questioning me about whether I was all right. After a moment of speechlessness, I got to my feet. I dusted myself off and shrugged.

"It's Africa," I said, as I remounted.

We rode on, into the wind among red-bush and velvet-leaved willows, past bridal bush in unseasonable bloom. We soon caught up with a herd of impala drifting through the bush and followed the oblivious antelope for a quarter-mile before we got to a place to take a shot.

The old elephant hunters might have shot from horseback; but after my recent experience with Saladin, I thought better of it. Tracy caught the reins as Ant and I dismounted, and I pulled the borrowed 308 from the "bucket," bolting a round and setting the safety. We stalked on foot now, closing to within 50 yards of a ram with short, gnarled horns that Ant wanted removed in the name of eugenics. Kneeling, I steadied the crosshairs on the shiny coat behind its front leg. Safety off, smooth squeeze, but no thwunk as the ram bucked. Ant knew, though; and we found the impala 30 yards from where he'd stood.

"Good to have someone who can shoot," said Ant, obviously a professional hunter easily pleased. I accepted his handshake all the same.

A week later, having taken a record-book blesbok, a cull wildebeest, and a gloriously grotesque bushpig, and after game viewing (leopard at six feet) at a reserve next to Kruger Park—and with a bruise spreading like a late-period Rothko study in blue across my rump—I moved on to the final African course: trout.

I met up with fishing guide Jonathan Boulton in the capital of South African fly fishing, the faux Tudor village of Dullstroom in the northern reaches of the Drakensbergs, the "Dragon Mountains," with a far better Zulu name: *uKhahlamba,* "Barrier of Spears." We were going to fish the Spekboom River, but first Boulton took me to one of his 15 still-water leases to take care of a small matter—for me to catch the biggest rainbow of my life.

Born and raised in California and introduced to fishing by rainbows, I came to South Africa to find the pure McCloud River strain, more likely to be discovered here than in their native range, where generations of hybridization have diluted the genes. They were brought from California in the late 1800s, fertilized eggs packed in ice in chests in sailing ships. Introduced initially to the Cape, they were eventually transplanted to flowing waters, and still-water ponds, throughout the country.

On a farm lake, one of Boulton's leases, we broke through shore ice; and I began casting and stripping in a green bead-headed Bunny Leech dressed on a no. 6 hook, Jonathan politely but firmly tutoring me on technique.

"Like the Interflora man," he'd say repeatedly, describing how he wanted my pose to look at the end of a cast, until he had me laying out lovely, looping 70-foot lengths of line. And before breakfast there was a six-pound, kyped buck in the net, a pound better than my previous best from Alaska.

Before supper we'd travelled 60 kilometers north of Dullstroom to a secluded manor on the Spekboom. The hills around were perfect leopard haunts and refuges for kudu; the river, filled with wild 'bows and browns, ran clear and cold below red shale cliff faces and abandoned gallows frames from old mines. The plan was first to bushwhack fish from cover, dropping a white attractor, with a bead-headed nymph dangling 18 inches below, on to their heads. If nothing fell for that, we'd switch to the "big gun," a Thomas & Thomas 5-weight with a heavy bead-head and a red-orange floating strike indicator.

The first night I landed only one fish using this latter method, but the next morning we had it down to a fair science. Action was slow on the dry, but at each pool I'd get three, four slashing, devastating takes on the big gun, turning the water to froth, before the trout caught on and clammed up. So onto the next pool, repeating the process until I'd taken 20 trout, including a four-pounder.

At the last pool of the morning, Jonathan had a go with my 3-weight G. Loomis, casting to one of the alarmingly large rainbows cruising in the lambent water. For a second the line was still, then it was unzipping the river, something rugby-ball sized airborne at its end. As Jonathan hooted, the trout slapped back into the water, making straight for a submerged limb to dally on it and break free.

"It's not whether you're going to land a fish like that," Jonathan philosophized as he wound the backing and line back onto the reel, "but how long you get to keep it on."

So, too, this trip to South Africa; more about adventures had than animals taken, dishes sampled than meals eaten. That evening I hooked my own titan—silver-white in the cold blue shadows as it left the river again and again, making me hoot and holler, "Who's your daddy?" and infuriating the hen into pulling free. Inspecting the partially straightened hook in the gathering dark, I thought how all the best things, whether dining, shooting, stalking, or angling, are always more recollection than possession.

Jonathan started to commiserate, but before he could say a word, I smiled my own half-smile.

"It's Africa," I said. And indeed, it was.

The President and the Pleistocene

Before . . .

AFRICA WAS NOT his only choice, but it was the one that most appealed to what has been called his "vivid . . . romantic imagination."

Over a century ago, in 1909, the war hero, outdoorsman, conservationist, and Nobel Peace Prize laureate, Theodore Roosevelt, after seven and a half years as the youngest resident of the White House, decided to honor the "wise custom" established by George Washington and declined to run for another term as President of the United States, an office to which he would have been handily reelected (and a decision he would regret). He had the opportunity, then, to run for the Senate or for mayor of New York or to become the president of his alma mater, Harvard College. But probably since at least 1906, based on his correspondence, he had been energetically cultivating the dream of going on safari.

From the presidential desk, Roosevelt penned lengthy inquiries to such notable Africa hands as the über-taxidermist and explorer Carl Akeley; the legendary hunter Sir Frederick Courtney Selous; Edward North

Buxton, author of *Two African Trips;* the Rev. Dr. W. S. Rainsford who wrote *Land of the Lion;* J. H. Patterson of the Tsavo lions fame and the chief game ranger in East Africa (and participant in the real-life *liaison scandaleux* Ernest Hemingway immortalized in fiction in "The Short Happy Life of Francis Macomber"); and the pioneering British East African colonial landowner and ostrich farmer, Sir Alfred Pease, 2nd Baronet of Hutton Lowcross and Pinchinthorpe and the holder of 6,000 acres of wildlife-infested land on the Athi Plains southwest of the newly settled town of Nairobi (more about that later). Pease is particularly notable because, having visited with Roosevelt in Washington in the last year of his presidency, he had offered assurances that he had a hunting lodge awaiting the president—except he did not. After Roosevelt decided his destiny lay in the British colonies of Kenya and Uganda, and the Belgian Congo's Lado Enclave, Pease found himself faced with the daunting task of scrambling to construct an edifice worthy of tenancy by a former head of state, a task he did manage to fulfill.

Seven weeks after the peaceful transfer of power to his handpicked (and later disappointing) successor, William Howard Taft, and after nearly a month-long ocean voyage disrupted by persistent seasickness, Roosevelt set foot on the shores of Africa in Mombasa during a torrential downpour. At his side was his "dreamy and interior" mandolin-playing second son, Kermit, having taken a break from Harvard to hunt with his father and act as the expedition's principal photographer.

Kermit, 19, was tall and slim, a lover of the Greek classics with a wide knowledge of languages. Roosevelt *père* seemed to believe that Kermit, who had never before hunted big game, needed a taste of the "strenuous life" that he, Roosevelt, so ardently advocated, to enable Kermit to "buckle down." By the end of the safari, Roosevelt was depicting his son as "an exceptionally bold and hardy sportsman" who had become "responsible and trustworthy" and "fit to lead." In fact, this may well have been wishful thinking on Roosevelt's part. By firsthand accounts, Kermit was an abysmal shot and even according to Roosevelt, "altogether too reckless." He may also have already begun exhibiting the distressing family tendency toward manic-depression, which later joined with alcoholism to lead Kermit to put a pistol to his head in an Army outpost in Alaska during World War II.

As for Roosevelt himself, he was a rather shopworn 50 years of age. A hushed-up carriage accident in 1902 had left him with an injured left leg that was chronically prone to abscesses. A boxing match with his wife Edith's cousin blinded his left eye. The arterial sclerosis that would ultimately precipitate his death at age 60 was well underway. And the physical inactivity of his presidential years swelled his waist to 47 inches and weight to 250 pounds, which, at his five-foot, eight-inch height, would classify him today as suffering from "severe obesity" (the Africans even labeled him *Bwana Tumbo*, "The Big-Stomach Master," and one commentator noted that his "bulk and conversational powers somewhat precluded" his stalking ability). Nevertheless, he felt his *toujour l'audace* "bully" approach to life could overcome any and all disabilities.

Roosevelt's initial intent was to hunt in East Africa in the rugged fashion in which he had, decades earlier, hunted in the American West. Then it had been a lone guide and he, sleeping rough on the plains under the stars.

He had hoped to do something similar with Kermit. They were to have a light, waterproof silk tent with telescoping poles (especially designed by Ezra Fitch, president of the famous firm of Abercrombie & Fitch); and a relatively restrained trophy list of game for the day; a minimum number of porters; and absolutely no professional hunter (to ensure that the only bullets to be found in the animals would be either Kermit's or his). It should have occurred to Roosevelt that for an ex-President of the United States this was an absurd and thoroughly adolescent proposition (and unfortunately reflective of his propensity for dashing headlong into adventures, which nearly cost him his life five years later on his ill-planned and outfitted Brazilian expedition). An English protectorate like Kenya would never allow such a potential diplomatic disaster—as the death or serious injury of anyone with the near-mythic worldwide stature of Roosevelt—to transpire upon its soil.

Roosevelt, finally, acquiesced to the practical wisdom of his African advisors and let them dictate the equipment and scope of the hunt. In Mombasa, Roosevelt, already costumed in his khaki Willis & Geiger safari-wear and pith helmet, along with Selous, the American naturalist, and former army surgeon, Dr. Edgar A. Mearns for whom the Mearns's or, "Harlequin," quail is named, and the Lieutenant Governor of Kenya, and a noted East African ornithologist, Frederick John Jackson, mounted a bench bolted to the pilot on the prow of a locomotive and rode the Uganda Railway into "the late Pleistocene" through the wild heart of Kenya.

When the train steamed into Kapiti Plains Station, 275 game-rich miles northwest of Mombasa, Roosevelt was greeted by his host Pease and a regiment of porters, trackers, and askaris (armed soldiers who were tasked with, among other duties, ensuring that the porters did not desert the safari), a 300-strong body of men second only in number to that which the "Colonel," as Roosevelt preferred to be called, had served with in Cuba during the Spanish-American War. And as with the Rough Riders, Roosevelt was again second in command, having accepted the services of a highly recommended Scots–South African "safari manager," R. J. Cuninghame, an expert elephant hunter. Cuninghame in turn convinced Roosevelt that a second professional was necessary for so large an entourage; and the crack shot and, more importantly, a man certain to stand his ground in the face of danger, Australian born Leslie J. Tarlton of the pioneering safari company of Newland and Tarlton, was engaged. Completing the dramatis personae were three naturalists, the 50ish Mearns and two thirtysomething zoologists, Edmund Heller from the University of California and J. Alden Loring late of the Denver Zoo, which had dismissed him for holding too grandly ambitious plans for the institute, certainly an attitude upon which Roosevelt would have looked with favor.

From a modest shooting party, Roosevelt's safari had morphed, in the Colonel's words, into "a full-blooded picnic," wrapped in the mantel of a major scientific collecting expedition under the auspices of the Smithsonian Institution, which bridled at the repeated descriptions of the expedition as "Roosevelt's," instead of the "Smithsonian's." For the collecting, tons of salt, skinning tools, traps (for large and small animals), shipping crates and barrels, and assorted other items were parceled out in 60-pound loads per porter. The silk tent was replaced with 64 heavy green canvas ones, eight alone for the riding horses, most of which died from tsetse flies. The food boxes, padlocked to discourage pilfering, contained everything from pâté to sardines, chutney, lard and tallow for cooking the lean game meat that would be the staple of the safari, liquor from England (the local spirits deemed "mostly poison"), canned pea soup, and 92 pounds of jam.

Among Roosevelt's personal accoutrements were, with much more, nine pairs of eyeglasses; custom-made rope-, rubber-, and hobnail-soled boots for his surprisingly tender feet; "spine pads" to button onto the backs of shirts to negate the effects of the equatorial sun's lethal "actinic rays"; complete changes of wardrobe for all possible weather conditions; six different hats, including a white military helmet in a tin case "for ceremonial occasions"; appropriate evening wear for formal dinners; and a lucky gold-mounted rabbit's foot from "one-time ring champion of the world" John L. Sullivan. And yet for all his personal impedimenta, he was, recalling the manly rigors of his Western days, slightly disdainful of the hovering presence of two tent "boys," two armed gunbearers, and two horse grooms, or *saises,* and especially of a canvas tub in his tent for regular hot baths.

Among Roosevelt's most vital equipage, though, were his guns and books. He brought a custom Army Springfield 30-'06 (a rifle he was instrumental in having the military develop after facing the withering fire of the Spanish infantry's Mausers with his Rough Riders), shooting army ammunition; a Winchester 405 (which he reported "did admirably with lions, giraffes, elands, and smaller game"); a 500/450 Holland & Holland double rifle (presented to him by a syndicate of English admirers); and a side-by-side 12 gauge compliments of the makers, Ansley H. Fox. For the reading he pursued as vigorously as every other passion in his life, Roosevelt selected 50 volumes and had them trimmed down for size and weight and bound in pigskin for durability. Packed in a "light aluminum and oil-cloth case" to make a load for one porter, the "Pigskin Library" ran from the Bible to the likelier more apropos than not *Alice's Adventures in Wonderland.*

Predictably, the expense of almost 11 months spent on safari in such a style was astronomical. Half of a one-million-dollar advance, at current values, that Scribner's publishing house paid him for a series of safari dispatches and a book, *African Game Trails,* was used by Roosevelt to cover Kermit and his private costs. (Roosevelt was hopeless about money; and his finances, especially because there was no pension, yet, for ex-Presidents, were always precarious, to his wife's constant anxiety.) Besides safari fees, these costs included (today) $5700 worth of licenses, apiece, entitling each hunter to some 50 head of game from elephant to rhino, hippo, buffalo, eland, other antelope, and cheetah (Kermit shot seven; Roosevelt, none), among others. Additional elephant were on license for $2000 each (Roosevelt took a total of eight; Kermit, three), rhino for something over $550 (again, eight and three), and $225 bought you another wildebeest or waterbuck. It was Roosevelt's good fortune that because they were classed as vermin, leopards and lions cost nothing: The most poorly concealed wish of Roosevelt for his safari was to come face to face with a lion in the African bush, and Sir Alfred Pease meant to see that wish granted.

Alas, lion hunting did not go off swimmingly. Never a patient hunter, Roosevelt was visibly frustrated after only a few days of potting antelope, with neither hide nor hair of a lion to be seen. At last, hunting with dogs down the thick cover of a donga on the spoor of lions, they "caught a glimpse of tawny hide" close by in the brush and fired into it, only to have two badly wounded cubs, the "size of mastiffs," come out the other side to be finished off. Luckily for Roosevelt, and particularly for Pease, later that same afternoon two large maneless male lions were put up and Roosevelt killed the first one. After fruitless, and disconcerting to Pease, 600- to 800-yard shots at the second, unwounded one as it ran off, the hunters belatedly remounted their horses and galloped after the lion, overtaking it two miles later as it loped along behind a herd of kongoni, and Kermit and Roosevelt combined in some truly hapless shooting to bring this one down.

The real moment of truth for Roosevelt came in June in the Rift Valley as he and Tarlton rode up on a "burly" and "savage" old lion with a yellow-and-black mane. Dismounting, Roosevelt fired at a distance of 200 yards, slightly wounding the lion, which ran off. Giving chase again, they caught up to it; and when Roosevelt once more clipped its hide, the lion came for them "steadily—ears laid back, and uttering terrific coughing grunts." Due to a badly sighted rifle, the usually reliable Tarlton missed with a shot, to Roosevelt's guilty "keen delight." Now, as he knelt, the bead of his Winchester's front sight solid on the center of the lion's chest, it was all up to the Colonel. The soft-pointed 405 bullet went "straight through the chest cavity, smashing the lungs and the big blood-vessels of the heart," the lion standing up, then pitching forward onto its head. It staggered to its feet, but could walk only painfully; and the two hunters put it down. This was the real dream that had brought Roosevelt to Africa, to be able to ride back to camp after dark, as he did that night, with "strange stars" shining "in the brilliant heavens, and the Southern Cross . . . radiant above the sky-line," bearing the hide of a freshly killed lion.

Within the first months of the safari, the hunters had taken so much of the game—black rhino (including the *keitloa* variation that's rear horn is longer than the front), hippos, Cape buffalo, giraffes, leopard, waterbuck, wildebeest, topi, antelope, and gazelles—which they sought for themselves and the Smithsonian, that Heller in charge of preserving the specimens, and his team of native assistants could barely keep up with the workload. To give Heller some relief, Roosevelt and Kermit began to intersperse their hunting with intermissions in Nairobi. Incorporated in 1904, the town was not dissimilar to the frontier ones Roosevelt was familiar with in the Dakotas in the 1880s. Residents drank, shot up the night, galloped their horses in the seasonally muddy streets, and sought the comforts of assorted multiracial soiled doves, while on the outskirts hyenas attacked the invalids in the sleeping-sickness isolation camps and scores of settlers killed by wild animals lay in the cemeteries. The better element, though, tried to keep up appearances with stately villas, men's clubs, foxhunting, cricket, polo, race meetings, cutaway coats and summer frocks, fêtes, and postprandial orations, of which the Roosevelts were obliged to be part. Roosevelt actually welcomed some of these hiatuses, though, after one-too-many meals of bush meat, and because they helped assuage the profound longing he felt for his absent wife, granting him at least the pleasant presence of women to converse with.

From Nairobi Roosevelt was also transmitting urgent appeals to the Smithsonian for additional funds to back the work of the scientists through the rest of the safari. The institution had already solicited contributions in the amount of almost three-quarters of a million of present-day dollars for the naturalists; but these, it proved, would only support the expedition half the way through. Another three-quarters of a million was required. Ultimately, the philanthropic industrialist Andrew Carnegie provided most of the needed extra money.

In August 1909, Roosevelt, with Cuninghame and Heller and their trackers, was following elephant trails and the rumbling noises of hidden pachyderms through the tangled wet jungles on the lower slopes of 17,000-foot Mount Kenya when he sighted a bull resting its heavy tusks on the branches of a tree, 30 yards away. When it turned its head toward Roosevelt, he fired to one side of the bull's eye, missing its brain but stunning it for a moment. Roosevelt's second 480-grain bullet from his 500/450 did find the brain, and "the great lord of the forest came crashing to the ground." Before he could even break open his rifle, though, a second bull swept out from the thick cover, passing within a trunk's length as Roosevelt dodged behind a tree to reload and Cuninghame fired twice at the elephant, turning it away to disappear into the bush.

For the next several months the safari seemed to meander like a fly on a window in the country around Nairobi. A becalmed Roosevelt celebrated his 51st birthday on the trail without firing a shot that day. Various *taka taka* species like oribi, reedbuck, duiker, and steenbok were added to fill specimen checklists or for rations. Kermit did take sable, oryx, roan, and kudu and became the first American to kill a bongo antelope, a feat not to be repeated by another American for almost half a century but Roosevelt seemed to be killing game to kill time as he awaited what for him was to be the grand finale of the safari, which came at the change of the year with the crossing of the great African lakes of Victoria Nyanza and Albert Nyanza and sailing, as Roosevelt read Edgar Allan Poe's demonic African fable "Silence," down the Bahr el Jebel branch of the White Nile to the Belgian Congo and the territory of the rare, and now virtually extinct, northern white rhinoceros.

On the west bank of the Bahr el Jebel lay the Lado Enclave, a portion of Anglo-Egyptian Sudan leased to King Leopold II of Belgium and to all intents lawless, making it a haven for slave traders and ivory poachers, such as the famed "Karamojo" Bell. It was here that Roosevelt went in pursuit of the white rhino, the last of the "heavy" game the continent had to offer him. Guided by the noted elephant hunter Quentin Grogan, Roosevelt and Kermit took nine of the rather placid creatures, bulls, cows, and calves. Worse than the calves killed was a half-grown one orphaned, in the belief it was "old enough to shift for itself." Roosevelt's motives for such behavior are problematic, if not possibly inexplicable. He fully recognized the perilous thread of survival by which the white rhino even then hung, stating in *Game Trails* that "it would certainly be well if all killing of it were prohibited until careful inquiry has been made to its numbers and exact distribution." And yet Roosevelt obviously felt this injunction was not applicable to his son and him. It can only be assumed that the putatively scientific significance of the safari granted him absolution in his mind for the "game butchery" he seemed to be committing, and in which he so strenuously denounced other hunters for indulging.

The safari, in fact, ended on a rather more sporting note when it reached the Sudanese trading post of Gondokoro. With all the professional hunters and scientists suffering from dysentery and fever, Kermit and the Colonel, who both enjoyed preposterously robust good health while in Africa, climbed onto riding mules and with 60 Ugandan porters struck off "alone" on "an eight days' trip after the largest and handsomest, and one of the least known, of African antelopes, the giant eland." After long, full days of stalking, Roosevelt ended up crawling after a fine bull, his rifle barrel heated too hot to touch by the broiling sun. Closing to within a 100 yards, Roosevelt killed the magnificent eland with a single shot, taking his last major big game animal on the continent.

On March 14, 1910, Kermit and Roosevelt landed in Khartoum, meeting Edith and daughter Ethel in a "hail of kisses," and greeting hordes of raucous reporters. Originally, Roosevelt had envisioned Kermit and his taking perhaps 64 different head of game. In the end, they took 512, including large birds, crocodiles, pythons, and a monitor lizard—the scientists collected thousands more of smaller mammals, birds, reptiles, and fish. Most of these animals were to feed the safari, and all but a select few went to museums, the two hunters retaining only a comparative handful of trophies for their walls. Roosevelt's book on the hunt ends curiously with his noting that he had consumed a mere six ounces of brandy from the camp bottle during the entire safari. This may have been a defensive assertion in light of his younger brother Elliott's premature, and tragic, death by drink.

However the tale concludes, though, it begins with Roosevelt's stating, through Shakespeare's "Pistol," that it shall be his purpose to "'speak of Africa and golden joys.'" And in that he succeeded, his story becoming the iconic saga of safari. Although the scale of his hunt is beyond duplication, it nonetheless created the template for all the safaris that were to follow. And all of us who have ventured to Africa since must acknowledge it is in the ineradicable footsteps of Theodore Roosevelt that we are following.

"A Suggestion of Grace and Poise . . ."

The 2000s . . .

A GAUGE OF the veracity of a hunting tale is a hunter's freely admitting his poor marksmanship ("liars never miss"). Rigorous honesty is never an acceptable apology, though, for an aim that is not true. Shooting is not all there is to hunting, not by a considerable margin; but it is the one skill a hunter cannot be without. When I was in Africa again, I wondered if it was a skill I still possessed.

At the start of another August in Africa, I began at the beginning, where the Indian and Atlantic Oceans marry at the Cape of Good Hope. The headland was covered in heathery *fynbos* ("fine bush"), the unique flora of the Cape. The fynbos was inhabited by native species including zebra, eland, blesbok, mongoose, and the always-delinquent Chacma baboon, while here were once numbered buffalo (the Cape giving them their name), Cape lion (*Panthera leo melanochaitus*—for its black mane), elephant, two rhino, along with the quagga (a larger, partially striped zebra) and the blaaubok (a shorter-horned sable-like antelope), both now long extinct. Even without those other

39

animals, I was seeing what was the premiere of Africa for many of the first travelers there, before the word "safari" entered the vocabulary.

From the fynbos I traveled with my wife and young son 500 miles east-by-northeast to the Great Karoo with PH Ralph Köster. It is always preferably "PH," rather than "professional hunter," though that's the meaning of the initials. In other parts of the world you may hunt with a *shikari, ghillie,* or guide, all of which cart about with them a certain air of something just a bit of the factotum.

Look at a "guide" in the movies: Invariably he is unkempt, foulmouthed, cowardly, treacherous, and ultimately a rube. It is a part tailor-made for Walter Brennan, without teeth—character-actor territory par excellence. The African PH, though, in the legends and Hollywood, anyway, has occupied a position somewhere between World War I flying ace and Lord Greystoke. The role of PH falls to Gable or Redford (perhaps out of the jumbled grab bag of reasons why safari movies aren't made anymore may be the absence of actors approaching the innate stature of anyone of the kind, above, Brennan included, perhaps especially so). In reality, a good PH is, rather than a matinee idol, a man of varied talents, from businessman to hotelier, never losing sight of his main occupation of reliable hunt organizer and practiced shot. When a good PH calls himself a "PH," it sounds a little self-deprecating. When a bad one—phonies, crooks, and assembly-line "truck hunters"—calls himself that, it rings with bluster.

Ralph did not look like Robert Redford; more like a young and sunnier Sterling Hayden. He was a good PH. He'd been at it for 14 years, since he was 20. For the last five he had hunted near the outpost town of Beaufort West (whose claim to fame was as the birthplace of the heart-transplant pioneer, Dr. Christiaan Barnard) in the Nuweveld Mountains in the Great Karoo. Here Ralph had a 45,000-acre hunting area where the Lemoenfontein River ran (when the rains fell hard enough).

Some 150 years ago (as this book is composed), a tubercular English gentleman, having made a long sea voyage to the Cape, made an equally arduous horseback-and-wagon trek inland and built a large wood-floored, high-ceilinged hunting lodge with wide verandas and wider sweeping views of the Karoo veldt, naming it Lemoenfontein Lodge. Each year he escaped the disaster that was the English winter to pass six weeks hunting the varied fauna of the area, before retreating to England. Over the years, the game faded from abundance and the lodge fell into disrepair. Not utter disrepair, though, because it still stood in Ralph's hunting area, fully restored.

Ralph's area in August was a cool, clear, dry winter country of mesa and rimrock, aproned by scrub plains. It looked most like Coues's deer country in the Mexican Sonora or the red Hole-in-the-Wall of Wyoming, with every bit as much wind (Ralph assured me this was an anomaly). The first morning we breakfasted—whole milk, passion fruit juice, haddock, eggs, bacon, sausage, cheese, croissants, toast, butter, marmalade, apricot jam: the healthy-eating menu—then went out to sight in the rifle, afterward to look for springbok.

Rowland Ward's Records of Big Game describes the springbok as "the well-known national emblem of South Africa" and as "the only gazelle [as opposed to antelope] found south of the Zambezi and in former times its numbers were prodigious." The word Selous used was "innumerable." The vast herds would eat out the veldt and swarm over the Boer farmers' lands in the proportions of biblical pestilence, in what the Afrikaners called the *trekbokken,* or "buck trek," said to trample underhoof whatever could not get out of the way, including humans. To carry the Wyoming analogy farther, they are the pronghorn of South Africa (capable of elegant springs, inelegantly called pronking, while pronghorn seldom leave the ground).

The farmers, of course, at one time did their level best to extirpate the springbok, in a fashion not dissimilar to the persecution of the pronghorn in the American West. The gazelle hung on, though, and today numbers in the millions across its southern-African range. (Worthy of note is that the two regions in the world where wildlife has increased on a large scale in the last century are North America and southern Africa, where conservation is built around hunting.) From among these springbok, Ralph wanted me to take a best-quality ram, one with heavy-based horns, like percontation point and question mark set side by side, that hooked back at the tip—achieving greater length.

After the rifle was zeroed, we had the luxury of looking at 1,000 or more springbok around the foot of the mesa. At about midday, Ralph spotted the one. We left the *bakkie,* as small utility trucks are called in South Africa, and stalked after the ram. Closing to within 150 yards, Ralph set up the tripod shooting sticks (the land is, again like parts of Wyoming, too flat to count on finding a natural rest); and I set the 7mm Weatherby Magnum on them. The wind howled, and I fought to get a steady hold; and there was the distinct sensation of opening-night (or opening-day-in-Africa) jitters. I should have backed off and waited to settle down, but I let off the safety and fired, instead. And missed. The springbok was unfazed, trotting off a little way and stopping; and I shot again and missed again. Matters continued in this doleful pattern for a troubling time, the ram after each plumule of dust spurted up near it drifting out to 200, 250, 280, and 300 yards, when something more troubling than missing occurred: I wounded the springbok in the hind leg.

We trailed the ram for two hours across the rocky plain, my feeling the wounded-animal sickness with each step. He kept ahead of us, but we kept him in sight. At one point, with the utmost indulgence, Ralph advised, "I know you can tell me a lot about writing [I wondered]; but if you don't mind, try to watch him drop in the scope with the next shot—don't lift your head—or we will be walking for a very much longer time." I knew all this already, but there seemed to be a disconnect between my consciousness and the motor skills controlling my trigger finger.

We got to within 175 yards of the gazelle, making for another tough shot in the wind. This time I kept my head down. The 140 grain took him behind the left shoulder, coming out at the point of the right; and he was dead—at last—before he hit the ground.

He was an older ram (one of the regular, "common," buff variety), his horns over 13 inches long with 6-inch bases. Ralph told me to kneel and smell the pronk, the fan of white hair the springbok carried on the rear of its back and "everted" when bounding in excitement. I thought it was some sort of gag, but I figured it was my turn to indulge him. Kneeling, I put my face against the sheaf of hairs and smelled a candy-shop smell. It faded as the springbok cooled, and I felt as if something perfervid in me had cooled. It hadn't.

The French, they say, have a word for it; but it seems Afrikaners do, too. For my condition, it was a word I heard Ralph using in a phone conversation with his parents that night, talking about the new hunter. *Bokkoors* was the word. "Buck curse." What we call plain old buck fever. Even though I had hunted big game since I was 16, I still got bokkoors, especially in Africa. And sometimes it seemed that the harder I tried to tamp it down, the more it wanted to push out of me.

I suppose I could have taken consolation in considering the way Theodore Roosevelt had shot in Africa—as a friend put it, "A wounding we will go." Robert Ruark was forthright about how badly he shot at the start of his first safari with Harry Selby; and even Hemingway, when not committing the "braggies" over some string of one-shot kills, reckoned as how his might not always have shot as straight as he could in Tanganyika. (While he admitted to missing a Grant's with "shot after shot," it was up to wife number two, Pauline, to record in her safari diary that something like 30 rounds were fired without effect at the gazelle by Ernest, whom she had never seen "miss so completely," though he "behaved beautifully," that grace-under-pressure thing.) I did want to shoot well (yes, a risible desire to have anymore); but I was not sure I wanted it at the possible total expense of ever knowing bokkoors again, to be filled with nothing at the shooting and killing of game.

The next morning, cold and cloudy and spitting rain, we drove to the top of the 1,900-meter mesa beetling over the hunting area, looking for black wildebeest. On top of the mesa, breath formed itself into white billows. The temperature, though, was not my worry.

Grinding up the rock-and-dirt switchback road bladed into the side of the mesa, we passed Cape kudu cows and klipspringer (Africa's miniature chamois, called *ko-ka* in the language of the Khoisan, from which Ralph took the name of his hunting camp, Ko-Ka-Tsara, "small buck's valley") perched on the rocks. On the mesa top the land was more lush, with tufted grass and heavier brush, and rockier than the plains below. Almost at once we began seeing the tan saddled, blue-black flanked, belly, stockings, blaze, and rump white as a starched linen cloth, ring-horned bontebok. When the quagga and blaubok were being shot from existence in the 19th century, the elegant little bontebok (reduced at one time to a total of 17 known animals in the world) nearly went with them. Hunting-based conservation (please see above; it cannot be noted too frequently) in South Africa brought it back, to the point where, although technically listed as endangered, it could legally be hunted and the trophy imported into the United States with the proper permits. They were beautiful; but it's an odd measure of game that some instills intense excitement, while others, perhaps not even so dissimilar, creates none. With bontebok, I could not muster much enthusiasm for taking one.

There were eland and gemsbok and blue wildebeest up here, too, in this dramatic hunting country; but we had come for black wildebeest. When the Dutch saw these absurd-looking antelope (bearded and hairy-muzzled with horse-maned neck and withers sloping Paleolithically to low hindquarters, a casque of a boss resting on its forehead as the horns grew down before turning up to long sharp points, and a light-colored flicking tail hanging nearly to the ground), they mistook them for a species of wild ox (*wildebees*), while the other name, gnu, also from the Khoisan, was imitative of their raucous snort. There was no doubt something off-putting to the Reformed souls of those early Afrikaners to see those animals cavorting on the plains in anarchic leaping circles, none coming forth to lead, and all refusing to follow. This impelled the Afrikaners to christen the black wildebeest "the old fool of the veldt." In truth, they were hardly fools, just sometimes inquisitive; but mainly they were wild, wary, fast, capable of aggression, and hard to put down if not shot right.

Ralph and I left the bakkie and stalked to the rim of a wide bowl. Ralph knew this place and that there was often a herd of black wildebeest here. When we crept over the rim, the herd was there, 400 yards away, with a very good bull in it. We made our way from brush to brush, then angled to a tree to cut the distance to under 200. Ralph set up the shooting sticks; and I tried to get a rest, remembering about seeing the animal in the scope all the way to the ground. I still felt rocky, but I got on him and tried to hold everything in as I squeezed off the shot. And hit him back, far enough for him to run off with the herd. More than an hour of blood-trailing and stalking went by before he could be caught up with and put down. He was an ancient animal with a massive boss and horns that ranked him high up in the record book; and I would have traded any ranking for a shot that was clean and quick, and not atrocious.

After we got the wildebeest off the mesa and back to camp, we went out to sight-in the rifle again, just to make sure. It shot right enough, of course, as I suspected it would. Maybe I was the old fool of the veldt; to know that for sure, I had to go on hunting.

In African hunting there is "new school" and "old." New school involved picking up a hunting client at the airport and getting him five assorted flavors of representative animals, by whatever means were most economical and expeditious, then depositing him back at the airport in seven days and reloading another client. Or make that a group of clients. Hunting clients bought into this travesty because they were 10,000 miles from home and were loath to return empty handed; nobody in their town was likely to distinguish a springbok from Johann Sebastian Bach, let alone a good springbok from a mediocre; and who, other than they, was ever going to know the circumstances under which they hunted in Africa? PHs, for their part, resort to new school because they've lost interest in real hunting (if they ever had any to begin with), because they didn't care whether or not their clients experienced a true safari. It was all about the money, it goes without saying.

Old school was climbing down from the bakkie and going out on foot for however long it took to hunt the best animal you could. It meant turning down all the immature game and the gimme shots—such as when you drove down the bend in the dirt road and found a better-than-decent gemsbok standing in the middle of it, when what you were out for that day was hartebeest. It meant meeting the animal on its own ground and giving it—to use a phrase anti-hunters delight in sneering at—a "sporting chance."

Ralph hunted old school. Shank's mare was what you rode to close the distance to game if you were going to hunt with Ralph, and he was not going to let you kill anything that was less than what he would want to put on the wall of his own home. Certainly, this was all quite admirable, though you did mull over if sportsmanship always had to be so damn bloody exhausting, not the least emotionally so.

Today the bets were on red as we went back onto the mesa to hunt red, or Cape, hartebeest. It is large antelope that in closely related species and subspecies, such as the tsessebe and topi, was once found almost literally from the Cape to Cairo. The Dutch settlers named it for its hardiness when they pursued it on horseback, flatly baffled that the dismal-looking 350-pound antelope could remain fresh during a long chase, when a hunter's horse would be badly "blown" before the trekker could catch up to the wild animal. The hartebeest galloped in an easy, ground-covering lope, its long mule-faced head up. The red in its hide was a dusting of cinnamon, shading to brick in old bulls, with patches of steel blue on the upper legs and face. The horns were maybe some of the most remarkable, if hardly spectacular, in Africa, thick-based, thick-ribbed hooks like quotation marks. And few antelope in the world had better eyes.

In the late morning we spotted a bachelor herd of six bulls, and in the herd Ralph sighted one of the best hartebeest he had ever seen. We went after the herd, but by the time we got around the side of the hill that the herd had walked over, the animals had run almost 1,000 feet above us, near the top of a high ridge on the mesa. There was really no way to approach the hartebeest without their spotting us, and the only thing was to wait for them to come down.

We made a *braai,* a barbecue, and ate lunch in acacia shade, and by half past one the hartebeest had fed down onto a small plateau a long way from us. We had to go on foot if we were going to stalk them without being seen.

It took almost two hours for Ralph and me to work our way up to the hartebeest. We were able to use the rolling terrain to hide our approach, the hartebeest preternaturally alert to movement. It was this alertness, and not as much about the horns, however admirable, or the size of the animals, that made them worth hunting. At one point we lay behind a rock pile for half an hour to keep out of the herd's sight while we waited for it to bed down. The winter August sun came down from the clear sky and beat on us as we waited. Then we got up and went on. The ground was a rock garden of oxblood stones shining in the heat. They could only be stepped over or on, never simply walked around. More than once I wanted to pick them up and smash them together into dust.

More than once, Ralph, perhaps sensing my frustration and tiredness, turned to say softly, "Let's keep on. I promise you won't be disappointed."

When we were 500 yards from them, we waited for a short while behind some more rocks, then crouched our way down to a draw and followed it up to the edge of a little plateau that sat on the big plateau of the mesa like an added layer, with the red hartebeest bedded on it. There was no cover, and we had to move slowly onto the little plateau to get in sight of the herd. We had a few seconds, once the hartebeest spotted us, for them to get to their feet and stand before starting to run. We eased forward, doubled over the tall grass that hid even more rocks underfoot, Ralph carrying the dreaded shooting sticks that I never seemed able to get the rifle settled on, but here the only possible rest from which to shoot.

As we went ahead, first we saw their horns, then their red bodies. Ralph set up the sticks and I lay the 7mm on it. We waited. A full minute passed, then another. A smaller bull stood and looked at us. Then the big bull stood—hindquarters first, then the front—just to the right of the smaller one, 200 yards from me.

I took a breath, eased off the safety, and held behind the bull's shoulder. At the shot, he leaped and the herd was up and running. The big bull swung wide to the right of the others and went straight away.

All I felt was anger. I already had another shell chambered and put the crosshairs on the base of his tail. The 160-grain bullet (switched over from the 140s for the heavier game) hit where I aimed; and the bull went down with a kick and lay still, the remaining hartebeest loping away.

"What the hell was that?" Ralph asked, shocked to see the bull lying on the ground.

"Portuguese brainshot?" I suggested. "Texas heartshot?" I wished I'd had a cleverer response at my fingertips, but I was just relieved that the bull was not still running with the others. And I let the anger bleed off.

When we got to him, Ralph was stunned. It was the biggest red hartebeest he'd ever taken with a hunter—23½-inch horns with 13-inch bases—good enough to blow past the Rowland Ward minimums. This hartebeest was definitely old school. The hunt had been old school. It was the school from which no hunters should ever let himself matriculate. Now I wanted one more shot to make it right—one shot only, at a kudu.

"There is nearly always a sardonic touch to the story of a kudu," wrote Ruark. Late on a bright afternoon, Ralph, his tracker and skinner Abram, my son Bryan, and I went off to the far north of Ralph's hunting area, to his "kudu haven" to see if we could find that touch of sardonicism. In the band around his hat, Bryan wore a white ostrich feather I'd found and given him, making him look like a definite Captain Kidd. He rode in the open back of the bakkie with Abram, plume fluttering, all of us looking for kudu. It was past four o'clock, and the sun was falling swiftly. This was when, according to Ralph, the kudu "let down their guards," as much as they ever did. As we drove slowly along a sandy road lined on either side by heavy thorn bush, Abram leaned down from the back and softly said to Ralph that there was a kudu.

Ralph and I looked, the bakkie still rolling, and even without binoculars we saw him standing stock-still, the angled light shining on the hard mirror-image helixes of his horns. When we got farther down the road, putting more brush between the bull and us, Ralph braked the bakkie and we dropped silently out of it while Abram swung down and got behind the wheel, Bryan still in the back. Abram drove the bakkie away; and Ralph and I crouched behind the brush, me with my rifle, and Ralph without the shooting sticks.

We had to stay in a crouch and move from bush to bush, Ralph expecting the kudu to ghost away at any second. But he stayed. Maybe it was part of what Ruark called the kudu's "perverseness, his consummate genius for doing the wrong thing always," except that it is almost always a wrong thing that inured to the benefit of the kudu. Ralph was able to glass him carefully and to tell me it was an old bull, his horns heavy and symmetrical all the way to ivory tips. There were longer horns in the world, he advised; but this was a fully mature kudu—past "mature," truthfully—whose horns would never grow any longer. Was I sure I wanted to take him? I nodded, and we crouched farther forward.

In the end we had to get on hands and knees and crawl through a gap in a bush so I could sit up on the other side and try to get the crosshairs on the bull. It was no good, too much brush in the way and not a steady-enough rest. I told Ralph I wanted to move to the next bush ahead of me, crisscrossed with thick dead branches, and see if I could get a shot from there. Ralph shrugged, telling me to go ahead, but more than ever certain that the bull would not stay. Ralph would sit where he was, though, where the kudu could probably see him, on the theory that even the wisest old bull antelope cannot count.

I made it to the bush and got to my feet, trying to see the kudu without his seeing me, and trying to keep down all the thoughts of all the bad shots. It was the gleam of the horns that showed him to me again. I lay into the bush, letting it take my weight as I slid the rifle ahead and rested it on one of the branches. I could see the bull facing me, through a halo of bone-white acacia thorns in the scope. I felt, in its inevitability, the bokkoors rising; but this time I didn't try to overwhelm it, increasing the pressure on it, just waited for it to ease and everything to feel right. I looked back at Ralph, sitting motionless, and he gave a little nod. I thumbed off the safety and held on the center of the kudu's chest.

I saw the kudu rock in the scope at the shot, then stumble and dive forward, the white of his scut curled convulsively over his rump, seeing it all in the ocular without moving my cheek from the comb of the stock. The bull went down behind big iron-colored rocks and green brush, and did not get up. When we got to him, the bright-white chevron of the Cape subspecies of greater kudu could be seen on his face, and he was gaunt and nearly toothless. He would not have survived the rest of the winter. The horns were far from "making book" but were what the antelope had spent a lifetime growing and were thick, double curled, polished, and capped in white. I had taken better kudu "heads," but none that meant as much. When Bryan got to us with Abram, I was glad for him to see that his dad could still shoot—sometimes, as atavistic as that may sound.

There would be better trophies and more clean shots to come. One was a very long shot at a lechwe that would not get up from his bed. The angle looked impossible; but somehow I put the bullet into his heart and lungs, and he did not move. Another shot was on a beautiful nyala, all draping fringe of long hair on his neck and chest, crest of white hairs along the spine, small hooves, stocky brown, white-striped body, and spiral horns rising above his head. He came out as the sun went down into a field of vermillion cactus creeping across the ground, covering it in a needled carpet, the sky growing to match the color of the cactus, the nyala barely there in the fading light; but the single shot at 175 yards brought the heavy antelope down. It was the shot on the kudu, though, that I remember far more vividly.

As an African sunset rivaling Capstickian prose—hemorrhaging "like a fresh wound"—painted the sky, I looked at this kudu bull and thought of the words of Sir Percy Fitzpatrick, written in one of the best of all dog books, *Jock of the Bushveld:* "There is a suggestion of grace and poise in the movement of the koodoo bull's head as he gallops through the bush which is one of his distinctions above the other antelopes." Even in death, you could see that suggestion in this kudu, that had stood there just long enough so the bokkoors could dissolve in me; and I could have my own suggestion of grace and poise, if for only that moment.

Arab Winter

The 2010s . . .

In the whole of Libya there is neither wild boar, nor
stag, nor wild goat.

—Aristotle

. . . and yet . . .

There is always something new coming out of Africa.

—Aristotle

THERE IS A yearning to romanticize the Sahara with images of white-
kepi-ed Légionnaires and blue-*cheche*-ed Tuareg. And difficult not to, as
behind you over the Tunisian sand dunes in the morning light glides a line of
wild camels, about to break into their high-kneed, feet-flipping trot. Three
things, it is said, cannot be hidden: love, the smoke of a fire, and a man riding
a camel, or a camel without a man, for that matter. In such surroundings you
want to add the words Balzac gave to one of Napoleon's aged "Immortals,"
who in campaigning around the world had never seen anything else like the
desert, where there was everything and nothing, like God without people.
But with wild boar.

Much of "Libya," the name for ancient Africa, would have been less new to Aristotle had he been more familiar with the rich panoply of wildlife along even the Barbary Coast in ancient times, and not so ancient. Until AD 1890 existed the formidable Barbary lion, with the last Barbary leopard reported to have been taken in 1949, though it is believed to carry on in vestigial numbers. Then there was, of course, the Carthaginian elephant of Hannibal, extinguished by Roman *bestiarii* in *venatio* performances in the arenas, and for the animal's ivory. The Atlas bear, genetically closer to the polar than the brown bear, faded away in the 1870s. Yet very much remains today, including the addax, scimitar-horned oryx, and ariel gazelle, and despite Aristotle's misplaced beliefs, the Barbary stag, the Barbary sheep (a sheep-goat), and the Barbary wild boar.

It is said that the Egyptian deity Set loved the darkness in which evil things abound; and it was while hunting wild boar with his dogs by moonlight that he came upon the coffin with the corpse of his brother Osiris, the king who taught the Egyptians to worship the gods and abandon cannibalism. In the telling, Set took the shape of a wild boar and rent Osiris's body into 42 pieces, one for every *sepat*, province, of Pharaonic Egypt. It was the (today) unfortunately named, heartbroken Isis, sister to both Osiris and Set, and wife of Osiris, who found the remains and knitted them back together so she could copulate with her brother and receive the seed of Horus, god of the sun. The wild boar then became the ritual sacrifice to the moon and Osiris, often offered up in the short days and long nights of winter, the death of the nocturnal boar forming a link to the rebirth of spring. Once roaming throughout the Nile Delta, the wild boar died out in Egypt over 100 years ago; and to find African wild boar, today, I went to extremes, in the form of Tunisia, North Africa.

When I landed at Aéroport de Tunis-Carthage in the heart of winter, the name reminded me that the "New City," founded by the Phoenicians, stood here from the ninth century BC, until sacked by Scipio Aemillianus in 146 of that era; and afterward the country that would become Tunisia was the breadbasket of the empire, thanks to Caesar's aqueducts and irrigation, only to see its agriculture dwindle in the centuries after the fall of Rome, though it remained a haven for *Sus scrofa*.

If I considered Africa as having four corners, then Tunis would have been my fourth, or close enough. To reach the east-west extremities of Africa, you journeyed to Pointe des Almadies on the coast of Senegal, then east to the headland of Ras Asir in Somalia, a distance of 4,600 miles. (For the life of me, having been to the former, I have never divined a purpose in venturing to Ras Asir, so I account Lamu on the coast of Kenya, a mere 4,100 miles from the point in Senegal, as my trek to the nearly-there easternmost reach of the continent.) From south to north would be the 5,000 miles from Cape of Good Hope, where the Atlantic and Indian Oceans marry, to Le cap Blanc on the Mediterranean, a span which, upon my arrival in Tunis on a January day, I had at last accomplished as I came in search of wild boar.

Splitters will contend that Africa major, with warthogs, giant forest hogs, red river hogs, and bushpigs, is bereft of true pigs; but northwest Africa retains a wealth of them. Nine-hundred miles west of Tunis, on December 6, 1942, General George S. Patton went hunting for sanglier at Sibi Sbaa, a forest ranger's station in Morocco. "There were 250 natives to act as beaters," half of them mounted; and the first drive "netted one pig and one jackall [*sic*]." On the second beat, Patton took two pigs and a jackal with what he acknowledged was exceptional shooting, with "a very fine over & under 12 gauge" belonging to his host.

"You use an expanding slug in the first barrel," he wrote in his diary that day, "and buckshot in the second. The slug is very effective and has a range of 100 yds. I killed one running pig at 90 yds. with a brain shot. The French thought I did it on purpose of course [*sic*] I just shot the pig," though ever the military tactician, Patton appears not to have disabused his hosts of their faith in him.

Now, I had come to Tunisia to hunt driven wild boar myself, in much the same fashion as Patton, who once hunted bigger game here in the Qasserine Pass. In my case, rather than an over-and-under, I used a semi-auto shotgun, reflex sight, and saboted slugs. I hunted with a group of seven Scandinavians and one English gunsmith from Lancashire, north of Liverpool. Our outfitter was Eric Eckhardt. From Sweden, Erik, now 74, had been a professional hunter in Tanzania for nearly 50 years, while working for the Tunisian game department in the 1960s when the rainy season kept him out of East Africa, and for 45 years had run wild-boar hunts in the northern country (and was one of the last living PHs to have worked on the film *Hatari!*, with recollections of the alluring Ms. Elsa Martinelli).

After clearing the firearms through customs at the airport, it was nearly sunset; and we drove 500 kilometers south in a small tourist bus in the darkness, stopping along the highway at a well-lighted cafe with tile floors, plastic chairs, oil cloths on the tables, and a photo of the head of state on the wall. Grilled whole fish (when in doubt, call it "dorado"), pommes frites, red-pepper relish, and the hallmark of civilization—warm flatbread. Then more hours on the road, until the hotel in Tozeur in southern Tunisia was reached, far from Carthage.

Tozeur now staked the southern boundary of the wild pig's range in Africa. In the daylight I found an oasis town where outside the butcher shops, from the awnings over the storefronts by way of advertising, hung the complacent severed head of a cow, or sometimes the doleful one of a fresh-killed camel. Many, but not all, of the women wore the hijab, but none the burka; you could quaff a beer in public without fear of incurring a fatwa; every sidewalk table with glasses of coffee was its own parliamentary assembly; and even the most civil of conversations resembled fistfights without fists.

Tozeur sat on the edge of the Chott el-Djerid, at 7,000 square kilometers the largest salt pan in the Sahara. This was Lotus-eaters' land where the wild ox, probably the Barabary aurochs that went extinct in the first millennium BC, had to graze backward because its long horns curved forward and downward and stuck in the ground if it tried to feed moving ahead. The chott may have been Lake Tritonis, named for Triton and described by Herodotus in his *Histories.* Around it, in almost every date orchard, every reed bed, every patch of scrub brush along a dry watercourse, lived wild boar.

In a string of Land Cruisers we drove out of Tozeur toward a line of rocky hills, passing Tunisians on motorbikes, the riders dressed in brown burnooses with pointed hoods, based on the Roman *paenula* (traveler's cloak) and billowing behind like sails filled in reverse. (In AD 850 Christians and Jews were required under sharia law to wear a white patch on their cloaks, shaped like an ape or pig, to distinguish them from Moslems.) After half an hour, out in the open desert, we met up with the Tunisian hunter Ghaouar Ammar and the beaters and dogs.

Tall and sharp featured with what is commonly referred to as an aquiline nose, Ammar was dressed in disconcerting American blaze-orange camouflage, carrying a side-by-side 12 gauge on a sling (for coups de grâce on wounded boar) and a small brass hunting horn in his jacket pocket. The beaters looked like agricultural workers, which they probably were most days of the year, and joked in the rough private way of working men. Along with the eight men there was a rotating pack of four dogs, dogs with the brown and white and black and white of pointer blood, the solid coats of retrievers, and the brindle of curs and terriers, all of them chased with the pink jagged scars of boar's tusks. All together, they travelled in two vehicles, a small pickup Ammar drove and a compact SUV, hauling a trailer for transporting dead pigs.

After meeting up with Ammar, beaters, and dogs, we fell in behind the two vehicles and drove to the base of the hills. Turning off the highway, we crossed open ground, dropping down into a large wash and climbing the other side. We came to a halt and Ammar got out and gestured back for me to follow him. We walked a quarter mile along a trail marked by scores of new pig tracks in the pebbly soil and came to an outcrop of rocks above a branch of the main wash. Ammar, who spoke no English, pointed to the ground at the outcrop, indicating that this was my peg, sweeping his hand across the slopes in front of me to show where the pigs would come. We nodded to each other, and Ammar left me to wait; and I took a seat on the rocks, loading the shotgun and switching on the red dot of the sight.

Scanning the terrain, I was reminded me of the bare rocky desert of the Mojave. I drove out there in December many years ago to look for a sheep-hunting camp and not finding it before dark, I slept on the front seat of my truck; and during the night, I heard from beyond the ridges the far rumble of artillery practice at the Marine base. When I woke up at dawn I got out of the truck; and looking up on the cliffs, I was surprised to see a band of pot-bellied desert rams, staring down at me. It was hard to imagine large wild mammals living out in country as arid and barren-appearing as this, but there they were.

I had, in spite of the evidence of the tracks, the same feeling in Tunisia, waiting on stand. I heard the beaters shouting as they were soon working through the hills, but was not expecting anything. And then there was a steam-engine chuffing; and over a crest, out of range, came a large boar, hobby-horsing down the slope and vanishing into a draw, leaving behind a kind of amazement that big game really did inhabit such seeming desolation.

In a short while, two smaller pigs ran down the slope in front of me. I debated for a moment whether to shoot. Then I thought I had never taken a wild boar in Tunisia before, never in fact had a chance to, and thought of something else. "Naturally," wrote Hemingway in the letter arranging his safari with Philip Percival's Tanganyika Guide Service, "would like to get better things if we could but this is a first shoot." This was a first shoot.

As it happened, I was spared the mixed emotions of taking small pigs by missing the running animals again and again. Waiting for a wild pig, driven by beaters, to halt and offer a clean standing shot was as conceivable as stacking BBs in a hurricane; but that was hardly an excuse for the dismal shooting I was exhibiting. The pigs crossed the draw and climbed out the other side, being missed by me some more. Finally, one scaled the rocks above me and despite my certainty that he would not, paused to look down, 15 yards away. But he was skylighted; and besides, I was too disgusted with myself to consider any more shooting under any circumstances—at least at these pigs. So I watched him amble off.

As the time passed, I heard away from me several hollow slams of slugs being fired, sounding like single, killing shots. After about an hour, I saw Ammar, the SUV towing the trailer, now sprouting hoofed legs, and the white Land Cruisers driving on the other side of the large dry wash. Unloading my shotgun, I headed back to them. When I got to the SUV, I saw the trailer with four pigs, three smaller ones and a genuine trophy boar taken by one of the Danish hunters, Per, the bristled hide dark and the long inches of ivory tusk curling out of the gumline. We had time for another drive before midday, and lined up across the bottom of a wide bank of alluvial stone just off the highway.

It took time for the beaters to drive the pigs from the rocky gray hills spreading before us and out of the draws, but I could hear shots from down the line of hunters as the wild pigs came into range. At the end of the drive, a big boar was running toward me across the line in the slanting winter light. When the chunky pig trot turned to a full stretched-out run, the long hairs of the crest raised, there was something in the snout-forward profile that made a boar look like an arrowhead or some kind of chert spearpoint, and moving faster than it actually was, but fast enough. But still not that fast. The hunter below me fired twice and missed twice, then I missed with two shots, and Richard, the English gunsmith beyond me, emptied his over-and-under at the boar, and in his own estimation shot two rather gaping holes in the ground. Then the boar was gone in a trail of dust.

We ate a late lunch at a long table in a date grove, sardines and salad, bread and cheese, stewed vegetables and grilled chicken, and sweet ripe oranges for dessert. Then in another part of the orchard we walked out on the grassy berms boxing the plots where the shading palms were planted and flooded, and Per killed a smaller pig that was driven straight to him at close range. The last drive of the day was under the high bank of a dry riverbed below another date grove. The beaters came on, unseen, whooping in the politically incorrect term of "like Indians," or at least like Indians in old Western movies. I heard the pig coming before it dropped down over the bank and ran across a small ledge on the river bank, an easy shot; and it kept running after I missed, Per in line beside me killing it. In the distance, the keening note of Ammar's horn signaled the end of the hunting.

On the road out from the drives, I looked back at the desert in the late afternoon, counting four horizons stacked in lines of palm green, foothills of blue, to farther taller hills of gray, to the distant dim gray of a mountain crest, the northeastern rim of the Atlases. Returning to the hotel with enough empty hulls to have taken a limit of greenheads, I sat outside at sunset after showering, listening to the muezzins' *azan,* the call to prayer, echoing from half-a-dozen minarets, each crier competing for recognition, creating a tournament of sacredness, a round robin of the devout, that was unanswerable, not ending until the last, most eloquent faded into silence. As I listened, I thought about what became of wild boar in a Moslem country. In this case, at least, there was a small local menagerie with lions, hyenas, and vultures; and since the qur'anic sura declaring the consumption of pork to be haram did not apply to lions, the animals would eat well for some time to come.

For the next two days, I shot every bit as abysmally as I had the first day, just seeming incapable of learning how to lead the damn things and missing a very fine boar at ridiculously close range on the third afternoon, after which while eating a delicious *deglet noor,* the translucent "date of light," fresh off a palm tree, I bit down cautiously to chew around the pit and still somehow managed to shatter a bicuspid with what seemed the slightest of pressures. Sigh.

We changed areas the next day, driving on the road across the perfectly flat dried-up Chott el-Djerid to the ancient oasis town of Kebili, which humans had been inhabiting, it was estimated, for some 200,000 years. The first morning there, meeting up with Ammar and the drivers where they waited around a small palm-frond fire on the shoulder of the road, we went out to a dry wash with shoulder-tall salt bush and got on our pegs. Between leaving the vehicle and waiting for the drive to begin, I wondered if I were ever going to be able to hit a running wild pig, not realizing how many more opportunities there would be; and like that blind hog, I was bound to stumble onto at least one.

I heard the dogs coming a long way away; and then there was the chuffing of the pigs, and a smaller one broke from the bush to my left. I waited until he was clear of the line and fired, and missed. Then a very big sow, as I later determined, running alone, came by; and as she passed and was quartering away, I fired, trying to hold the red dot a little ahead of her and following through; and she started up a large berm pushed up at the edge of the dry watercourse, then stumbled at the top and seemed to go down as she topped the berm; and I saw dust rising on the other side, but from one place, not the trail of dust of a running animal. I had reloaded then, and wanted to go over to see if the pig was down but knew I could not leave my peg until the shooting was finished. Then another big sow came out, this time running back up the wash with the dogs behind; and I fired at her. She ran out of sight, but in a few minutes I heard the dogs barking excitedly and fading squeals coming from her. The drive and the other shooting was done after that; and I climbed over the berm to see the big sow on the other side, lying on her side, dead.

I walked over to her, making sure she was finished before unloading the shotgun. She was over 200 pounds, and even had visible tusks. While I waited beside her, four of the beaters crossed over the berm, carrying the second sow, a little smaller, each beater with his hand around a trotter, leaning out as if he were counterbalancing a heavy bucket. They lay this pig down beside the first one. Looking at them, I saw that both sows were dry. We never saw piglets during the hunt; and though I assumed that wild pigs bred wherever and whenever the mood struck, it seemed as if we were probably in the pre-rut for the hogs.

One of the beaters had a small tuber he had dug up and was brushing the sandy yellow soil off it. He cut slices from it and offered them around. I took one, and began to chew. It was like a watery piece of horseradish, and the beater made me to understand that it was good for the stomach. Then the SUV with the trailer came up, and we loaded the pigs.

We hunted the rest of the days in and along washes, in salt-grass marshes, around beds of 10-foot tall phragmites topped with waving white tassels where you could see the progress of the drivers by the parting of the reeds, and in date groves where the windfall fruit stuck in the cleats of your boots, Sahara swallowtails fluttered, and the date flies circled your head. The beaters shouted, made their versions of pig snorts, swung sticks, drummed together empty plastic bottles like noisemakers at football games, and even sang as they drove the wild pigs, in the afternoon the muezzin's call, from somewhere unknown, drifting eerily through the palms, punctuated by the sound of shotgun fire.

In the first part of the hunt, except for Per's trophy boar, all the pigs seemed to be sows and small boars. In the last days, though, we began to take one large boar after another. Ove, an octogenarian butcher from

Copenhagen, took one boar that was better than 310 pounds, weighed on scales, with long curved tusks and black bristled winter hide you could bury a hand in. Richard made an excellent long shot on another big boar, despite being wracked with pain from a severe attack of sciatica running down his back and legs, so that he had to travel lying across the rear seat of one of the Land Cruisers, or not go out hunting at all. The other Scandinavians, too, started killing big wild boar, until almost everyone had one.

On a morning drive out of the phragmites out onto a dry lakebed, the take of pigs was extraordinary. There was shooting going on all around; and as I stood on one side of a canal half filled with clear water, I heard behind me the barking of dogs that had run out of the reeds; and I turned to look. Lit from in back by the sun, the dogs were on an average-sized boar who dived into the canal and came out the other side with three of the dogs pursuing him, shaking off water and baying as they went. The boar was hobbled from a slug and the dogs kept worrying him as they ran together across an open plowed field, when the pig ran into a bush and squared around to face them.

I started hurrying down the canal, looking for a place to cross, until I was opposite the dogs and pig. The pig was bristled up, keeping his haunches on the ground to prevent an attack there, and fought the dogs for many minutes, standing and turning and squatting down again, catching one dog with his snout and tusks so the pointer-looking dog cartwheeled end over end through the moted air. I was about 40 yards away, blocked by the canal; every time I tried to get my sight on the boar, he got into a dog, or another grabbed him from the opposite side. Finally, one of Ammar's assistants, carrying his own shotgun, got up to the boar and finished it before any of the dogs were seriously hurt.

By the last afternoon of the hunt, I was prepared to go home, satisfied with two large sows, though wishing I could have many of my missed shots back, especially on the large boar. We had spread out around another reed bed with the beaters coming toward us, the old man Ove visible off to my left and Richard to my right, Richard bent over to tolerate the pain. I could just begin to hear the beaters when the big boar came out of the reeds toward me, running on the sandy ground.

I couldn't help feeling excitement as he came, his ears straight up and hackles raised. Everything about him looked big. I shot too soon the first time and heard the sickening whine of the slug ricocheting off the soft soil like a stone skipping off water. Now I waited, and he turned; and I had a hard background behind him; and I hit him back, enough to break his stride. He angled past me toward a fence of palm fronds at the edge of a date grove, heading obliquely in the direction of Richard, when I led him enough and my third shot took him through both shoulders; and he rolled like a barrel, his trotters kicking in the air. I was reloading as he stood again.

He was sick; but he kept running, and I took a fourth shot as he turned at the palm fence and began running directly at Richard. He may not have been charging, at first, just wanting to get away; but as he got closer to Richard, and could begin to make him out, he clearly meant, at the least, to run over him, rather than swerve around. Richard, watching the boar, reached onto the top of his over-and-under and detached the scope he carried on it from its claw mounts, dropping it gently onto the sand, then lifted the gun and lined up the sights. I yelled at him to shoot, but he kept waiting. He explained later that he had not wanted to damage my trophy by shooting too soon and perhaps hitting the tusks. Only when the boar seemed to be at his boot laces did he fire at the crown of its skull.

The boar sommersaulted, and Richard went down. I was going to him, thinking he'd been struck, when the boar started to stand again. I yelled again to Richard who was trying to get up as the pain of the sciatica shot through him; and from his knees he managed to lift the over-and-under from the sand beside him, break it open, replace the empty 16-gauge hull in the top barrel, and shoot the massive wild boar in the head, once more, then collapse face down in the sand as the wild boar kicked out its last breath beside him.

I made it to him as from somewhere one of the dogs came up and began tugging at the pig-scented hide on the boar's ham. One of the boar's top tusks was broken, but it was an old break and had nothing to do with Richard's shooting. The pig had not touched Richard, but he had thrown himself out of its path and was now in excruciating pain. As beaters and hunters began to come up, I unloaded my gun and picked up his over-and-under and scope for him, breaking open the gun, noticing that it was a combination gun with the barrel under the top smoothbore chambered for a rimmed 30 Blaser, the reason he had stopped to reload being that he hadn't wanted to "spend" a more costly rifle cartridge on the boar.

I was feeling bad about Richard and ashamed about the ricocheted slug and apologized to everyone, even though I'm not sure there's any way to do that after the shot's gone off; and some accepted it right away, and others did not. It took Richard 20 minutes before he could stand and with help walk even the short distance out to the Land Cruiser on the highway shoulder and to our lunch, that Richard ate without getting out of the vehicle.

We made one more drive in Tunisia, my peg on the edge of a date grove and the beaters coming out of the phragmites. We were a long time, waiting on stand, the drive taking over an hour, without seeing a pig, until I figured we were done, the beaters long past, and walked out through the cool shaded orchard. I met up with Richard where he had been standing at his position, and he came over to me and shook my hand. I saw he was standing upright, and smiling.

"You don't know why I'm shaking your hand, do you?" he asked in his Lancastrian accent.

I had to tell him that I did not.

"Jumping out of the way of the boar," he said, giving his feet a little tap in the sand, "cured my sciatica."

The hunting part of the trip ended after that, with tips handed around in dinar, a currency based on the 2,200-year-old Roman coin, the *denarius,* hands shaken, and *shukrans* spoken. For me, a further ending came some weeks later, back home in a dentist's chair, an oral surgeon breaking off pieces of the shattered tooth, drilling, probing, pulling, until he had all the fragments out, to his satisfaction.

You'd be just a little crazy not to wonder about traveling these days to the Maghreb to hunt. You don't have to be Prufrock to worry about bad things happening, even when you only dare to eat a peach, or a date. I guess I could have played it safe, or anyway what I thought was safe, by staying home and not going to Tunisia, not to touch this extreme of Africa, to have avoided any threat—from wild animals, the kind of people armies are hunting now throughout the region, or stone fruit. But then, I would have never seen a tusked wild boar charging, or tasted the sweetness of a ripe deglet noor, fresh from a palm tree and filled with light.

De Rebus Africanis

Sept. 14, 1974

Welcome to the wild. How did it come to this?

A clearing's being hacked from the bush and all these black guys, blacker than any black guys I've ever seen before, are pitching these olive tents, and this lividly white guy, with blond curly hair and a nose broken into about three incongruent planes, is pouring gasoline down all these holes in the ground, then squinting into them. I've already been warned about the oleaginous little creek behind camp, that they call the Njugini River. Crocs.

So I ask the white guy, whose name is John Fletcher—who has been a professional hunter since the 1950s, after he was a volunteer in the "pseudo-gangs" during the Kenya Emergency, prepared to disguise himself as a Mau Mau and infiltrate the insurgents, seriously—about the gas; and he says, "Cobras." Is this what I had in mind?

"Nasty piece of business," he adds, dropping lit matches into the holes. The whooshing flames should drive them out, though I am tactful enough not to inquire where they might be driven to from out of dark holes in the ground, in which I am happy for them to remain.

63

This evening in Kenya I'm 22 years old and throwing money at a problem by taking all that I have, and probably ever will, and throwing it directly at Africa. My friend, Bill Cullen, is along with me, not to hunt but to see. We have driven all day in the Land Cruiser, followed by the green Bedford lorry, seeing towering giraffes off the tarmac, then on dirt roads through small villages, all the roads evaporating into trackless cross-country journeying, sticking the lorry at a ford of the bigger Rombo River and winching it out, coming at last to where a camp can be raised.

In the hotel room the day before—after having picked up thousands of Kenyan schillings in bundles of dog-eared bills from an Indian jewelry *duka* in a sketchy neighborhood, part of a highly speculative transaction over discount airline tickets that began with a phone negotiation to somebody with a Punjabi accent in Vancouver, Canada, caught up with us in London, and came to a dubious settlement in a shop in Nairobi with an enormous truncheon-wielding African guard at the door and wide drawers stuffed with flimsy currency filed like documents—not realizing we were on the verge of nervous collapse from our abrupt advent in Africa, we were rearranging our "kit" to take what we required into the field, and to leave behind what was unnecessary, when we heard the woman's screams coming from the street below through the open window.

Looking out, we saw a white woman floors below being hurried onto the sidewalk out of the crosswalk by her companion, his arm around her shoulder, a genuine mob gathering about an isolated black man, pleading his complete innocence. Deadly violence seemed preordained, but the man made his desperate case and was released, hurrying off with his head down and not looking back. Leaving us lurching around the room in the grips of savage panic, some monkey demon having flapped its invisible way through the room on leathern pinions, its scent of sulfurous corruption filling our nostrils and triggering near hysteria. By morning we were calmed, and hungover, enough to leave Nairobi gladly behind.

To return to the question, I don't think I can truly say why I'm here except that I've always wanted to hunt something more than the deer and birds I've known at home, and that seemed to mean Africa—after years of dreaming the place, now's my chance to meet it in the flesh, and blood. (No, I can say why, its having to do with the head of an African buffalo, even if only a dwarf forest one, seen hanging on a wall when I was no more than five and seeming unfathomably wondrous; and there it was, an ember that never was extinguished, our most lasting desires traceable back to such ages.)

At this late stage of the game, though, exactly who goes on safari in Kenya anyway? Safari. What an odd sounding word in this day and age. A month of hunting. Hunting, hunting, hunting till hell will not have it.

How had I wandered this far from home?

Sept. 15, 1974

Is this what I had in mind?

I didn't sleep last night, my first with only canvas between me and whatever the hell is out there in the bush of Africa. Either too many wild sounds and wild voices, or not enough, silence here as unnerving as roars.

On the way out to sight in the rifles we find a very large, very fresh leopard pug in the dust of the two track, and I put my index finger into the center of its pad mark, feeling a shiver run through me clear to my foppish desert boots. Then, having zeroed in the guns, Fletcher and the trackers and I head out into this Rombo Kuku country to find camp meat, and I guess what for me could only be termed "first blood," vis-à-vis Africa.

We spot a herd of hartebeest (*kongoni* in Swahili)—a hypothetical animal designed by Cubists—and I fire my first-ever shot at the game of Africa. And sail it clean over the back of a big bull. The herd detonates and my second shot kills a cow through, it would seem, no particular fault of my own.

Somewhere this side of Tanzania we come across some Grant's gazelles, and I hit a fine buck too far back and the Samburu tracker and I have to run after it till it falls.

Is this really what I had in mind?

Sept. 16, 1974

Eggs, tea, and toast and then we drive out in the morning past the *manyatta* where the Maasai live—only Maasai don't live here anymore, rings of white ash the only evidence of their recent occupation. Fletcher says somebody died in this place and the Maasai burned down all the stick and cow-dung houses and moved on.

Today I have to shoot a waterbuck again after it gets up after my first shot. Then I go on to miss a zebra clean, and another kongoni, too. Hear my first lion roaring, along with the trumpeting of elephant. These scrubby yellow plains are filled with animals; and most of the time they act as if we're not here, like it's a time before we ever appeared on earth. Until I open fire on them, of course, throwing lead as if it were rice tossed at a bride and groom.

Sept. 17, 1974

Today it's a fringe-eared oryx's turn in the barrel.

Fletcher and I stalk to a termite hill and he urges calm deliberation—and for Christ's sake shoot straight. I know, this time, that I will kill this animal absolutely. I squeeze the trigger . . . and squeeze . . . and squeeze some more.

Nada. I am clueless. Fletcher sees that I'm starting to melt down and obligingly points out to me that I've neglected to take off the safety. Now I jerk the trigger and gutshoot the oryx. We trail the bull all morning until we lose his blood and tracks on bare rocky ground.

At noon we meet up with another safari car. We lunch with a Mr. P., of a famed newspaper family, his entourage, including a young woman not his wife, and his professional hunter. While I turn away, pretending to be engrossed in peeling a hardboiled egg so no one will see my face, Mr. P., in his tailored Palm Beach accent, tells us all what a ball this hunting is. Just a ball.

Running oryx are all I can see.

Sept. 18, 1974

What'd old Ortega y Gasset say, about how in our stupid time, hunting is not considered a serious matter? Serious as a heart attack's what I say. Maybe more serious than I'm ready for.

So here's to a frivolous day. *Callooh!* And, to be sure, *Callay!*

Spend a whole bunch of it moving lava rock from off the unbeaten path to make way for the Land Cruiser. Run across our first black rhino, *kifaru*— which is one animal I don't think I can, in good conscience, shoot anymore— who squints in amorous prehistoric dimness at the Cruiser while the trackers whistle and snort invitingly. See where the Maasai goats and sheep have grazed the land down to bare dirt. Even spot one herdsman and his goats across the line in the national park, Tsavo, illicitly helping themselves to the grass there.

Kind of fun playing tourist all day, not having to fire a shot. Not having to be serious about hunting anything.

Not watching anything run away, wounded.

Sept. 19, 1974

Another day when nothing gets hunted.

Spot a herd of elephant standing like red-gray boulders this afternoon in the shade of an acacia tree. Fletcher carries his 500 Nitro double, and I my 35mm single-lens reflex camera, determined to be just a neutral observer. We stalk to within 30 yards of the herd. All cows and calves. Elephant hunting is closed, but Fletcher shows me where you shoot to kill an elephant, as a point of interest. I snap a few pictures as quietly as I can, and we duck-walk our way out. About 100 yards from the elephant we stand, and I take maybe three steps before I hear, behind me, Fletcher say that I should run. I look back while running to see him leveling his double at a cow as big as the Ritz, coming at him with her ears flapped out. Fletcher doesn't even twitch, and things sort themselves out with no shots fired.

I'm not even hunting and I can still get killed, and an elephant almost killed, because I wanted to take her picture! Somehow that possibility is never mentioned in the brochures for photo safaris.

After barbecued lamb for dinner tonight, Fletcher informs me we're almost out of meat, which is something that hasn't occurred to me: that we will be living off what we (I) hunt. He says the "lads" were looking forward to me hunting more so they'd have plenty of meat (*nyama*) to dry and take home after the safari. Wives, kids (*watoto*), that sort of thing. Says he can radio Nairobi and have them send out more meat. Or we can buy some sheep, or perhaps a goat, from the Maasai. Or I can hunt something for us all to eat. Entirely up to me, of course.

Of course.

Sept. 20, 1974

Woke this morning with fever and chills. Not life-threatening, just a pain in the ass. Or arse.

Heading back toward where we saw Mr. Kifaru day before yesterday, we sight a herd of zebra (*punda milia*, "the donkey with stripes") in the distance. Fletcher says we should take one and gets his 375 and tells one of the trackers to hand me my "three-oh-oh." He tells me to carry my rifle across my shoulder, like a Maasai carries his lion spear, and we can walk up close to the zebra. About 300 yards from the herd we go behind some brush and use it to stalk within 150 yards. Fletcher looks over the herd and tells me to take the big stallion with his head turned toward us. I'm having trouble holding the crosshairs on him; but I take a breath, let a little out, and when I have the two wires crossing over his heart and lungs, fire. The zebra's tail shoots straight out, and as the rest of the herd gallops off through the heat waves, the stallion runs with them. Fletcher just turns and walks away, whistling.

I call to him in distress, "I couldn't have missed," wondering to myself how the hell I must have. It's then that the stallion peels out of the running herd.

"No," Fletcher says, putting on his sunglasses. "You killed him."

The zebra raises dust circles as the herd vanishes, then falls, stands, falls, brays, and is still.

"Lady of Spain, I adooore you," sings John Fletcher, lying on his back on the hood of the Land Cruiser, one bare leg crossed over the other.

Sept. 21, 1974

I try to puzzle why I am here. What I have is the child's memory from when I was five. It is night and there is a small wood-paneled den and the smell of tobacco and bourbon. On the walls are the head of an elk, a wild boar, a red dwarf forest buffalo, and a pair of rose-ivory tusks, the last two having come from French Equatorial Africa. The man whose den it is will teach me to hunt and come to mean more to me than my own father, whose life is mostly self-inflicted torment I had every desire not to replicate. And those animals on the wall, especially the buffalo head and the elephant tusks, map the trail that has brought me here. Somehow it's not always great trauma or spectacular events that map us. Sometimes, it's a head on the wall of the house of a man you know.

I'll wait till tomorrow to record what happened today.

Sept. 22, 1974

Yesterday: I killed the leopard in the morning, and then the lion in the afternoon. Big maned male. Spotted him late in the afternoon in the brush along the river bank. Fletcher and I dropped out of the Land Cruiser as it drove on, and crawled to an old log where we lay for hours, watching his maned head in the brush, ticks scuttling in over our belts and rambling inside our pants. At almost last light the lion stood and walked out into the open. When he got 75 yards from us, Fletcher said take him, and I felt all the tensed muscles in my face relax as I put the crosshairs of my "three-seven-five" on the lion's shoulder. He went over with a roar and lay still and I jumped up to run to him, but Fletcher jerked me back, getting right in my face and hissing at me, "It's the dead ones kill you."

Now, this morning after the night before, the sky is blue with high thin clouds, and my entire skull throbs like a purple bruise as I try to swallow some orange juice and aspirins.

When we agreed to finish off the cognac bottle, I remember Fletcher saying, "Good you killed your lion now. Lions are for young men."

And today could be spent in good conscience shooting sandgrouse. Big fun on the Rombo!

Sept. 23, 1974

In camp by lantern light this morning the skinners and trackers are divvying up the lion fat that's been scraped from the hide and carcass so they can take it home to rub on their watoto when they get the croup. Sandgrouse today for Fletcher and me under the most azure sky I've ever seen. The sun rises through the thorn scrub surrounding the water and the brownish birds come in high, laying back their wings and losing altitude, little feathered quanta of both kinetic and potential energy. It's pass shooting along the vertical axis, and Fletcher shoots quite well, and I don't shoot too bad, either, and we're done in time to make it back to camp for breakfast.

On the way in we pass an unburned manyatta, the sod roofs green with clumps of grass. A small pack of Maasai dogs comes out to bark at us, their leader a bony, scruffy bitch with nipples pendulous. In the afternoon we glass for lesser kudu from a hill and plan to hunt greater kudu somewhere up north—after we deal with buffalo.

The tubes on the single sideband glow this evening as Fletcher runs through the dial, picking up random communiques from camps and ranches. He stops on one where a worker is listing supplies he needs brought out.

"Tep," the long-range voice says in his Kenyan accent. "We need tep."

"I am sorry," comes back the English *mzungu* voice. "What do you need?"

"I need tep. For the pipes."

"What is 'tep'?"

The Kenyan worker is raising his voice now.

"'Tep.' Tay-a-pay-a. Tep!"

"I am not understanding you, I am afraid. You are saying 'tep'?"

"Yes, tep!"

"I don't know what you mean."

"Tep. Tep. For the pipes."

"'Tep,' you said?"

"Yes. Yes. Tep!"

"Tep?"

Fletcher snatches up the microphone and presses the key.

"Tape," he shouts, "you bloody jackass! Tape!"

"I say," comes the *mzungu* voice, "who's that on the radio?"

Fletcher has already hung the mic back up, and I toss the ball to 'Because' in center field.

Sept. 24, 1974

Pteroclididae (so my field guide calls them) once more at dawn when the air is soft as brushed suede. Back at camp, as we breakfast, three Maasai *morani* appear, having heard that I've killed a lion. Their polished spear blades are shards of light, their hair greased and plaited and ochred. They are all about my age or a little younger, but in their red togas seem as stately as praetorian guards. Nodding in approval when shown the lion skin, they grip our hands and then head off, waving as they go.

Later a golden cloud of dust rises on the horizon, and in a few minutes a small Datsun, beaten into scrap metal, arrives. A tall figure contorts himself out of the car, and I meet another PH, Abdullah, grandson of the sultan of Zanzibar, who has come to scout the area for his next safari. After coffee, Abdullah, who speaks like an Etonian compared to Fletcher's colonial-cowboy accent, departs on his "recky," and I realize that it's going to take more time than I have to get to know any of these Africans well.

In the afternoon we spot three big crocs beached like driftwood on a river bank, and they vanish at the speed of saurian thought when they spot us. Hunt lesser kudu in the thick brush, finally spotting one. He's in range, but after studying him carefully, Fletcher says his horns only make a little more than one spiral, instead of the two full turns we're hunting for.

More elephant at the end of the day, and at last light I drop a decent oryx bull at 200 yards with my first shot, more meat for dinner and for the staff. We break camp tomorrow and head for buffalo country to take a couple of bulls quickly, then off for greater kudu.

Sept. 26, 1974

Sitting at the sidewalk cafe outside the New Stanley Hotel, amid the ugly city bustle of "Nairobbery" redux, trying to catch up this journal before lunch with Fletcher, who is out resupplying us.

Break camp yesterday and drive to Amboseli to spend the night at a lodge. At the entrance a moran, dressed in photographic costume, stands with a spear polished to a quicksilver sheen. In English he asks Bill, seated in the left-hand passenger's seat, if he would like to purchase a picture. When Bill declines, the moran goes back to polishing his spear with a cloth, smiling enchantingly as he says to Bill, "You are terribly white."

To the pool for a dip and find two European girls there, one very pretty. Am forced to enter the water to disguise my admiration. Then a neurasthenic-looking boyfriend appears. Spend the afternoon touring the yellow circumference of Amboseli with a game ranger. Against the snowy backdrop of Kilimanjaro the ancient lakebed is marked with herds of wildebeest and zebra, buffalo, rhino, elephant, and a lioness asleep on her back, paws limp in the air. Nice, but I believe what I most want to do is climb out of the Land Cruiser and walk among the animals, which is prohibited.

At dinner Joy Adamson herself circulates among the tables, working the crowd. ("For Christ's sake," Fletcher advises, soto voce, "don't tell her you killed a lion.") Fletcher heads for his room after dinner, and Bill and I discover the two girls in the lounge, with boyfriend. Boyfriend (who is not surprisingly not feeling well) leaves, and we find ourselves in conversation with the girls. They are Swiss. Cousins. The pretty one is Ruth ("Root"). She does not like Switzerland—too restricting. She wants, she says, to be "*frei.*" What a coincidence, I tell her. Frei is what I want to be, too. I ask about the boyfriend. Oh no, she laughs, he is just a traveling companion.

"I do not think he is very . . . suitable," she says, smiling at me. Then he reappears, telling the girls that it is very late. Ruth shakes my hand as she goes.

At daybreak as Fletcher and I are leaving, Ruth appears beside the Land Cruiser, smiling, bidding me goodbye. Fletcher stares openly. As we drive away from the lodge, I see the faux boyfriend in a gift-shop T-shirt, kowtowing to take a rock's photograph.

"You some kind of hero to her?" Fletcher asks, arching an eyebrow. I simply smile.

Two miles down the tar road, outside the reserve, we pass the most magnificent lesser kudu ever seen, two-and-half spirals of horn. He stands on the shoulder, watching us go.

Sept. 28, 1974

Hyenas howl outside the tent tonight. First time I've ever heard them. Time to backtrack.

Poisoned at lunch three days ago at a steakhouse in Nairobi. (Tip for Travelers: Think twice about sauce béarnaise in an equatorial zone.) As the dodgy whiff of the sauce boat passes by my nose, I note the Kenyan gold-medal miler, Kipchoge Keino, elegantly besuited, taking a seat at a nearby table. Spent the night in bed at Lake Naivasha hotel, clutching my stomach and flopping like a gaffed fish. Meanwhile, back at the bar, Fletcher was "chatting up" an American bird, inviting her to join us on our safari. Actually, to join him on my safari. Awfully decent of him.

Yesterday we traveled past Maasai Mara and across the Rift Valley. An orphaned elephant calf ran in front of us before turning off into the grass. Lion meat.

We climbed the Escarpment in a cloudburst and found a campsite in Block 60A, one of the most beautiful places in Africa. Ineluctable greenness and tangled bush ("Right sporty for buffalo," Fletcher enthused). As soon as camp was up, I swallowed a handful of sulfa pills and went to bed.

This morning I feel well enough to hunt in earnest. We spot a bushbuck, brown as cocoa powder, who vanishes before we can even begin a stalk. See some eland later, and stalk them, too. We crawl the last 50 yards, lying behind a small hillock, the eland very close. A large aquatinted cow walks within 20 yards of us, staring hard at our motionless figures. She makes a loud, hoarse bark and moves off from us. Catching our wind, she trots away, drawing another eland cow with her; and we peer over the hillock, seeing the rest of the herd a few dozen yards away, but no big bulls. Just beyond the eland there is a good kongoni bull, and I take him through the shoulder. We skin and quarter him and hurry into camp ahead of more rain.

After lunch the sky clears, and I go for a walk, unarmed. I kick up oribi and warthogs. Then something huge and unseen begins roaring in the heavy bush, the ground literally vibrating, so I mosey back to camp, making it in alive. Hot hors d'oeuvres ("toasties") and whiskey on ice around the campfire at sundown, then kongoni fillets wrapped in bacon for dinner. Hope this buffalo hunting doesn't take too long.

Sept. 29, 1974

At dawn three buffalo bulls are at the edge of a thicket. They spot us and move off. We follow on foot through tall grass and suddenly there is a rhino less than 100 yards away, drifting past. Everyone freezes, thumbs on safeties. The kifaru moves on by, and we creep forward until we come to a solid wall of bright green leaves into which the mbogo disappeared. We can hear them bedded in there, rumbling and grunting, and I pray, Please, don't tell me we're going in there. And without my saying anything, Fletcher says, No, we'll come back in the late afternoon.

Which proves to be something far worse, because I have all day to think about it. I hardly see the country we move through until we find our way in the last hour of light back to the thicket. The trackers pick up the spoor and we follow it into the bush.

Inside it is not as impenetrable as I thought, 40 or 50 feet of visibility around us. Maybe this won't be so bad. Then in the next instant there is a terrible crashing and grunting, the sound of trees splintering and limbs snapped off by horns and bosses. We can see nothing except the shaking of the bush, and nobody knows which way tons of stampeding buffalo flesh are headed. The noise begins to fade, finally becoming total silence, broken only by a soft, anonymously voiced, "F——."

There is lightning in the Rift Valley as we drive through the darkness. We come across a band of morani and they ride with us for a few miles, before jumping off to walk away into the night, giggling. Fletcher drives nervously, scared to death of running over bunnies caught in the headlights. I slump in the left-hand seat, scared to death of something of another order all together.

Oct. 1, 1974

Fletcher is displeased with the size of the buffalo we've seen (many very small—*kidogo sana*—bulls), so yesterday we broke camp and moved to another spot about 10 miles away. Here it is more of the same: mbogo in the open by the dawn's early light, then they move into the bush and we follow.

It is cool inside the bush, the ground covered in leaf litter. Enormous elephant tunnels drill through parts of it, the elephant tracks filled with muddy water; invisible bushbucks bark like dogs within feet of us; the sound of rhino entirely too close for comfort ("Be ready," Fletcher whispers, nodding toward the 375 in my hands); 400-pound giant forest hogs mistaken for buffalo; and always buffalo when least expected, crashing off, or worse, slipping away warily, alert to us, but not in the least intimidated.

I do kill an excellent warthog today, the curved ivory of his footlong tusks clean and white and clear, his mane of bristles draping thickly over his neck,

Tonight Fletcher tells me that the trackers have a name for me, *Bwana Cheka,* the "laughing bwana" (Bill is *Bwana Fisi,* "hyena," for his apparent willingness to eat virtually anything). They find me amusing, while mostly I'm sort of tired of getting the piss scared out of me.

Is this what I had in mind?

Oct. 2, 1974

Early this morning I flat miss two easy shots at a good bushbuck before he springs back into the bush. I stand there in silence. Fletcher stares at me in silence. The trackers study me in silence. I don't know which silence is the worst.

Later in the cool, cloudy morning, from the top of a green hill of Africa, we spot four very distant buffalo bull's, too far to stalk. Walking back to the Land Cruiser through a swale, we see a defassa waterbuck rear his magnificent head out of the tall grass as he moves uphill, away from us. He halts, skylined, about 200 yards away.

"Take him," Fletcher whispers.

I hold just behind the waterbuck's shoulder, just above the top of the grass. Now I shoot carefully, and at the sound of the rifle the waterbuck just disappears.

"Safety on," Fletcher commands, and we sprint up the hill. Just on the other side of the ridge we find him lying in the grass, his 30-inch horns wide-flared, the 300's bullet having passed through the top of his heart.

The afternoon is all buffalo stalking, all the time. Doubled over, stomach and back muscles aflame, I stalk two bulls with Fletcher through lightning and lashing rain, only to have them prove kidogo sana, their hides bald in big patches, as buffalo hides are wont to be. Then we cross the slick mud of a gully and go after a large herd on our hands and knees, crawling around an elephant cow black from the rain (which also soaks through our clothing), finally getting close enough to the buffalo to see that they are all cows, calves, and young bulls. The wind swirls our scent to them and the herd runs and wheels, then halts. For a moment the question is, Are they going to charge or not? as all the buffalo stare back at us with their heads held high, their hides shiny and wet, my heart thudding like a two-stroke engine. Then a flash of lightning lights up the world and at the thunderclap the herd gallops off, leaving us to head back to camp to warm and dry our soggy frozen asses. Or arses.

Oct. 4, 1974

Yesterday we moved camp again. Drove through a dusty village, Kilgoris, whose largest building is the Nylon Bar & Hotel, then many miles beyond it to a new campsite among tall trees. We're becoming a bit like gypsies here in Block 60A, striking the tents at a moment's notice and loading up the lorry to shove off in search of someplace greener, someplace we hope at last to call home. But all we seem to find is more of the same when it comes to buffalo.

This morning, cool enough for a sweater, we crawl through tall grass and fresh steaming buffalo *mavi* to get up on a herd at first light, only to have them slip into the thick stuff on us. So, of course, we follow. As usual, we find ourselves in the middle of a whole damn herd, buffalo slowly lowering their heads beneath the leaves to glare at us, then the herd stampeding, the effect probably equivalent to having a line of boxcars derail around you.

In the afternoon we find a couple of morani who'll show us the country. They take us through a densely foliated draw where we find the day-old track of an enormous bugger. Then there is a deep ditch to be crossed, and the morani and Fletcher drop down and climb out of it; but when it's my turn, I have trouble dragging myself out. Which is when our Samburu tracker, who has not crossed yet, begins to snap his fingers softly and whisper loudly, "Mbogo, mbogo," pointing down the ditch. I look up at the morani, and they are holding their right arms cocked back, their left arms stretched out in front of them, preparing to hurl their spears, and all I can think is that I am about to be trampled to absolute death right here in this gully. Somehow or another I am up the sheer bank of the ditch in a twinkling and standing ready, my 375 at port arms. The stampede does not materialize, though, and easing forward we find the hoof print of the giant forest hog at the root of all the commotion.

I am disappointed, more than I might have expected. I'm beginning to feel that I'm getting the hang of this buffalo hunting, and that, all told, more of the same may not be so bad. Curiouser and curiouser.

Oct. 5, 1974

Regrettably, as I take pen in hand by lantern light, I find I may have dined somewhat too well.

Get this close today to a huge bull. *Mbogo mkubwa sana.* Mbogo. Mbogo. Old Maasai tells us where some are. And there they are, feeding. In the open! Five bulls with one very big one. We crawl up on them through the wet grass, knowing that this is finally going to be the one, when they all turn and trot into the bush and keep going. We look around, and there, 50 yards behind us, is the old Maasai standing in the wide open on an anthill, craning to get a good look at the running buffalo. Fletcher goes up to him, furious, chastising him for spooking the big bull; but all the Maasai hears is "mbogo mkubwa sana," and nods with satisfaction. I told you, he says. And what can you say?

Hunt through some more thickets, but all we find is the rotting, vulture-shit-spattered carcass of a small elephant, the tusks chopped out.

"They're really starting to hammer things," Fletcher says, meaning poachers.

Get back to camp in early afternoon, and we decide to have a drink. Then decide that all this buffalo business, and the wasted elephant, is simply too much. One thing leads to another. Holding a glass of white rum against his chest, Fletcher worries out loud that if we don't find a bloody buffalo soon, we won't have time to make it over to the greater-kudu country.

How can there be a time limit to Africa? To hunting?

I want a room by the year at the Nylon Bar & Hotel and an open *pombe* tab there. I want to wear baggy shorts all the time, own a beat-up Land Rover, carry a double with the bluing worn where I've held it by the barrels over my shoulder. I might even want to wear a goddamn gardenia behind my ear. I want all of this to stay just the way it is.

I have most definitely dined too well.

Oct. 7, 1974

I feigned sleep when one of the camp staff came to my tent at dawn yesterday to light my lantern and serve me my morning cup of chai. One look at me was all he needed, though, to sigh and turn off the lantern without attempting to wake me. But I had to get out of bed to pee and Fletcher called to me from the dining tent, "Feel fit to hunt?" Of course, I lied, feeling worse than death.

The day was pure hell, but (luckily) we didn't find any buffalo big enough to concern ourselves with. I am never going to hunt in this sorry condition again, he said.

Today is immeasurably better. Pick up another moran guide and I take a good topi and one more black-and-white punda, again right through the heart. We drop the moran back at his manyatta, giving him the fat and some of the haunches from the two animals.

In the afternoon we spot a large buffalo herd at the edge of a thicket, and as we are stalking them we hear a simba grunting, very close. The mbogo hear the lion, too, and quickly bunch up, edging into the bush. We move to an anthill near the bush, and we can now hear something going on in the thicket. The bush is shaking, leaves trembling, the cracking of trees and buffalo bellowing as two bulls battle, unseen. If they come out fighting, Fletcher says, he'll tell me which one to take, and I am ready, elbows locked over knees, 375 at my shoulder.

The sound moves away, dimming. We circle the thicket, then move in, twisting and winding on the buffalo's trail through the dense bush. Very boggy and slow going. We hunt through the bush and back out into the open without finding the buffalo. Once we're in the open, though, the herd emerges 30 yards behind us, and we drop to the ground and watch them pass, not a bull in sight.

Fletcher tells me tonight that he thinks kudu are out now. I'm not sure I mind that much. I want to see this Cape buffalo hunting out to the end.

Oct. 9, 1974

One more camp, probably the last of the safari. A thin ribbon of a creek trickles through it, the water cold and drinkable, this creek absolutely too small for crocs.

Hunt out of camp late yesterday afternoon on foot. Find a clearing with fresh buffalo sign, following the tracks into a muddy thicket where we soon hear the all-too-familiar ruckus of buffalo dashing away when we get close to them. It's only a matter of time before one of these herds runs the other way.

Last night there are mbogo walking through camp. A warm breeze washes over us as we hike out before daylight, heading back for last night's clearing. We pass two manyattas, fast asleep, except for a couple of Maasai who come hurriedly out of the second one, wrapping their robes around themselves and telling us that three bulls feed every morning in a clearing just past the next thicket.

We hurry now, and there are indeed three buffalo bulls, one of them very respectable, his horns 42 or 43 inches wide. The bulls are grazing away from us, but haven't gotten our wind yet. Fletcher glasses them for what seems forever, then says, Yes, that one, the one in the middle.

I sit and try to get a solid rest, try to watch my breathing; but in the end I just pull the trigger. And hit the bull. He starts to spin slowly, and the other two bulls turn and run in our direction, their hooves spraying the dew from the grass as they angle past us. There is altogether far too much shooting, all around, before the very old and wall-eyed buffalo is dead.

Asante sana, the trackers politely say, thanking me for the nyama as they shake my hand. But nobody's genuinely smiling.

I have a buffalo, but everybody knows that this is not the way it should have been. Whatever way it should have been ought to be different from this.

Oct. 10, 1974

No time left for greater kudu now—just have to come back again (though who knows, as the herders expand the ranges they graze their herds in and the poachers step up their activity, and as this country and the whole damned world change, how much longer there'll be any of this left to come back to?). There may still be time enough to do it right with buffalo, though.

Chase a herd into a thicket this evening, circling around the bush to catch them as they come out, and have to stare down a cow. There are shouldered rifles and safeties off, until she lumbers off blackly into the spreading night with the herd.

"Well done," Fletcher says, resetting the safety on his 500, noting some unaccustomed grace under pressure on my part.

As I thumb back the safety on my 375, the Samburu tracker offers his compliments. Only after it is all over does my heart begin to beat just a little faster.

Oct. 11, 1974

Hunt in the thickets again this morning with the usual results. Eat a cold lunch from the chop box in the shade of a tree. Another moran has joined up with us.

While Fletcher retires with the bung wad, the Maasai and I engage in a contest of spear throwing. These six-foot lion spears are even heavier than they look. The moran dashes out to retrieve one of his extended throws and peers at the ground, waving to me. I walk over and he points to the thick, coppery body of a snake lying in the grass. Like little kids, we toss sticks at the snake, trying to get it to raise its head. Maybe it'll even hiss at us.

Fletcher wanders back and comes over to see what we're up to.

"Ah," he remarks with the appreciation of an Ionides, "a spitting cobra." Outstanding.

In the afternoon we jump a bushbuck who plunges into a small patch of bush. When the trackers circle around, trying to push him out, I hear him break from cover behind me. I turn and he's already 50 yards away, stretched out in a full run. In another 50 yards he'll be behind more bush. I bring up my 300, thumb off the safety, and swing the sights through him, like leading a bird. When the sights are just in front of his chest, making sure not to halt my swing, I squeeze the trigger, and the bushbuck kicks out his hind legs as he disappears behind the bush.

I hear an intake of breath beside me and Fletcher saying, "Good shot, lad!" I'm not so certain, but we run to where the bushbuck went out of sight and find a wide blood trail in the grass. A hundred feet along it we find the buck, shot through the heart. I kneel and run my hand over his white-marked brown hide, soft and long as dressed fur.

"Right where I was aiming," I tell Fletcher, who refrains from telling me exactly how full of shit I am.

Oct. 12, 1974

Tomorrow's it, and this morning, just for laughs, we crawl after buffalo again. And guess what—they get away!

Lunch in camp is the finest impala curry of my life. Then a nap. When I awake, I lie on my cot, staring at the leaf shadows dappling the tent canvas, and think how I could live 1,000 days like this.

In the afternoon, Fletcher sends the trackers one way to scout for buffalo, while he and I hike back to where we saw the buff this morning. As we near the place, a Maasai watoto appears, asking us if we're looking for buffalo.

What comes of it is a tricky stalk, some tense moments, and a perfect shot that sends the bull collapsing like unreinforced masonry in an earthquake.

After dinner tonight, Fletcher raises his glass of cognac and says, "Very well done, indeed."

This buffalo is the way they should always be.

Oct. 13, 1974

Spend this last day walking around the country, hunting with my eyes. Plenty of nyama now for everyone to take home, so it's time to put up the guns.

Tonight there's no wind and the olive canvas of the tents hangs slack in the dark. It feels goddamn cold out here, even with hundreds of fireflies in the air. Funny how it could feel this cold in Africa. Everybody else is asleep, but I've pulled my camp chair close to the fire. The wood's burning down, and the smoke'll probably shift into my eyes in a minute. But while yellow flames are still leaping from the wood, I don't want to sleep, not yet.

I don't really know what else to write about what I've learned. I probably haven't learned a thing (a "bloody" thing, Fletcher might say), at least not anything I can put into words, no wiser now than I was at five in my father's friend's house. As I watch the fire, I feel myself sort of falling into it. In Swahili, Fletcher says, they call it *kuota moto*, "dreaming the fire." Swahili's the trade language the old Arab ivory traders invented. I like the la-la sound of it. I guess there's a lot of other things I like, too. But, as I say, I don't think I can write them down. I guess I'll just go on dreaming this fire until the flames all burn away. And wonder how I can bring myself to leave this place that seems to be where all the maps have led.

No, this isn't at all what I had in mind. And what I want is more of it. What else is there to write?

Tiger, Tiger

The 1990s . . .

*M*OSIATUNYA, "SMOKE THAT THUNDERS." Or is it "mouse that roared"? Either way it's Dodge, so get the hell out of it.

A decade and a half before, this town of Victoria Falls was mostly broiling tin roofs, stunned lizards appliqued to whitewashed walls, one very colonial hotel in which to take a gin of an afternoon, and Africans in shiny black pants and tire-tread sandals squabbling in broken English over who was to porter the bags out to the battered safari car. It was where ruddy hunting clients arrived to go a-whacking outsized quadrupeds and Katherine Hepburn doppelgängers materialized with Tilley hats and field guides. That was when it was still old Africa.

This time around the decor was pastel, the new airport had arcade ceilings and indirect lighting; earth-tone knits and silk shirts had replaced shiny black pants and white shirts, and basket-weave Gucci loafers supplanted sandals. The English was decidedly unbroken, as was the French, Italian, and Japanese being spoken into cell phones no bigger than sparrows. With a Rolex on every wrist, Africans in Mercedes vans idled in the white zone (For The Immediate Loading And Unloading Of Passengers Only), waiting

to collect their Banana Republic–clad, adventure-traveling charges come to Whitewater, Balloon, Honeymoon, all of which are capitalized verbs these days. Forty-five minutes of cooling my heels there in another August, searching for a bush pilot to enable me to escape new Africa, made me welcome that fact that I was packing only fishing rods and not my 375. This is how international incidents are averted.

Africa this time meant tigerfish on the Zambezi River in Zambia. Salmon-shaped and silver-sided with broken black horizontal stripes, soft dorsal fins, a swallowtail the color of gill filaments, a hinged upper jaw the better to eat you with, and a toothed grin right out of *Alien,* the tiger, a relative of the South American piranha and dorado, is regularly acclaimed the "supreme sporting fish of African fresh water." Various species of *Hydrocynus* ("water dog") are found in rivers throughout the continent; the largest, the Congo's *H. goliath,* grows to six feet and over 100 pounds, with the all-tackle record settling in at 97 pounds. Voracious, cannibalistic, and said sometimes to hunt in packs, goliaths will attack anything in the water, including crocodiles.

They have even taken chunks from humans. British angling writer Jeremy Wade (who with the appositely named Paul Boote co-authored the renowned fishing book *Somewhere Down the Crazy River* before going into TV) has given goliath the title "the most horrifying freshwater fish in the world." The somewhat smaller (all-tackle record, 35 pounds 7 ounces; the fly record, 22 pounds 8 ounces) and much more common *H. vittatus* of the Zambezi is also horrifying, just less so (the IGFA records book lists only "Vacant" under fly-caught entries for *H. goliath*, and rightly so).

The primary thing I found horrifying about tigerfish was the insistence from my fishing companion, Jonathan Boulton, a well-known South African angler and guide, that we go after them with fly rods alone. Or at least he insisted he would. To me this fishing a fly for a heavily toothed fish, said to hunt in packs, smacked of the angling equivalent of not using anywhere near enough gun. At the least it meant work and wading; and given all those teeth and the various ill-tempered fauna that also call tigerfish country home, there was an element of risk as well, work and risk two attributes I generally prefer to exclude from my angling. However, if this was the only way of escaping Vic Falls International, I was nominally in favor.

And escape we did when the bush pilot (definitely ruddy, the barroom tan of his forsworn drinking days still in evidence, someone definitely old Africa) appeared in the afternoon, loaded Jonathan and me and our gear into his Cessna and carried the two of us 250 kilometers northwest through the hazy air up the Zambezi, erasing 15 years and then some. We flew to where the silty Njoko flowed into the green of the Zambezi; where the thatched-roofed *ronadavels* were not tourist "chalets" but the real homes of real herdsmen and farmers; where the airport was a strip of dried grass without a control tower in sight; where during the dusty, open-car ride to Mutemwa Lodge, owned by ex-professional rugger Gavin Johnson and his wife, Penny, we passed basketball-size lumps of elephant dung and tracks as big as hubcaps; where the accommodations were canvas; where in lieu of a floral arrangement a croc's three-foot white skull centerpieced a table in the alfresco dining area.

Jonathan wasted no time getting us out on the river, even though I had no objection to sitting in a folding chair with a sundowner, contemplating the afternoon light and being back in Africa. But we got aboard a small pontoon boat with our Lozi guide Lifuqe (to be pronounced with some care), and motored upstream; and as soon as Lifuqe cut the engine, Jonathan was in the bow, barefoot, lashing the water with an 8-weight shooting head. He made powerful side-to-side false casts, then sent 90 to 100 feet of line out into the Zambezi, quickly tucking the rod grip under his arm and stripping line with both hands so fast it sang, a fine mist spraying from it. Lifuqe, nattily dressed in designer jeans, shirt, and cap, clucked his tongue at Jonathan's curious behavior and handed me a spinning rod with a blue Rapala dangling from it. I wrestled with the fly-or-conventional-tackle question for the better part of three seconds.

On my third cast I hooked the first tiger of my life, all 13 ounces of it. Held in the air, it looked far too mean for its own good. I slid it back into the water and returned to tossing the Rapala, while Jonathan kept casting his big streamer. Later he landed a seven-pound tiger and was, of course, thoroughly chuffed, as they say.

The next morning, the tea tray was set outside the tent flap in the dark; and I sat outside with it, wrapped in a blanket against the soft chill, drinking tea while the sky behind the trees across the river lightened. At dawn we went with Lifuqe in a small outboard downstream to a set of rapids where hippos snorted and rumbled and blew and the white heads of Cape clawless otters bobbed out of the water. This was what Jonathan liked, scrambling out onto the farthest rocks to make the longest possible casts and, I suppose, to get closer to the hippos and crocs. His bravado shamed me into breaking out my 7-weight and an intermediate sinking line.

With only a midday intermission for a shore lunch with Gavin and Penny, I spent the day trying to make long casts of my own (Jonathan, as he passed en route to some other half-submerged rock—ambulatory amuse-bouche for crocodiles, as I saw it—exhorting me to extend at the end of my casts so I resembled "the Interflora man," his name for Hermes in that god's classic, outstretched pose).

By sunset Jonathan had caught several good tigers, while I had none. From some Lozi fishermen in a hollowed-out *makoro* we purchased red-breasted bream to cook that night over leadwood (more poetically *hardekool* in Afrikaans) coals. On the way back to camp the dark carried the fast-food scent of potato bush and the rotting-meat smell of a poached elephant's carcass. Jonathan, who was young, insisted on spotlighting crocodiles all the way to camp, just so I would not forget they were there.

We switched camps the next day. Jonathan was up again before light to cram in as much fishing as he could before the Cessna arrived, while I preferred to lie in bed and watch through the mesh the sun peeking above the trees on the other side of the Zambezi and hear the birds awaken. The bush pilot flew us nearly 1,000 kilometers downriver to Mwambashi River Lodge in Lower Zambezi National Park. Here the river flowing in was the Mwambashi, the Mombashi, or the Mushingashi, take your cartographic pick. Brobdingnagian concrete-colored baobabs grew here, their bare branches looking like root networks threading into the sky; tasseled phragmites reeds lined the shores; and we had to wait for the Cape buffalo to clear the dirt strip before we could land. The lodge sat in a grove of tall, shady winter thorn trees; hippos and buff regularly wandered among the tents at night; and a few days before a herd of 150 elephant had rambled through the grounds. Jonathan had us out fishing as soon as we put down our bags.

The young guide, Kelly, born in then-Rhodesia and a member of the Anglo tribe, rigged me a spinning rod baited with fillets from a small tiger, while he plied his bait with a free-spooling center-pin English coarse–fishing reel mounted on a fly rod. Jonathan remained true to his fly fishing–only creed, hooking into a good tiger on a streamer and shouting "Inside!" (Saffa code, apparently, for "get into the net!") as the fish came out of the water like a fanged tarpon. As he landed it a disgruntled elephant bull, standing nearby on a reed-covered island, flapped his ears and flung clots of mud at us with his trunk.

Even bait fishing takes a certain finesse and patience, in that you must allow the tiger enough time to get the bait down deep before setting the hook, and my general lack of both virtues lost me several tigers. I did manage to land several more that first afternoon and evening, none of any real size. Then one hit, took, and proceeded nearly to spool me before straightening the hook and releasing himself. One in 10. That's what experienced African anglers figure for the ratio of tigerfish landed to tigerfish hooked.

The next day, my finesse and patience improved overnight, I did manage to land some decent ones, seven-, eight- and nine-pounders. Kelly hooked one on his center pin, and amid the sound of the reel handle cracking against his knuckles brought aboard a 15-pound slab of tiger. The spell of the fly rod soon fell upon Kelly, and by noon he was asking Jonathan to show him the way. There seemed no alternative but for me to join the party, too.

I could see the sport in it, to be sure. Choking a tiger on the flesh of its own kind is effective and even somewhat restful, but there is something to be said for convincing one to hook itself on a fly. The work part was clear: all that casting. The risk part came from the 70-some hippos per kilometer in that stretch of the Zambezi, often swirling below the boat; then there were the elephant, which sometimes were in the river, though not usually in sufficient number to pose a hazard; and there were always crocs, Kelly advising me as I waded barefoot not to stay in any one place for any extended period, which gave them time to triangulate one's position.

The main problem with fly fishing, though, was the intense, blinkered concentration it demanded, something Africa kept getting in the way of. Trying to think about my back cast, I would be distracted by a colony of carmine bee-eaters nesting in tiny burrows in the high bank like a curtain of red Christmas lights; a flock of black-crowned night herons perched dazedly in a thorn bush during the day; a herd of buffalo bulls with horn spreads beyond reason grazing on a grassy flat; a six-foot monitor running along the river's edge, its tail waving like a strap of gunmetal-colored leather. I wanted to stop and look, but realized that going after tigers with flies meant being as single-minded as Jonathan, every inch the New African.

Late on the last afternoon, in another country on the other side of the Zambezi, I stood in the tethered boat, wondering if crocs might be venturesome enough to muster a boarding party and tossing out my fly. Kelly and Jonathan were a little downstream, flogging the river relentlessly. By now my casting was looking good, except for this one time when I piled the line and the fly off the side of the boat, not really fishing it. And had a boil right where the fly landed. I jerked the fly back and wondered out loud, "Wuzzat?"

"Flip it in again," voices cried. I did, and nothing happened; so I returned to the long, mighty Interflora-man casts I had come, every once in a while, to perfect. Then I fumbled a cast and piled the line up beside the boat again, and I had a take. I tightened the line, and a three-pound tiger cartwheeled out of the river.

"Inside!" I yelled, for Jonathan's benefit.

I fought the tiger fast to keep it from beating itself to death, beached it, slipped a finger carefully under its gill cover to lift it and had my finger slide through to its jaws, which it promptly clamped down. I had my tiger on a fly, though, and once its teeth were out of my flesh and it was back in the water

I could enjoy the view as the river turned from mercury to rose to black with the sunset.

That night, gin and tonic in hand, shredded index finger throbbing, I sat in a folding chair beside the campfire talking with the 30-ish woman who, with her husband, managed the camp. Hearing the hippos making their throat-clearing sound and the roar of lions from across the water, I thought how this was a good part of the Africa I remembered, the old, slow Africa, where what mattered was the quality of the adventures you had, not the new, vulgar, accelerated Africa where what counted was how many leopards you saw, rivers you ran, or miles you trekked, all crammed into seven-, five-, or even three-day "safari excursions." There were times when the best part of Africa was the one without any adventures at all, and that was the part that seemed to be getting lost, turning the Dark Continent into every other place on earth where tourists went for cheap thrills.

That's what I was thinking as I sat adventure-free, when the woman standing in front of me at the campfire took a drag from her cigarette, exhaled, and in the mildest of voices suggested, "Don't move."

There are places in the world where those words might mean little or nothing, but Africa is so seldom one of them.

"Wuzzit?" I croaked.

She tilted her head slightly, as if to get a better view, then with a hint of a sigh said. "Buffalo."

I heard the crunching noise behind me. I turned my head oh so very slowly to the right and looked over my shoulder at the shape black as the suit of spades, looming 15 feet away. The bull was munching down the seed pods fallen to the ground from the winter thorns as if they were cocktail peanuts, working his way into the firelight. The woman went on smoking; and I cursed myself for being sunk into a low-slung canvas chair, as prepared for a fast escape as a tortoise flipped onto its back.

When the bull came fully into the light, he lifted his head and fixed us with one of his huge round baleful eyes, and the planet ground to a standstill on its axis. Then he dropped his head and went on feeding until the darkness surrounded him and the earth began rotating again.

"That was interesting," I said, letting out my breath.

"Funny thing about them at night," the camp manager said placidly. "If this had been day, we'd be quite dead right now."

I manipulated myself out of the canvas chair, drank down the G&T, and set the empty glass on the camp table. I walked calmly to my tent without a flashlight, having to circle around to the back to avoid the herd of buffalo bulls lying on the river bank right in front of it. In bed in the tent, the lantern extinguished, I listened to the sounds of the insects and amphibians, the contented grunts of the buffalo, the manic noises of hyena, and lions roaring in Zimbabwe. Down the Zambezi lightning flashed, too far for thunder. And then I slept in Africa, neither old nor new, but something that in its heart could never change. And where the laughs just never seem to stop.

Seeing the Elephant

Before . . .

EVEN THOUGH THEY weren't, call them Ahab.

"Ahab" does not fully explain the why of all the men who set off during the 19th century, and startlingly far into the 20th, to follow the elephant's track. Few if any were as existentially obsessed as the good captain with the "whiteness" of the elephant they chose to pursue for their ivory, but they were every bit as interested in those tusks' commercial potential as the old New Bedford whalers were in their particular quarry's oil and baleen. Rare among these men was one who was in it purely for the "sport," however imposing. There was undoubtedly as much exhilaration and awe and, frankly, joy in stalking the largest animal who walks upon the earth's face, while armed with a smooth-bore gun of dubious merit, as there was to be found in bracing yourself in the front of a twin-bowed whaleboat driven by a handful of other men straining at long oars, waiting for a barnacled back to rise like a reef to the surface of the sea so you could set the iron of your harpoon and commence a Nantucket sleigh ride over the green swells. That would be all mere sidelight, though, to the commerce at hand. Because commerce it very much had to be, and the elephant hunters of the past were

as much whalers of the green hills of Africa as Ahab was of the blue water. And something more.

Ivory tusks were the obvious desideratum of the sometimes cruel, sometimes scoundrelly, sometimes maudlin, sometimes romantic, sometimes clever, sometimes imprudent, sometimes timorous, sometimes undaunted men who trekked after *Loxidonta africana* and *Loxidonta cyclotis*. Yet those tusks are no more than the elephant's exaggerated upper incisors, carried by both the male and female of the African species and by most of the males of the Asian, and were known in the ivory trade simply as "teeth." Covered by a compact outer layer of cementum, the inner dentine that is the actual ivory derives its beauty and worth from the ease with which it can be carved and by the bright rich polish it will accept. There is also the "touch" of it, the smooth coolness it has without ever growing chill.

Prized beside gold, ivory was fashioned into the thrones of the kings of Etruria and King Solomon. Elephant tusks were delivered as tribute to the Persian kings by the Egyptians. The galleys of ancient Tyre were outfitted with ivory benches, as was the Roman Senate, while the bon vivant Emperor Caligula presented that special horse of his with an ivory manger. The Renaissance saw the wide use of ivory in religious carvings, and the Japanese have long used it for their *netsuke* and seals. As time passed, more and more domestic applications for ivory were found, from combs to knife handles to toilet seats to billiard balls to those ivories on the piano that just cried out to be tickled. (Among the largest purchasers of tusks during the 1800s and early 1900s were the ivory-cutting companies along the lower Connecticut River, producing piano-key veneers, hair combs, and billiard balls.)

The earliest humans to hunt elephant were little concerned with the ivory of their prey, except perhaps for such utilitarian odds and ends as fish hooks, arrow straighteners, or harpoon heads. They wanted meat in tribe-sized portions. From the Pleistocene on they collected it by digging pitfalls or ringing an elephant herd with fire in the tall grass and spearing to death the smoke-damaged animals as they tried blindly to exit the flames.

They might rig a heavily weighted, broad-bladed lance between two trees across an "elephant road": When an elephant passed beneath the dangling lance he would trip a cord, releasing the lance to fall between his shoulder blades. Bows with a draw-weight of 100 pounds or more were, and still are, used to propel poisoned arrows into elephant; and Pygmies (a term said to have been reclaimed by many tribal peoples of Central Africa, despite its racial-sounding origins) to this day creep to within feet of an elephant in the thick cover to spear him in the belly, decamping from the vicinity to return to take up the blood spoor and usually in a few hours discover the elephant's dead body. In the least complicated of ploys, an army of spearmen would manage to encircle a lone animal separated from the herd and do him in by a frantic rush. (One visualizes ants attacking a grasshopper, or honeybees swarming a bear.)

The 19th-century Bagheera people of Abyssinia brought unmistakable panache to their elephant hunting. Stripping naked so their garments could not be caught on thorn trees or wait-a-bit bushes in the event they had to beat a hasty retreat from the field of honor, two men would mount double on a horse, a broadsword in the hand of the rear rider. Then they trotted out across the rough, broken ground until encountering an elephant. Running head on at him, they issued boisterous challenges ("I killed your father . . . and your grandfather . . . and I am now come to kill you . . .!"), that were essential if the proper form was to be maintained, until the elephant could be provoked into charging this pestering horse and its cargo of yammering humans, who had to be nimble enough to avoid the grasp of its trunk if the contest was to continue. After a charge or two had been gotten out of the elephant, the horse was galloped up from the rear and the armed rider dropped off; and while the elephant's by-now infuriated attention was fixed upon the horse, this *beau sabreur* deftly hamstrung the bull. Then the horseman circled back to retrieve his accomplice, and they would ride after any more elephant there were to be had, returning to the hobbled elephant later to conclude the spectacle with javelins. That was how, from the Bagheera perspective, events were supposed to transpire, though more than one speedy elephant managed to catch ahold of the horse and cast it and its riders to earth, rendering them all into hyena kibble on the Abyssinian highlands.

While the finest ivory comes from Equatorial Africa—the tusks usually blackened on the outside by the long use to which their original owners had put them—even there the material meant virtually nothing to Africans before Arabs and Europeans came and got around to suggesting that it might be something of value. After all, tusks could no more be eaten than the elephant's bones, though as with the marrow in bone, the large nerve in the tusk could be extracted and consumed. The most sensible course, after perhaps removing the nerves at their roots, was simply to leave the tusks behind with the rest of the bones for rodents to gnaw on. When they were brought in from the field, tusks might be made into bracelets or armlets or necklaces, but were as likely to become fenceposts or chopping blocks or stools. There might be so many tusks in a village, collected over who knew how many years of hunting, they would initially be set on end (perhaps just to see how that looked), then laid flat, then heaped around some wooden idol or over a chieftain's grave, then perhaps scattered idly about like so many tons of giant Lincoln logs or even used as pilings to set huts upon. As a trade good among Africans themselves, ivory could seemingly demand a price no higher than firewood's. (Two tusks totaling 141 pounds were once exchanged with Europeans for the munificent sum of eight pounds of beads and two bullets.)

The ivory trade among non-Africans had been carried out since Roman times and probably well before. Twenty centuries ago Chinese merchants traded with Siberians for the ivory the Siberians dug out of the ground, it being the product, it was believed, of a giant subterranean rat, *fen-shü* in Chinese, who was said to die instantaneously upon contact with air or sunlight. To the Mongol tribesman of Siberia, where ivory continues to be unearthed, fen-shü was known as *mammut,* and we know him today as the vanished "mammoth," though with today's reproductive science who can say what might someday be resurrected from the DNA of this creature.

The Arabs who sailed in their dhows to Zanzibar 10 centuries ago also traded with the mainland for the tusks of elephant, and the Portuguese fairly exhausted the accumulated stockpiles of ivory to be found in Angola and Mozambique soon after they took up residence there. Then the Dutch landed on the Cape in the 1600s and once again a new supply of ivory was brought to market.

All of this was ivory collected from around the barest rim of Africa, but it was enough to spur such an intensified demand that between the years 1788 and 1798 approximately 192,579 pounds of ivory was imported into Great Britain each year (in another 60 years this yearly figure grew to 1,000,000 pounds). When imports dipped 118,000 pounds by 1827, it was time to venture into the interior of Africa in search of new lodes.

The first non-Africans to explore and "discover" in the heart of the Dark Continent were not, as the view made popular in 19th-century England would have it, resolute, staunch, indefatigable Britons like Speke or Burton or Grant or Livingstone or Baker or Stanley—whose declared goals were to settle age-old questions of geography or bear the word of the Lord or "rescue" the seemingly lost bearers of that word or nobly inflict education, law, and "humanity" upon "savages"—rather they were Arab ivory traders.

Almost anywhere in Central Africa that the great British explorers went (and despite the inflationary spiral their achievements experienced back home, most were in the end genuinely great in a quixotic, somewhat addled fashion in conjunction with which we would scarcely dare to use the word "great" today), they found Arab merchant princes already firmly established with their settlements, business organizations, and harems.

At first the Zanzabari Arab ivory sultans, reacting to the clamor raised by British, German, and Yankee traders for more ivory, chose to deal utterly scrupulously with the native chieftains of the interior from whom they collected it. They readily paid the agreed-upon *hongo,* or ivory tax (often some ludicrously small amount), and hired the necessary porters to transport the tusks to the sea. Many Arabs borrowed money at 100 percent interest to finance their expeditions; but ivory was then the only product in Central Africa that could "pay the cost of its transport," according to one author; and a tidy profit was more than likely realized. Matters progressed agreeably enough for all concerned so that as late as the 1840s it could be said of any Arab that he could "walk through Africa armed only with a cane." Then the African chieftains wised up to the genuine worth of ivory, and the Arabs got guns.

Hongo now came payable in black powder. At dawn the Arab ivory raiders and their armed band of Africans mercenaries descended upon a village whose ivory they desired and torched the huts. As the villagers fled their burning homes they were shot, clubbed, knouted, and lashed with hippopotamus-hide whips until the survivors could be strung together in a coffle, each handed a tusk and marched to the Indian Ocean or the Nile River at Khartoum. One in five made it. At journey's end, instead of having to provide severance pay and letters of recommendation, the Arabs merely had the porters lay down their burdens at the ivory warehouses and then deliver themselves directly to the slave markets: a business proposition as eminently neat as could be.

One of the premier big-game hunters of his time, Sir Samuel White Baker, born in 1821, was also an ardent foe of such slaving, even though a discernible racist. His convictions even led him in 1870 to accept, along with a salary of £10,000, the command of a force of 1,400 men sent into the Nile basin ostensibly to stamp out the practice—as well as, if at all possible, to annex the entire territory for Ismail Pasha, the profligate Turkish viceroy, or *khedive,* of Egypt whose wretched excesses (£5,000,000 lavished on his harem alone) would in due time resoundingly bankrupt the entire nation he was supposed to oversee. Baker's distaste for slavery, aside from being the "correct politics" of the day, was no doubt abetted by the fact that a decade earlier he had purchased his Hungarian mistress, and eventual second wife, Florence, at a slave auction in the Balkans, rescuing the then teenaged girl from that fate worse than death—if it did not, of course, involve an Englishman.

No conventional Victorian, Baker was the eldest son of a prosperous banker-shipowner-colonial planter, but was himself a rover and, though in later years a linguist and author, no fan of schooling or discipline. His only love was for the hunting, and the polite society of England constricted him fearfully. Marrying his first wife when just out of his teens, he had soon taken her off to Ceylon where he spent eight years hunting the tuskless rogue elephant who pitilessly trampled the crops and broke down the dams and irrigation tanks of that island.

Baker probably killed more Asian elephant than anyone before or since, hundreds of them. His favored technique was to shoot the animal at 10 or a dozen paces as it was charging him, making the, for him, certain frontal brain shot. He was one of the most knowledgeable sportsmen of his day on the subject of firearms, being a vocal advocate of not only rifles (versus smoothbores) and "plenty of powder," but of sights as well—apparently a controversy of the moment. For all his hunting he preferred a matched pair of 15-pound Reilly No. 10 (10-bore) polygroove rifles that handled seven drams, or nearly 200 grains, of powder without "disagreeable recoil."

In 1861, after the death of his first wife and his acquisition of Florence, he resolved to fulfill an old dream of seeing the elephant of Africa and exploring for the source of the Nile, the great quest of the day. To his battery he added a 20-pound 2-bore which the native Arabs he encountered in Abyssinia eagerly proclaimed "Child of the Cannon" after they found there was amply room to slip two fingers down the yawning muzzle. Baker simply called it "Baby" and described it as an "instrument of torture" to the shooter. He actually feared to use it, noting that when he fired it, it spun him around like "a weathercock in a hurricane." (He assigned his gunbearers to discharge the weapon when the regular interval for cleaning it came around.) Its sole saving grace was that any elephant he hit with its half-pound projectile perished without fail.

Baker had significantly less success with his close-range brain shot on the African elephant he faced, due to the structure of their skulls being appreciably different from that of the Asian. Still, when called upon, Baby carried the day. Most of the elephant Baker killed on his four-year journey to discover Albert Nyanza, the freshwater inland sea of Africa through which the Nile flows, were to provision his expedition. Perhaps the truest hunter of his time, he found in the African wilderness among the elephant a place where he could live a life, with the doughty, and far from British, woman he loved, that was impossible for him in "civilization."

The foremost popularizer of the professional elephant hunter's way of life for the Victorian audience was one Roualeyn Gordon Cumming who pursued the animals with horses and dogs to good effect in southern Africa during the 1830s and 1840s. Author of *A Hunter's Life in South Africa,* his book inspired future elephant hunters from Baldwin to Selous to Bell to forsake the humdrum, and very real comforts, of England and strike off into the bush—in much the same way the writings of Jack London inspired my grandfather's generation to go before the mast, or the writings of Hunter S. Thompson sent so many of my own generation careering off in search of "king hell" highs.

When it came to the actual shooting of elephant, Cumming was, to judge by his own words and at a time when the term sociopath had not been coined, either a bumbling incompetent or a thorough-going swine. He once spent from before noon to the setting of the sun to pump 57 balls into a single elephant before it succumbed to his attentions. He was apt to begin laying down his barrages out at 100 yards or more (a range Baker would have found despicable); and in an oft quoted passage, he blithely describes bringing up lame the largest elephant bull he ever happened on with a shoulder shot. As the elephant leaned immobilized against a tree, Cumming unsaddled his horse in a shady spot, built a fire, brewed up some piping-hot coffee, and hunkered down to contemplate this "noble" animal at his leisure. Finally he resolved to conduct his own science project and began to probe methodically for the bull's vitals with rounds from his "two-groove" rifle. A cure for cancer could have been found in less time than it took him to dispatch this weary creature.

William Charles Baldwin followed in Cumming's unspeakable wake with his own book, more a journal, *African Hunting and Adventure.* A parson's son, Baldwin was another rover whose father was determined he should become a clerk at 16; but William Charles soon found himself better suited to "sport, dogs, and horses" than "quill-driving." When his subsequent effort at "light Scotch farming" degenerated into nothing more than an excuse for running game on a daily basis, and Baldwin saw "no earthly prospect of the command of anything like a moor or a stud in the old country," his thoughts turned to Canada and the American plains, both then awash in wildlife. Then came friends' and Cumming's stories of southern Africa, and with an accompaniment of seven deerhounds and a volume of Byron, Baldwin arrived in Natal in late 1851, aged 24, to commence an eight-year career of professional hide, ostrich-feather, and ivory hunting. His first expedition was to St. Lucia Bay for hippopotamuses (or "sea-cows" as they were called there and then), and seven out of 10 of his hunting partners died of fever and various illnesses.

It was not until 1858 that Baldwin finally killed his first elephant at 15 yards with a 5-bore round in front of six drams of powder, dropping the bull a witch doctor had prophesied would be his. He went on to kill considerably more, to be sure, his wagons sometimes bringing out 5,000 pounds of "white gold" at a safari's end. On a whim, seemingly to break the drudgery of his hunting, he once marched all alone to the Zambezi River to become the second European, after Dr. Livingstone, to view Victoria Falls; he was overcome by their magnificence—though not to such an extent that he was unable to note that the "baboons here are out of all number." Yet after almost a decade of being chivvied through the African bush by belligerent *inthlovi,* he was to conclude that elephant hunting was "the very hardest life a man can chalk out for himself," and retired to England on his ivory money, never to return.

Some of the more noted Southern African ivory hunters harassed the elephant in large squads, employing as assistants African hunters, such as the ex-jockey Cigar whom both William Finaughty and Frederick Selous hunted with and made famous, or as family parties, such as Henry Hartley & Sons who tallied 1,200 animals in 30 years' work. Finaughty took most of the 500 elephant he accounted for in his nine years of professional hunting in Matabeleland and Mashonaland on his own. Born in South Africa in 1843, and by his own description a "harum-scarum from youth," he was also a total abstainer with a wily Roscommon face, a relentless gambler, a good horseman, a fair shot, a gunrunner, a freebooter, and a looter. On one two-month hunt alone along the Umfuli River in 1868 ("the two finest months of my life") he took 95 elephant and numerous rhino, the ivory fetching 6s. 10½d. per pound, while the rhino horns brought £4 apiece.

Finaughty, like the Blackfeet, refused to hunt in any manner but from horseback, his cherished bay mount Dopper having trained itself to lower its head and hold its breath whenever Finaughty leveled his ponderous muzzleloader. When in the mid-1870s, with the elephant driven into "fly" country where horses could no longer be used, Finaughty abandoned hunting in favor of other forms of roguery.

On one of his last hunts, Finaughty used one of the "newly-invented" breechloaders, a trifling 12-bore, to kill half-a-dozen or so elephant in a single day; but even in a gun as "light" as this, the recoil was such that recalling it 30 years later still made Finaughty's "eyes moist." The punishing recoil of the enormous big-bore weapons they used was a topic all elephant hunters got around to discussing at one time or another. Selous, who hunted all his elephant on foot, explained that his first pair of cheap 4-bores— actually waterfowl guns—when loaded with a "handful" of "common trade powder" (approximately 20 drams), "drove better" than more expensive guns he acquired later, but kicked so unmercifully that his nerves were utterly destroyed by them and his shooting was affected ever after. The recoil of most elephant guns was such that the stocks invariably had to be bound in the green skin of an elephant's ear and the skin let to dry like "iron" around the wood to keep it from splitting when the gun was discharged. (Selous once touched off a 4-bore that had accidentally received a double-charge of powder, the resulting detonation cartwheeling him backward and splintering the stock to smithereens.)

Frederick Courteney Selous's advent upon the African scene occurred in 1871 at age 18, and for 20 years he followed the "free-and-easy gipsy [*sic*] sort of life" of Cumming and Baldwin in the wild country between the Limpopo River and the Congo Basin. An ethnologist and naturalist besides, Selous contributed vitally to the outside world's knowledge of the area's flora, fauna, and native cultures. He hunted widely around the globe and become a great friend of Theodore Roosevelt's, organizing, as we recall, Teddy's 1909–10 East African safari; in 1917, while a 65-year-old captain with the 25th Royal Fusiliers battling German guerrilla forces for nominal control of the inhospitable Tanganyikan bush, he took a sniper's bullet in the neck. And back in his ivory-hunting days, he could express genuine regret over having to kill elephant for just their tusks, yet pointed out the basic fact known to all those in his chosen field, that ivory was the sole item obtainable in that wild country "with which to defray the heavy expenses of hunting." Ivory paid the way for Selous to hunt and to live his life in Africa, where he lies buried beside a tributary of the Rufiji River in the 21,000-square-mile Tanzanian game reserve that bears his name, established by the iconic game warden, C. J. P. Ionides.

Baker died in Devon in 1893 in Florence's arms, dreaming of lion hunting in Somaliland. By then in the scramble for Africa, the concerted European powers had all but demolished the vast Moslem empires the Arab ivory-slave sultans had constructed in the interior, including that of the greatest of them all, Hamed bin Muhammed bin Juma bin Rajab, or Tippu Tib (meaning either "the sound of guns" or a reference to a nervous blink, depending upon the authority one cites). A charming, intelligent *gentilhomme* or a ruthless, blood-thirsty corsair, as circumstances dictated, Tippu met and aided during his life both Stanley and Livingstone, and others of their ilk, while going on to gain harsh control over 100,000 square miles of the Upper Congo Basin. In time, even he was made to see that the game was up and retired to Zanzibar to die of a fever in his late 60s in 1905, a modestly wealthy man.

It was to fall, then, to a pale imitation of Tippu, one Shundi, who terrorized the area around Kilimanjaro for a brief period with his ivory-gathering activities, to collect the grandest prize of all the elephant hunters. One day in 1898 at the base of the snow-cowled mountain, one of Shundi's armed slaves caught sight of a small-bodied elephant bull with high shoulders and a sloping back, the "like a hyena" elephant the old Zanzibaris contended always carried the heaviest ivory. When this one fell, his *el Hadam,* "the servant," tusk—the one more worn due to greater use because of right- or left-"handedness"—weighed 228 pounds, while the other came to 232. Each was 12 feet long. No bigger elephant ivory has ever been found, and none is ever likely to be.

Nonetheless, there were more elephant to be killed, an estimated 30,000 a year in the period between 1905 and 1912, and more men to kill them. Arthur H. Neumann was one of them, using a, for then, laughably puny 577 to gather the ivory needed to recoup the cost of his following his "bent of wandering in the most remote wilds" to be found across fin de siècle Kenya, as far as the northern shore of Lake Rudolf. He donned gloves at the equator because his "small bore" 577's recoil tore his hands to shreds, and when not hunting elephant he collected butterflies. Once terribly wounded by an elephant cow, he lay in the bush for several months, fed a diet of milk by his porters who titled him *Nyama Yangu* ("my meat") for his prowess in obtaining game for them. The scope of his hunting restricted in time by colonial authorities, Neumann returned to England and died.

Captain "Jimmy" Sutherland, who because of his services to the German government during the Maji-Maji Rebellion of 1905–06 was given free rein to slay elephant in what was then German East Africa, was another who employed the 577. Safari-ing after ivory with a virtual municipality of porters—1,000 men, women, and children—he was conveyed along in a swaying hammock borne by relays of runners and slept in tents of silk. He was the acknowledged first, in that phrase that sounds as if it were taken from the Book of Samuel, to "have shot his thousand" singlehandedly. Yet he was never confident of his ability to halt a charging elephant; and so his unease was somehow communicated to his prey, as often happens, and he was charged again and again. Yet his demise on safari came not by elephant but by native poison, perhaps administered by disgruntled hammock bearers.

Then, of course, there was the famous "Karamojo" Bell of the 1,011 documented bull elephant and the "tiny nickel pencil-like" 275 bullet he used to dispatch an inordinate number of them. As a solitary boy in the 1880s, he dreamed of going off to hunt the bison of North America, not realizing that the buffalo were already long gone by then. Then he was to hear of Africa, and it was he who was long gone. It did not end with him, either, because even into our lifetimes there were the likes of "Pondoro" Taylor, Wally Johnson, Ian Nyschens, and the notorious Zimbabwean Shadrek Muteruko, in their own wild wrinkles in time, still practicing the very hardest life a man can chalk out for himself as the greatest wars were fought and space explored. Yet perhaps not so ironically, it was when these lonesome outlaws (far more pilgrims than imperialists) had finally passed from the scene that the armies of organized poachers marched in with their Kalashnikovs and Chinese buyers in Vietnam and began to persecute the elephant more heartlessly than any of the old ivory hunters ever had in their blackest dreams.

What could they have all been seeking, those singular men, as they went about cutting off the tails of dead elephant to mark the kills as theirs and burying tusks to keep them from burning like "candles" in the all-too-frequent grass fires? No white whale, certainly. And probably since they had to walk, it is calculated, an average of 100 miles for every large bull elephant they killed, surely the ivory alone could not have been inducement enough to set them seeking.

It must have been, I think, the search itself that drew them to the life, the absolute freedom they discovered in those places so far from the orderly cities and citizens they had put behind them, learning "the joy of wandering through lonely lands" that Roosevelt so profoundly knew. In a real sense, they ruled those lands, being their self-crowned monarchs (Ahab, remember, is also the name of a king). Lonely monarchs, yes, lonely hunter kings. Perhaps lonesomeness became their true Moby Dick, leading them on long after more conventional, and mundane, men would have abandoned such a quest.

I think, unlike Captain Ahab, they must have finally come to love, even more than the hunt, the elegant isolation itself of that empty country where, as their eyes circled the horizon, the only other living creature they might behold would be—look! there—an elephant.

The One

The 1970s . . .

THE GREATER PART of a lifetime ago, red volcanic Tsavo dust displayed for me a track like an impression incused in metal with a die. When new, the edges and outlines were sharp as stamped steel, so that a hunter could hunker down and touch his finger to the pugmark and feel the mass and energy of the animal whose paw imprinted it. In my case, I first felt a frisson traveling up my spine, then an unsightly grin spreading across my face.

We found the carcass of the impala ewe hauled into a tall tree near the Njugini River the next afternoon. I had killed a ram that morning, and now we hung its forequarters from the limb as well, saving the better haunches to eat. We built the blind 20 yards from the tree, weaving it from cut brush—a curtain with loopholes. That night in camp we dined on peppery slices of impala rump roast. And thought about leopard.

Before dawn, Jbwani came to my tent with the tea tray. Ten minutes later I was eating breakfast with Fletcher under the propane lamp in the large dining tent. Thirty minutes after that, the night seeping from the sky, John, his gunbearer Mmaku, and I dropped from the Land Cruiser and crawled to the blind as the Toyota drove off. The Maasai herded cattle

and goats in this Rombo country of southern Kenya, where Kilimanjaro bulked on the horizon; and as we sat motionlessly in the blind, flat on the ground, we could do nothing about the ticks affixing themselves to our skin. Fletcher had his 375, I my 300; and Mmaku had the 500 Nitro Express double, loaded with the 578-grain soft-nosed bullets. No one, ultimately, can define what is "too much gun" for a leopard, because the idea is to slam and bolt a door between you and it if it charges.

When in the first light only a few minutes later a leopard walked around the edge of the blind and stood two dozen feet from us, staring off in the direction in which the Land Cruiser had driven, I was the first to see it. I moved only my eyes, but was able to see with absolute clarity the black rosettes charred into the golden hide, and how the lithe, female line of the cat's body was broken by loose white fur hanging along its belly. Mmaku beside me did not see the leopard until I touched his leg. He hissed across me to John.

"*Chui.*"

"Do not move," John ordered without turning his head to look at the cat, his whisper raspy. Move? I went on sitting here, watching this first leopard I had ever seen in the wild—who because we were motionless could not identify us—until the ticks made a dry husk of me. Then the leopard snapped its head toward us, perhaps having detected the flick of an eyelash; and I was staring into bottomless panther eyes. The cat was frozen there for a full minute or more before crouching and spinning and rustling off through the tall dry grass.

We saw the leopard an hour later, stretched out on the limb bearing the impala.

"She-leopard," the PH said after studying her for a few minutes through his binocular. "And there's a cub." I reset the 300's safety. For the next two hours, until the Land Cruiser came back for us, we watched the cat in the tree, she with her big cub curled near her in the crotch of the limb. A fish eagle circled, whiffling down toward the carcasses hanging on the limb, opened talons outstretched. The she-leopard watched the raptor with entranced attention, until the bird was about to close its scaled yellow feet on the impala; then she shot out the limb to the end, the claws of one paw sinking into the wood, clenching it, the other paw swiping through the air as the eagle urgently backstroked its wide wings.

The next blind was a cavity cut into heavy brush. It was so big inside that four of us could stand and walk around, like those women coming and going, talking of Michelangelo. We hung the hindquarters of a Georges Braque kongoni in a small acacia in front of the blind. By the next day the leopard who left the pugmark was feeding on it. We were in the blind in the late afternoon.

The trouble with leopard blinds is that when properly constructed, not only can leopards not detect you in them, none of the rest of Africa's dangerous game can either. This has led to everything from lions to elephant stumbling onto hunters who were minding their own business in leopard blinds. Fletcher, back when black rhino were numerous enough to be nearly a nuisance, had once had to kill one in full charge at the entrance to a leopard blind, while the gunbearers forcibly detained the hunting client as he tried to hare away from cover. This afternoon, I sat in the blind until it was too dark to shoot, careful all the while not to move even my eyes unless a flash of white could be detected, wondering what might stumble onto us.

As we waited in the darkness for the Land Cruiser to return at the appointed hour, I heard the leopard come to feed on the bait. I heard meat being torn from bone, then bone being cracked by teeth. Small bumps rose on my forearms. It was something primal, something heard 1,000 generations ago when the earth was so silent that sounds like that might carry across distance and transmit the information that a predator in the darkness had killed again, while we huddled together on rock ledges. Then the Land Cruiser's lights began to play through the grass and trees and the leopard receded into the night and in a little while we were riding back into camp.

John hunched forward in his camp chair, a drink of rum in his hand, and stared into the fire, "dreaming" it, as the Maasai say.

"We could have had a light out there tonight," he spoke to the flames. "A light doesn't matter to a leopard. He'd have just gone on feeding. Lots of other professionals I know use lights," he added, leaning back in his chair, a conclusion reached.

"I hope I never become that kind of hunter," he said, swirling rum up the side of the glass.

We used no flashlights to cover the last half-mile to the blind on foot the next morning, still night under the bright equatorial moon, the two stellar bears, major and minor, lying beyond the northern horizon, replaced by the Southern Cross as the vicinity of a lodestar. Africa at night is true Africa; Africa at night, campfires and safari cars left far behind, is truest. It's puzzling the way darkness strips the layers hiding the heart of the land: In daylight the dazzle and clarity are distractions, rather than enhancements. During the day, I might not feel my soul crouching as it did in Africa at night, ready to spring out of me with each step I took, no certainty whether that heart belonged to predator or prey.

Then we entered some brush, and I found myself inside the large blind again. In the darkness I felt for the rest for my 300 and set the rifle in place. I took a knee and waited. I did not see, so much as feel, the dawn spreading outside. The feeding sound came again.

"The leopard's here," Fletcher whispered. I took up my rifle slowly, like raising a shotgun on a turkey. The big male leopard, his head short and square, his thick muscles defined, was standing on his hind legs in the tree, his front claws in the kongoni and his jaws tearing at the flesh. He chewed, then took his claws out of the carcass and dropped back down onto the limb. He stood with his head pointed down and tail curled up. I laid the crosshairs on the center of his left shoulder, and gave the trigger a straight-back squeeze to break the sear, a dull yellow flame licking toward him.

When we return to camp that morning the Turkana tracker will sing a warrior's chant that will echo in my heart, Jbwani will race around the tents to meet me with a glass of straight bourbon whiskey in his hand, the skinners will painstakingly scrape all the clean white fat from the cat's hide and body so they can take it home to rub on their children's throats in the rainy season when they come down with the croup, and there will be pale pink leopard meat to cook and eat. Now, though, as we drag the cat's heavy body out of the deep grass at the base of the acacia and the PH and the gunbearers clap me on the back, I just want to look at this leopard, to run my hand over his warm fur, to spread open his sharp claws, to see that my single bullet passed through him, killing him on the way, and to touch my finger to the center of one of the black rosettes on the golden hide.

The PH, older than I, smiles and says, "Good shot, lad!" as I lift the leopard's paw and hold it to the palm of my own hand. "Well done, lad!" There is no frisson now. We have already met.

Half a life on from that dawn in Kenya, a Zimbabwe professional hunter at a game convention is trying to sell me on a leopard-hunting technique he's devised. In Zimbabwe, cat hunting at night with artificial light is legal. So he hung a shop lamp in a tree above a bait, wired it to a battery and a rheostat. When the leopard is heard feeding on the impala quarter in the darkness, the PH in the blind with his client, stealthily dials up the light until the cat is illuminated as if it were break of day, the leopard completely oblivious.

For some reason, I have stopped listening. Maybe because I have the only leopard I can ever want.

Something Borrowed

The 1990s . . .

IN THE END, you keep what you need.

"Ant" Baber had a ranch in Africa, "Ant's Nest" in Limpopo Province—
then the Northern Province, having been Northern Transvaal and the
Transvaal before. Ant's lay in Limpopo's Waterberg Mountains, a massif of
bluffs and buttes where on its highveld *Homo erectus* once scavenged game
in the heat of summer. Afterward, Bushman came, then Bantu; and some
of the first Europeans were Cape Dutch who reached it on a pilgrimage to
Jerusalem, miscalculating the distance and mistaking the Waterbergs for
Egypt. And it's where I borrowed a rifle to hunt a blesbok.

Seldom the object of safari tales, the blesbok is a horse-headed, medium-
sized antelope, high-withered, bay-bodied with white belly and stockings,
named for the white blaze (*bles*) on its face, and crowned by lyre-shaped
ringed horns that curve back in shallow S's with 15 inches being record class.
It's native to South Africa and found elsewhere where it has been introduced.

The blesbok's larger, smaller-horned, and more dramatically colored
cousin is the bontebok (the "parti-colored buck"). Much rarer, too, living
in that Mediterranean fynbos habitat of the western Cape, where it was

ranked a pest and shot near to extinction by white settlers. A few farmers and ranchers in the mid-19th century ultimately gave shelter to the remaining handful. The blesbok, that subsists on short grasses across a much broader territory, has enjoyed far greater success than the bontebok that survived only because of an 18,000-acre national park created for those final 17 of the animals placed there for preservation in 1931.

The first afternoon at the Nest, Ant ground the Land Cruiser up a treacherously steep and rocky road, the road named for his Kenyan-born wife, Tessa. She and Ant had a genuine Hollywood "meet," Ant opening the door to his ranch house on a night when the rain was pelting down, to find a beautiful young blonde standing there, having come down in the lorry that carried a string of new horses to Ant. When a beautiful young horsewoman comes in out of the rain, you take it as a sign; and they were married and worked the ranch and stock and wildlife together, happy ever after.

At the top of the road, we ran along the ridge, rocks grinding under the tires, the sky, with the sun setting, that particular shade of Africa-orange from woodsmoke and obscured by the soft evening haze. Out on the plains of the ranch giraffes paraded like tall, mobile honeycombed beeswax candles.

Coming around a bend in the road, I saw a folding table caparisoned in a starched white cloth, bottles of brown and white liquor, small pebbled-glass bottles of tonic, beer, soft drinks in cans, ice, and plates of simple hors d'oeuvres set out on it, the table oriented to the sundown. Here we toasted the end of the day and that start of a hunt, returning to the ranch buildings in the dark.

It was chill that night at dinner inside the *boma* beside the main lodge. As the servers brought out the different dishes, one slid a shovel into the red-orange embers in the fire ring and placed half a blade of them on the bare ground under each canvas camp chair, the warmth bathing the calves of our legs and rising to the seat, a trick worth remembering.

The next day, I went out to shoot with Ant's rifle. A keen professional hunter who grew up on the large cattle ranch near Ant's Nest, Ant began hunting when he was nine, purchasing his first rifle at 11. It was a Musgrave Model 80 308 Winchester, a push-feed rifle built in South Africa. With a plain wooden stock and three-position safety, it was nothing custom in the least. The scope was a fixed 4X Stirling—not the highest resolution scope ever built. From the bench with 150-grain bullets it grouped within two inches at 100 yards, or perhaps it was meters there in South Africa. In his early 30s, then, Ant had used the rifle for over 20 years, and it was a firearm, in a phrase from the honky-tonk stage, that was ragged but right.

After seeing how it shot off sandbags, I rested it on crossed sticks on the ground and fired it at lifelike animal targets Ant painted. He'd found that having his clients sight in on animal portraits gave them a far better notion of where to place shots in the field—especially when he had drawn vital organs on the reverse side of the target, to show his hunters where their shots landed.

After a few shots, I found I could hit where I aimed even if that (to my chagrin) didn't always turn out to be where the heart and lungs happened to be on the target. Still, the next day, I made that very credible shot on the cull impala, and then the day after we went in search of a trophy blesbok.

Ant believed in hunting on foot. During the morning, we drove the dirt vehicle tracks to a couple of likely jumping off spots, then went out walking, even bringing Rufus, Ant's big black Lab, with us. Toward the end of the morning, we were thinking of heading in for lunch, having seen only a few small blesbok rams, but struck off on one more walk.

Ant had no sling on his rifle, so I had to carry it in my hand, muzzle down to prevent glare. He preferred me to keep the rifle loaded, with the safety on, because there was no way of predicting what we might come upon at any given moment. As we walked, I looked down at the rifle and noticed the bolt handle had lifted up, and the bolt itself had slid back an inch, drawing out the cartridge with it. I asked Ant about this, and he assured me that while the safety was too worn to keep the bolt locked closed, it still served its function of keeping the trigger locked so the rifle could not fire.

A few minutes later, apparently in an effort to test Ant's assurance that the Musgrave was entirely safe, I managed to put my foot wrong and twist my ankle (adding insult to the injury I'd already suffered in falling off Saladin), pitching forward in an unintended and far from graceful break-fall, the rifle muzzle jamming into the ground as I went. As I regained my feet and dusted myself off, Ant picked up the rifle, unloaded it, and examined the plug of red dirt up the spout. So much for this hunt. There seemed to be no choice but to return to camp and clean the rifle, then hunt again in the afternoon. We could still press on just a little farther, though, to see what we might see; which, a quarter mile farther, turned out to be an old, fine blesbok in the middle of a large plain of yellow grass.

We squatted in the tree cover and debated. The more we debated, of course, the more we knew there was only one answer: If we waited till the afternoon to come back to find the blesbok, we never would. Ant, therefore, set to the blocked muzzle of the rifle, picking out as much dirt from it as he could with a twig, then removed the lace from his boot and triple knotted one end, pushing the other end through the barrel and out the muzzle. Pulling the knotted lace through, he looked down the barrel and saw a bore clean enough to shoot. He reloaded the rifle and handed it to me.

By now the blesbok had drifted off about 300 yards from the edge of the trees, farther than I felt sanguine about trying to shoot with a borrowed rifle—this borrowed rifle. To close the range at all, we had to cross the open at an angle to the ram to reach another lone thorn tree out on the plain. We walked through the grass, not attempting to hide, pretending we had no interest in the blesbok or even noticed his presence, the rifle carried down along my leg. Reaching the tree, I quickly got a standing rest across one of the branches and found the blesbok, now about 150 yards out, in the sights. I flipped off the safety, and as I started to squeeze I leaned into the butt of the rifle, pushing the muzzle right, in front of the ram's chest, the shot going wide.

The blesbok ran a dozen yards and stopped. Now I was starting to get flustered. I jacked the bolt and set the safety, then moved around the tree to where I got a clearer shot at the blesbok, forgetting in the process that I had reset the safety, then trying to shoot the rifle without taking the safety off, only to have the increasingly more nervous blesbok run back those several yards toward us.

I had to change positions again. Now I flipped off the safety, put my finger on the trigger, and hit the ram higher than I intended. Luckily, the bullet caught the spine, dropping the blesbok. But the ram kept trying to get up until Rufus, let slip by Ant, barreled into it well ahead of us and took it by the neck. Then it was over, the ram turning out to be something more than exceptional, his unusually wide, very white horns—no, translucent, like the nail on a finger—going well over 15½ inches.

Bringing back the bakkie, we loaded the bull into the back and drove it to the skinning shed. My young son Bryan was there to see the blesbok when it came in, and watch with determined fascination as it was skinned and quartered and hung up to cool before butchering. I brought him to Africa for the first time, and he would return.

That is what is called to mind when I look at the head of that blesbok on the wall of my home, now years later. The rifle was borrowed, but the memories and emotions remain all mine.

Big Running Mean

AT LAST, IN the entirely uncalled-for heat of December that hunkered down upon the northwestern horn of Zimbabwe and refused to leave until the wet season's rains broke, there were elephant to see again. Black from the mud of the river, they glided together across the harshly green flats beside the Zambezi west of Victoria Falls, retiring to the relative coolness of the gusu woods above, moving as smoothly and steadily as large structures raised up on wheeled carriages and drawn in stately procession down the boulevards of a city in triumph.

This Zambezi River—whose upper reaches the Glasgow-born Dr. David Livingstone first saw very near here at the Zambian town of Sesheke in 1851, and the Portuguese slave trader Silva Porto saw some years before, and Africans had known about all along—came out of a bog near Kalene Hill in the far north of Zambia. It passed through Angola before re-entering Zambia, then constituted a portion of the border between Zambia and Namibia, flowing next past the single point where the maps of Zambia, Namibia, Botswana, and Zimbabwe converged. Establishing then the boundary between Zambia and Zimbabwe, it ran east to where

the falls of Mosioatunya cut a 100-yard-high and 1,900-yard-wide slash across its bed. In late 1855 Livingstone, completely alone except for the presence of 114 African porters, came upon these falls and named them in honor of Victoria Regina. Farther east, today, there were hydroelectric dams, impoundments, Mozambique, and the Indian Ocean. Which paled in comparison to elephant black and glistening in their coats of river mud.

It may be one's honest intention to see Africa just once in one's life, to get the chasing of its game out of one's system; but if you find yourself enthralled with hunting in Africa, it is an intention almost impossible to carry through on. Once seen, Africa demands to be seen again. And again.

Two years before—as I'll tell you—during a rather long and quite curious safari in the Central African Republic, what I had missed most was the sight of elephant. Other than their tracks, all I had seen of them there were their skulls every so often, white and massive and smooth as polished marble, the milestones of poachers. But here, encamped beside the Zambezi in the 1.2-million-acre Matetsi Safari Area in the Wankie District, one of Zimbabwe's largest safari concessions, there were elephant galore, along with Cape buffalo, sable antelope, greater kudu, lion, leopard, southern impala, warthog, bushbuck, and numerous other species. I felt myself, not against my will but perhaps against any possibility of my ultimate control, sliding in that burning December back into Africa, like an apostate returning to the faith with new-found zeal.

That I was there in December to begin with was fair measure of just how badly I wanted to see Africa again. Only a certifiable lamebrain or a hopeless addict knowingly ventured after game in Zimbabwe then. December is an appalling time to hunt there, first, because of the shimmering mad-dog heat; second, because all the bush as far as the eye can see is leafing out into a verdant curtain impossible to spot animals through; and third, once those rains—already long overdue—did break, they would fill every pan and depression, allowing the wildlife to spread out over the land in a thin, almost transparent film, instead of forming huntable congregations around a few permanent waterholes. All this I knew; yet when offered even this imperfect opportunity to see Africa again, I went for it like a trout for a fly that matched the hatch . . .

. . . And so found myself on my first day of hunting stalking a young elephant bull standing in the shade of a tree at the brow of a hill. We had driven along one of the concession's dirt tracks in an ancient pumpkin-colored Land Rover—branded with those resolutely British names, "Solihull, Warwickshire, England"—doing all those things you do on the first day of safari. At the margin of a waterhole we found the tracks of a "dagga-boy" buffalo, one of those old mud-caked bulls who chart a solitary, disgruntled course through life. In a long valley of beige grass we saw two giraffes galloping, as they always galloped, like building cranes making a break for it. Standing together in the Land Rover's open back, hanging onto the roll bar, my professional hunter, Sandy, and I got to talking. In his mid-30s and bearded for the very pragmatic reason that it lent him an air of authority, a touch of the patriarch in dealing with his trackers and staff, Sandy had left his native Canada years before and spent the time since in wild locales where the important cultural headlines of the West were not readily available.

Were, he asked me, the Grateful Dead still performing? It was my painful duty to detail for him the pathetic spectacle of superannuated flower children in French-tailored blue jeans, work shirts, and bandannas, along with hordes of bike messengers, filling concert halls to hear them. What was Dylan up to? Who, in fact, could say? What about Hendrix and Joplin? Perhaps he should sit.

Then we had spotted this dark-as-gun-bluing elephant, his short tusks clean white, and decided—as who would not?—to see how close we could amble up to him, solely to see how close we could. He looked wrinkled and myopic and drowsy. All the same, though, I chambered a 300-grain solid into my new 375 as Sandy did into his old 375, one with iron sights and a grip wrapped in black electrician's tape, the previous owner having cracked it, literally, over the head of a charging warthog. As we eased uphill toward the elephant, who stood showering himself with dust thrown up by his trunk, I wondered how fast he could charge down on us, if he were to take such a notion. There was a photographer with us, my friend Dan Hernandez, and as we drew closer I kept a weather eye on the bull as the motor drive on the camera clicked, to my ear, as loudly as a hydraulic press in a stamping factory.

We got to within two-dozen yards before the elephant suddenly stood alert, his ears fanning out, and stared in our direction. We froze. The bull raised the great pyramidal slab of his forehead, the effect evocative of a steam locomotive about to pull out of the depot. Then he came, splintering a rotten stump in his path, scattering us screaming like ninnies to the four winds. Some distance downslope, I threw a glance over my shoulder and saw him running away from us over the crest, and realized how lovely the rump of a departing elephant always was. Now this was the proper way to commence a safari, running from elephant one of my favorite things.

In the kiln-hot days that followed, the tropic daylight seemed to mail everything in a thick metallic dazzle. We found no game, only their tracks, but got to see the country of the Matetsi. Its "Kalahari sand structure" soil was quite fertile, and decades earlier quasi-heroic efforts were made to turn it into something "beneficial" and "productive." This meant trying to kill all the animals off thoroughly excellent game lands and turning that ground with the plow. Naturally, the animals tolerated such folly only so long and in the end reclaimed it all.

Today what remained of the "improvements" were vague dikes and ditch banks subdividing the river flats, and in the hills overgrown tobacco patches and the ruins of drying barns and abandoned whitewashed farmhouses. In place of cash crops, the gigantic elephant-gray baobab grew. In dense brush that had once been cultivated fields impala bucks gave startlingly loud warning snorts. Atop the old earthworks on the flats stood waterbucks, with lyre-curving horns and the bodies of elk, all the plowshares gone long ago to rust, or perhaps beaten back into swords for the hands of war veterans, Mugabe's useful fools.

The camp and outfit was run by one Green Torto, a former alumnus of Rhodesian detention with the President, back in the day, making him a very important person for the time being. During my third night in Matetsi, a new-moon night, there had been the not-so-distant roaring of lions outside my green tent, and on the dirt road we followed from the camp the next morning we found the tracks of a large pride. This gave the day some promise.

We crisscrossed the country in the Land Rover, seeing the requisite elephant or two (*zhou* or *nzou* in the native Shona language). Then there was a fine big warthog, *njiri;* and we set out after him on foot. He moved off, tail high, and the trackers trailed him across the broken volcanic stone, up a small draw, and over the brow of a rise where in the pale papery grass I saw his warty, ivory-tusked profile. I took a rest on my shooting stick and put a 270-grain soft-nosed through the grass and just behind the heavy boar's left shoulder. He bolted across a dozen yards of broken ground before collapsing, and that night in camp we dined by lantern light on warthog chops.

More sweltering game-less days came after. In Africa one can never say what any day may bring, but the uncertainty only adds to its attraction. It was the sixth morning, and as we came out onto the dirt road above camp again, heading for the "tar" road that slices across the upper rim of the concession from Victoria Falls to Botswana, Cape buffalo were in the tangled cover below us, returning from the river and their nocturnal waterings. Sandy, his tracker Enoch, and I went in to look at then, paralleling them as they moved in a black wall through the thicket, trampling trees and bushes. At first they went slowly, nervously, knowing we were there and uncertain yet which course to follow. Then they stampeded. Sandy, Enoch, and I ran with them, no more than 20 yards from the column. I could hear bovine grunts, horn bosses cracking against limbs, hooves splitting deadfalls, the continuous hollow thump of big running mean colliding with other big running mean, and above it all the beating of my heart.

Then the stream of 100 or more low, squat, round-bellied herbivores, their square-muzzles thrust forward, broke uphill and headed for their home ground in the vast area of trees and savannah that spread to the south, coming almost near enough for us to put a hand on them as they passed. There was nothing "shootable" in all those buffalo—the best bulls tend to stay by themselves. Panting, I watched them running off into the trees, thinking, damn, that was fun!

That same morning, some miles farther on, I killed an old sable bull. We had turned off the tar road and followed one of the sandy tracks that looped around the concession, when we sighted three sable ahead. One was worth a look, so Sandy and Enoch and I again mounted a stalk. We slipped from tree to bush to tree until we came to a downed trunk, the sable moving 100 yards in front of us. *Mharapara* in Shona, the big hippotragine antelope walked with his black-and-white-masked head tucked down, like that of the Darley Arabian's in an oil portrait, as if an invisible bit were held by the reins in the hand of an equally invisible groom. This gave his neck, with its clipped ginger-and-black mane from which the finest of paintbrushes are manufactured, a bow whose line the arcing black horns carried on into the air—all of this creating in my mind the most fundamental of African antelope.

He had a graceful substantialness not seen in the almost too aesthetic gangliness of the kudu's fringes, spirals, and funny ears. The sable is a no-frills antelope. As he walked in the shaded gusu woods he was all clean lines and smooth power and one of the main reasons I was here. I steadied the crosshairs, and my bullet dropped him as he walked.

When I came up to him I saw he was an old bull, his horns worn back to 39 inches, but the bases heavy and thickened by secondary annular rings.

His head was marked by many old scars. He was the best kind of bull to have killed, in the last years of his life and past his breeding prime. Now with all the njiri eaten, we would have mharapara. I felt very good about this bull, the feeling lasting until I wantonly squandered it all in the heat of mid-afternoon.

He was an old dagga-boy along the Botswana border, completely alone at 2:00 p.m., and his horns were respectable enough for Sandy to reckon that we could do worse than to use one of our two Cape buffalo permits on him. He moved off when we began to stalk, but halted out 90 yards from us, showing me the point of his left shoulder—the same target a giant eland had given me two years earlier in the C. A. R. I held on that point and, expecting the buffalo to collapse with the shot, squeezed the trigger.

The bull bucked when the bullet struck, and he began to run. My first mistake was that I have obviously not hit bone. The second was that we did not give him time to lie down, but rushed after him, jumping him a few hundred yards into the brush and pushing him away before I could put a solid into him.

For an hour-and-a-half we followed a trail of blood drops the size and bright color of salmon eggs. From behind every bush, tree, or tall termite hill, I simply knew he was going to rise up, the anger in him fiery as burning brimstone.

Early on, Sandy whispered to me to breathe through my nose, not my mouth, to prevent dehydration. There was no telling how long we would be out here, and we had hurried off without water. The next thing he whispered to me after an hour of my waiting to be murdered, or at least severely walked upon, was, "Oh yes—be alert." He fairly twinkled from behind his beard when he advised this.

Be alert? Alert? I am the Alert Man from out of the pages of Ortega y Gasset. I can see every movement, hear every sound, smell every scent. I feel like a walking satellite dish receiving all transmissions. I am not feeling the least drowsy.

Then a lone bull was directly ahead of us in the direction the blood spatters led. He was 200 yards out, walking slowly with his head down, and neither Sandy nor I hesitated. He had gotten away once already, and we could not let him get away again. We both raised our rifles and fired almost simultaneously. Then, just like ducks popping up in a shooting gallery, buffalo come out of the grass and brush everywhere and charged off, the wounded bull falling behind.

What the hell?

Circling widely around us, the herd, 50 or 60 strong, slowed, then halted in a milling knot, trying to ascertain where the shots came from. The bull was moving very slowly now, and I crept up to a sapling to take a rest against it. I held the crosshairs on the knobby part of his shoulder, and the 300-grain solid sent his legs out from under him, his head twisting up and his huge black body slamming to the ground as the herd galloped off.

Here was a dead bull buffalo, but was it the right dead bull? It certainly looked right, but to make sure we went back to the place where we had shot when we thought he was alone and followed out the blood trail. Its logical conclusion appeared to be none other than the dead buffalo, with blood leading to him and none continuing on with the herd. There seemed to be a tight fit to the pieces.

I said that we should make one more cast, one last sweep to see if there were any other signs of blood at all. So we did; and in the opposite direction from that taken by the fleeing buffalo I heard Enoch, bent low to the ground, uttering distinctly what could have only been the Shona equivalent of "Uh-oh."

It looked as if the wounded *nyati* had led us into this herd and passed through, trying to lose his tracks among all the others. We three stared at the blood and one another. It was impossibly hot and there was no water and we had been chasing that buffalo hard now for seven or eight miles. We had one on the ground who was a good one, and no one would ever be the wiser. No one but us.

As we trailed after him from there, the wounded buffalo's tracks never slowed. At each increasingly infrequent, rusty, dime-sized drop of blood on the reddish dirt I considered what I was feeling. Pity for the bull, to be sure. Remorse for not having killed well. But what else?

In hot pursuit of an animal widely known "to run both ways"—at you as well as away—particularly when injured, my most sensible emotion should have, as my thumb lay moist against the knurled safety of my rifle and my eyes bored ahead, by rights been one of witless terror. Yet I could not honestly say that it was. I assuredly had no desire to be maimed or killed, but in a rather baffling manner I was enjoying this nonetheless. I never would have intentionally created this situation—as much for the animal's sake as my own—but now that I was in it, all the more prosaic concerns of life were cleared from the table. I did not have to worry about what bills to pay or errands to run; I did not have to think about dentist appointments or deadlines or being sure to behave engagingly. In this fierce state of freedom the only obligation I had was to stay tuned for the abrupt manifestation of something quite large, black, horned, and infuriated, and to kill it when it showed up. Yes, I was enjoying this, certainly more than I should; and the conclusive discovery of this fact scared me more than any buffalo ever could, with the thought of where such enjoyment might lead in life.

We were swiftly losing the light when the bull's trail meandered through a grove of trees and we found where he had stood long enough to bleed onto the ground a pool of blood the size of a saucer. It might be lung blood, but that might mean he was hit in one lung only, probably the left from the angle of the shot, and only one lung gone might not be sufficient to bring him down. Or he might be hit high in the shoulder, that shot probably not fatal. He had gone on from here, but we had to go back three miles or more to quarter up the other bull and fetch the Land Rover to load him into and carry him back to camp. As we walked out, Enoch broke off green leafy branches from the bushes he passed and tied the long grass into knots along the trail to show us the way back to the spoor. We would return in the morning.

Back at the dead buffalo, we dismantled it as you would an old Ford and stacked the parts—protein-rich quarter panels, fenders, and front hood—into the Land Rover, filling it so we had to ride on top of the meat. In equatorial Africa the sunset had no denouement, light and dark a process of input and output. As I rode back in the night, seated on the buffalo's polished horn boss, every jolt of the rutted dirt track was transmitted through it to me; and I wondered what I had lost out there on the trail of that wounded buffalo, or what I might have gained. These days one did not admit to feelings of bloodlust or the "thrill of the chase"—far too impolite and barbaric, far too "male privilege"—but there it was. I guessed I was going to have to find a way to live with it. The Land Rover bounced hard, and I held onto the curved horn tips for dear life.

We planned to go out late the next morning to give the vultures ample opportunity to ride the midmorning thermals into the blue sky and locate the buffalo for us. We wanted to find him down and as we approached to see the vultures around his carcass lift up in a flapping of wings that would have the dry sound of newsprint fluttering in the wind. We did not want to believe that he could still be going on.

But he was. For four hours we trailed him, past dry pans where the baked mud was as white as newly cast aluminum; through thorn-bush coverts where he could have lain up and run amuck through us when we stumbled over him; and finally into a bachelor herd of buffalo, Sandy and Enoch, and I bellying to within 15 yards of them, our belt buckles scooping up dirt. We glassed them all fastidiously.

One bull was sheer enormity, over 45 inches across the spread of his horns; but neither he nor any of the others showed any wounds. So we stood; and the bulls stood with their scenting noses held high, peering at us in the simmering shade the trees gave, then ran. In a few hundred yards they joined up with a breeding herd with hundreds of animals in it. We drove them all ahead of us, watching for a straggler, until we reached the tar road, having crossed much of that wide buffalo land of trees and savannah; and the buffs trotted across it and into the timber on the other side. Then there was no more spoor to follow.

The Department of Parks and Wild Life (as their shoulder patches read) was notified of the dead bull and the wounded one who was still at large. Both, as they should have been, were marked down against my two buffalo permits. Then Sandy had to leave and the rains broke and the green became unbearable to behold.

We drove into Botswana to spend the night in a game lodge in Chobe, to get away from tent camping for one day. There was a bar along the road for a beer, and at the end of the bar sat two Botswanans, both with watches the size of grapefruits on their wrists, half-a-dozen empty cans in front of each, holding the same conversation drinkers do around the globe: "I hear this drought will last another 10 years."

Back in camp, Dan for his first time on safari or in Africa was taking to it, perhaps too well. Seated in his canvas chair under a thatched-roof patio, he called out, "John! Pepsi!" And John promptly appeared and handed Dan an open bottle of cola, taken from the propane refrigerator positioned two feet behind where Dan sat, his maybe looking a little too close to Kurtz for comfort.

Coming back from Chobe, we met a group of Irish nurses with backpacks, walking the road from the border crossing, and invited them to have dinner and spend the night in our camp. Despite the tawdry dreams of then-bachelors, there is little to report. Except Dan's coming down with flu-like symptoms that left him prostrate on his cot, and which to this day he claims were the result of a mysterious bite inflicted by a deadly poisonous scorpion.

I hunted out the rest of the safari with another hunter, Sten. Born in Sweden 67 years earlier, he had for his life's resume one much more audacious and far-flung than the progressively drearier regimentation of this century seemed to allow: officer in the neutral Swedish Army during World War II; gaucho in South America; merchant seaman; Green Beret in the U. S. Army during the Korean War; game catcher; hired to work on the filming of *Hatari!*; and a professional hunting career in Kenya, Uganda, Sudan, Tanzania, Zambia, Botswana, and Zimbabwe. He had been tossed by buffalo and rhino, been shot at by armed men, could still walk down an elephant, and his greatest joy was rowing out into the Indian Ocean off Malindi in Kenya and fishing for big fish. I asked him how he could have ever devised such a fanciful life.

"I read too many books," he answered quietly, staring off into the gusu, his well-used 458 laid across this shoulder.

With Sten I hunted greater kudu, but all we were seeing aside from a multitude of tracks heading into the densest of cover along the Zambezi were cows and immature hulls. One gray afternoon as we traveled along a ridge near the old tobacco barns, Sten spotted an exceptional impala standing out from all the leaves. We left the vehicle and stalked toward the buck. He was about 60 yards away, looking in our direction. I had to stand to shoot over the brush, working the bolt of my other rifle, the 270, as I rose from my crouch. I had not forgotten the wounded buffalo, and I wanted this shot to be right. Firing offhand, I took him cleanly through the shoulders. He ran a matter of feet and fell. His horns were ribbed and long and black, his coat a reddish-buff, and I knelt beside him to move my hand over his hide.

As we drove down the tar road a little later we sighted three mature kudu bulls slipping into the gusu woods. Sten, his tall tracker Richard, and I struck off after them. Sten's elephant hunter's legs ran me to a frazzle as we chased the braiding and unbraiding of the kudu's tracks in the sandy soil. One set of tracks split off, and we kept on with the two that stayed together;

and it all ended with my standing behind a tree, rifle braced against the trunk and crosshairs on a long gray neck, before passing up the bigger bull, that was only fair.

The rains, having broken, fell constantly through the last days in Matetsi; and there was to be no last-minute 60-inch kudu bull for me in those particular green hills to "reward" me for the one I passed up—but then, I hadn't expected there to be. I sat beneath the thatched roof of the dining patio in the afternoon, drinking tea, watching the rain mark the Zambezi and remembering Africa before I had even left it, savoring it while it was still embracing me.

I remembered the heat of midday when all movement ceased with the finality of a fan engine seizing. I remembered the calling of a dove in the evening, and the softness of the chill-free dawns and the pleasant walking until the morning grew too warm. I remembered the flash-freeze of a gunbearer as he was about to put his foot into the disquietingly fresh track of a black rhino, and the feel of the sweat trickling down my spine. I remembered the ludicrously rapid trotting of helmeted guinea fowl; the high bounding of escaping impala; a young lion coming out of a dry donga, looking back over his shoulder, his jaw slack but eyes hard; and hippos with the jowly faces of middle-aged barflies—"Set us up another one! And they say this drought will last another *20* years."

I remembered Africa as the tartness of the sour plums I plucked from the bushes as we chased ghosting kudu, and as shit and blood and flies and striped-legged ticks and cobras and wait-a-bit thorns like no. 12 hooks and tremendous dung beetles whirring in like gunships when we gutted an animal, with the vultures still circling overhead, awaiting our departure from the scene. I remembered Africa as lightning over Zambia, the barking of poachers' dogs in Botswana, and gin after sundown in Zimbabwe. And most of all, as the *éminence grise* of elephant striding round-footed through it all, a sight I traveled around the world to see once more.

Finally, Africa was far more than memory. It was about being, the truest kind of being I ever knew. Is-ness. It was why I would continue to return, why I had returned before and would return again, each time leaving behind some incremental portion of myself—as I had with that buffalo and that kudu—until there came a day (I sincerely hoped) when I would dissolve entirely into Africa, consumed by it, run to an absolute frazzle.

That was Africa. More than memory. Far more than a dream.

As for that wounded buffalo, game scouts found a carcass some weeks later in the area, likely pulled down by lions and cleaned by hyenas, jackals, vultures, and storks. It looked like the head we had described. So they gave it to Green Torto, who put the other permit on it, and sent it to me. I've never quite known what to make of it, what kind of omen it may be. Whether of good, or bad. Or maybe something of both. Or neither.

The Great Koodoo

The 1990s . . .

WITH KUDU, AS it is with Africa, first impressions are largely wrong. In Africa, in our minds, to begin with, it is all dangerous game, good ol' nature red in tooth and claw. Our thoughts go first to lions, leopards, and those "thick-skinned" beasts whose entire *raison d'être* is, we have seduced ourselves into believing, to take our lives, even though they so seldom ever seem to (but thanks for thinking of us, all the same; and where the fatal threat comes from is where least expected—take that charging wild boar).

In fact, the hunting of dangerous animals can be far less fascinating than might be imagined: Cape buffalo are hardly a threat until one sets out to kill them; leopard hunting condenses into sitting in silence, waiting for public transportation that seems to take forever to arrive; and hunting elephant is about the same as genius—99 percent perspiration. There is considerably more to Africa than death, in any particular length of grass. There is, after all, that greater kudu.

With the kudu the misconception is one of fragility. In Venice, glassblowers craft miniature animals that must be packed in cotton-lined cardboard boxes and carried gingerly home where they are showcased on

shelves behind the closed doors of vitrines, lest they shatter. And when you first see a kudu, in that fleeting glimpse he gives you, he makes you think of something delicate glass menagerie. Upon closer inspection, though, a kudu creates another impression altogether.

It takes a long time of looking to see the kudu as it is in real life. And what you do see, instead of something frangible and gazelle-like, is an animal sturdy as an elk. One of the largest antelopes in Africa, second only to the eland, greater kudu bulls weighing 700 pounds are not unheard of, the tops of their high-crested withers reaching to over five feet. Blue gray and white-striped, a white chevron marking the face, a fringe of hair hanging beneath the almost too-long neck, ears too big by half and shaped like the spade on a playing card, the kudu carries above all this the greatest spiral of dark-brown horn carried by any animal on the continent (among the very greatest in the world, as it happens), mirror helices in some cases exceeding 60 inches in length. "Elegant" is the commonly accepted word for the kudu—a kudu standing still, perhaps, in a certain light. An actual kudu on the run—who when pressed can take a 10-foot barrier in a bound—moves like nothing so much as a sack of used auto parts tumbling down a ravine. "Gawky," or "disjointed," would be the most generous characterization— though obviously that is another false impression, the kudu nimble even on rocky slopes.

In my real life it took me quite some time to be able to look carefully at a kudu. But then, it seems to take everyone a fair amount of time. The English explorer and hunter Frederick Courteney Selous had been in southern Africa for several seasons before he killed his first "koodoo," judging it to be possibly "the handsomest antelope in the world." Theodore Roosevelt never killed one of the (for him) "stateliest and handsomest antelope in the world," while his son Kermit managed to kill two of the "great koodoo" during their 11 months in Eastern and Central Africa.

Ernest Hemingway famously spent the final two of the 10 weeks of his safari in Tanganyika in 1934 hunting kudu (somewhere between Roosevelt and Hemingway the spelling was streamlined), not taking one until the very end, when he found his bull in "country the loveliest that I had seen in Africa"; and all he wanted, afterward, was to come back so he could "hunt that country slowly, living there and hunting out each day," to "lie in the fallen leaves and watch the kudu feed out and never fire a shot" unless he saw a better head than the one he took. By the time he did come back to that country it was too late for him to save himself; but he did write a book about the first time, *Green Hills of Africa,* for which his hunt for kudu was both armature and beating heart.

Robert Ruark also wrote a book about his own first safari to Tanganyika, titled *Horn of the Hunter.* The 15 days he spent hunting kudu on that safari were not, though, the centerpiece of his book. They were, instead, an interim of comic exasperation in which kudu eluded him at every turn. In the end, kudu for Ruark were no more than "an impression . . . a gray blur, partially seen, swift to vanish."

"A kudu," wrote Ruark, "is definite only when he is dead."

It took me quite some time to learn that was not precisely true, but it does seem to be the case that kudu hunting owes more to vagary than most other forms of the chase. There never seems to be any such thing as a kudu hunt that qualifies as "typical." Either kudu slip away again and again, ghosting through thorn bush that leaves pursuing hunters tattooed from cheek to shin, or at dawn a bull beyond imagination is standing beside the ashes of the campfire. I met one hunter who just happened to shoot a bull (whose horns went some impossible length beyond 60 inches) while he was in Africa on a bird hunt; while a friend of mine, after weeks of hunting kudu almost desperately, at long last took a bull with one horn well over 50 inches, with the one on the offside barely 40 inches and curled tight as a pig's tail. Even when you "win" with kudu, the victory is often illusory.

My own history with kudu extends back over four decades to Kenya in the early 1970s. There I went through, as I've said, the requisite business with the big cats in a great tumble of luck, and so the plan then called for us to move north to the mountain terrain near Isiolo, where we would have to use horses to get into the kudu country. All we had to do first was stop off in the western Maasailand on the way there and pick up a Cape buffalo. That was all. So of course, what should have been four or five days of buffalo hunting turned into over two weeks; and with all my time and all my money gone, I never got to see the kudu country of Kenya.

Then one afternoon in the mid-1980s I was jogging through the gusu woods of Zimbabwe's Matetsi, following the racing shadows of three kudu bulls, leaving bits of myself on the thorns as I went. It was a hot gray summer's day in December, and as the trotting across the sandy soil stretched into miles, I wondered if I would ever get a chance to see a kudu in real life. When, on the move, we saw from their tracks that one of the bulls had broken off from the other two, so we guessed that the two together would be an older bull and his younger guard, the askari; and we stayed on their trail, moving deeper into the woods, until 250 yards ahead of us, partly hidden by the thick trunk of a tree, there were kudu legs and kudu ears, kudu eyes and kudu horns. We lowered to the ground and crept to the base of a tree where I got a fixed rest and put the crosshairs of my rifle's scope on the farther tree, watching the elements of kudu shift nervously behind it, waiting for a kudu to step out whole.

The air was absolutely still as the sky gathered into clouds of rain, and after about five minutes one of the kudu, the larger of the two, eased out from behind the tree so that I saw all of his head and neck and shoulder. And then I saw in what way Ruark had been wrong; because as indistinct as kudu may seem when you are in pursuit of them, at some point when they stop and you catch up to them, they are there as definite as a tree or rock or sunlight or the moon in a cold black southern sky. Some animals—nyala and giant eland are two—are almost never there, not even when you have them in your sights; but when a kudu stands he seems set in bedrock. And now here was one standing before me, and the professional hunter, Sten, was studying him carefully through his binocular as I watched him through my scope. After several seconds Sten whispered to me that this bull, a young one, was just fair, maybe 44 inches around the spiral; but he might also be the only kudu we saw before the seasonal rains hit and hunting would become almost impossible. So it was up to me.

I watched the kudu for a few seconds more, then lowered my rifle. And then he and the other kudu were not there anymore; and I knew that while I'd seen kudu at last, I still needed to see more. The 1990s, then, found me in the Northern Transvaal for one reason, and that being that the Northern Transvaal is where the largest greater kudu in the world are.

On the July day that I at last got to see kudu long enough in real life, I first got to see the sun rising redly through thorn trees, which is the logo Africa seems to stamp on every dawn to let you know where you are. Where the professional hunter Bruce and I hunted that day, the leaves of the red-bushwillow trees—one of the favored foods of the browsing kudu—were all brown when they should have still been bright green. This was the height of a dozen-year drought; and Bruce worried that there would be no feed left for the kudu by September, and that more kudu would die than would survive.

Early in the cool morning, though, we spotted a pair of kudu cows moving off into the bush; and Bruce and I trailed after them on foot. The trailing was made difficult by all the dead leaves that had begun to carpet the ground, but through the bush we saw the gray, white-striped kudu, now become a small band, moving ahead of us. They did not know we were there; but when we tried to circle around them to see if there was a bull in the group, a cow gave a loud, hoarse bark, and with tails raised in white flags they were gone.

There was a chance that the bulls might still be with the cows, even though the breeding season had been over for many weeks; or they might have moved back into the rocky hills, or *kopjes*, where the biggest bulls liked to live; either alone or in small bachelor herds, until the breeding season again sent them back to the cows. But except for one immature male, there were no bulls we could see with any of the cows we spotted or trailed after that morning.

During the hottest hours of the midday, we ate lunch and rested in the shade of trees growing out of a concrete-hard termite hill, watching a waterhole 70 or 80 yards away. Kudu come to water, but only when it suits them, at any time of the day or night. Still, the majority of kudu are taken from blinds, and while we watched from ours, there was the sound of a woodland kingfisher calling, and doves, francolins, and guinea fowl; and warthogs came to the water. But no kudu, and in the afternoon we hunted on.

Traveling down one of the soft sandy roads, we saw a kudu bull appear 100 yards away in the bush on a hillside. In the afternoon light he looked ingot-like, bright as pewter or steel. Even his dark horns were silver; and as he stared at us with his head lifted, he carried those horns laid back so we could not see how far they spiraled. Then he turned his head and we saw that those horns, rippled like a set of polished Malay krises, ran back nearly the entire length of his body. And before I could get down and creep away from the vehicle and find a place to get a shot at him, before Bruce could even tell me what I already knew—that this was a good bull very worth taking—the kudu was gone, like a lantern blown out.

We went on hunting as the daylight was going. In the sun of the late afternoon we spotted two aardvarks, "earth pigs" (looking supple and round as very large, very well-stuffed leather duffels), out feeding—a strange occupation for these highly nocturnal *Orycteropodidae,* but maybe another sign of the drought's effects. There were also bushbabies in the trees, and then five kudu cows 200 yards away, jumping a fence, one at a time. We watched them jump, Bruce telling me I had to shoot the bull as soon as he stepped out, because he would not wait, but would jump the fence and disappear again into the bush at once. But after more minutes of waiting we decided there was either no bull with the cows, or he simply chose not to come out. With kudu there is often no plausible explanation.

Now it was the very last light, and we had time to check just one more waterhole. As we drew near, kudu ran from the waterhole across a stretch of open ground. The kudu stopped at the edge of a stand of thorn trees about 150 yards away, and Bruce, glassing it, said, "Cow." I glassed it, too, seeing the kudu-ness in the gray shadow. And to the left of it I saw another gray shadow, larger and even more kudu-like.

"There's the bull," I whispered to Bruce.

I sat on the ground at once, wrapping a hasty sling around my arm, elbows locked over my knees. When the bull turned, his horns stretched back the length of his body, and Bruce did not even bother to tell me that this was a good one.

The kudu ran into the trees several more yards and stopped, quartering to the right, sharply away from me. I made myself not look at his horns, only at the spot behind the high, narrow, white-tufted withers created by the vertebrae of his spine. Ten long white stripes marked his flank, and sunset light lined his back and neck and horns; and I held the crosshairs of the variable scope behind those high withers, about halfway up his body from the bottom of his chest. I eased off the safety on the 300, and at the instant I fired the bull vanished.

The cow, now joined by two others, ran off to the left; but none of us could see if the bull was with them. Not even Bruce, who had his binocular on the bull when I fired, was sure where he went, though Bruce was certain my shot was a hit. So we sprinted for the trees, Bruce ahead of me; and then he stopped at the spot where the bull was standing when I fired, looking at the ground; and in a step or two more I saw the spiral of black horn in the air, and when I was 10 feet from Bruce I saw the entire bull lying at his feet, the hole where the 200-grain bullet entered showing no blood at all, the bull having fallen dead at the shot as if the earth had opened beneath him, not even staying on his feet long enough to bleed.

Running up breathless, I shouted at Bruce, "Can you see where he went?" and he turned and smiled at me out of his red beard.

Now I had time enough in this real life to look at this "fragile" kudu, which I saw was the toughest and oldest possible of bulls, a couple of inches broken off the tip of his right horn and a patch barked off the front of the lower spiral, all from fighting to keep his harems over the years, as were all the scars that jagged across his body like lightning strikes and formed an almost solid mass on his face. His left ear was split and his left hoof injured, the mane on his throat worn short, everything perfect.

The sole signs of daintiness anywhere on him were his tiny hooves, made for carrying him awkwardly but quickly over rocky ground. And his body, though thin, was huge, like some great bony horse's. The bases of both horns are 11 inches around, and the broken one was 51 inches long, while the perfect, ivory-tipped left one was 54 around the spiral. Aged and gaunt and relentlessly noble, he would not have seen another breeding season, with or without me.

I hunkered down and put my hand on the longer horn, warm still in the spreading darkness. And that was where I stayed, seeing him, the great "koodoo," as he really is, until there was no more light at all.

That night in camp when we brought the kudu in, one of my friends who had come for the first time to hunt them stared at this bull I have been waiting 20 years to see, and running his hand along the horn, told me what the truest impression of kudu is.

"So this is why we're here."

Perfect Game

Yesterday, Today, Tomorrow . . .

A FEW FAR from final words about Cape buffalo.

In a frame on the wall, the yellow stub has printed on it in black and red letters, "Field Box, $3.50, Chicago CUBS vs. Los Angeles DODGERS, DODGER STADIUM, THU. SEP. 9, 1965." There was no place else on earth quite like Dodger Stadium then, especially for a 13-year-old. It was another day when Walter O'Malley owned the team and kept his rampant polar bear mount on display in the Stadium Club. With its wide band of upper-deck seats painted a shade of aqua, like seawater over a bottom of marled sand, and with banks of halide lights creating an artificial sun, stepping into the stadium somehow gave the sensation of venturing into a marine environment, like wading out onto the flats to fish. As unequaled as the stadium was maybe the team itself, with Drysdale, Wills, and the Davises. And that Thursday night in Dodger Stadium there was absolutely no other figure in sports even the remote rival of Sanford Koufax.

It wasn't supposed to be a pitching duel, something you might expect from a, say, Juan Marichal–Koufax matchup. The Cubs starter

was another southpaw, Bob Hendley, who would have only a seven-year career with lackluster teams, and a middling win-loss record; and he would be facing the "Left Arm of God," even though Koufax was already experiencing the arthritis that would rob him of his meteor fastball. Hendley, though, would pitch the game of his life; regrettably, for him, so would Sandy.

In the stands the fans tuned in on their pocket transistor radios in the September night when the breeze off the ocean carried away the heat of the summer's day. It wasn't a Dodger game, even sitting in the stadium, without Vin Scully's calling it. Hendley was losing 1-0 on a walked batter and an error, giving him a no-hitter into the seventh when Dodger left fielder "Sweet" Lou Johnson hit a bloop double that had no effect on the scoring. Now, at the top of the ninth, Scully was at his eloquent best. He was also violating the unwritten rule of never speaking the words "perfect game" before it was complete.

"Three times in his sensational career," said Vin over the air, the tinny echo of his voice rippling, just audible, throughout the stands, "has Sandy Koufax walked out to the mound to pitch a fateful ninth where he turned in a no-hitter. But tonight, September the ninth, nineteen-hundred and sixty-five, he made the toughest walk of his career, I'm sure, because through eight innings he has pitched a perfect game. . . ."

Koufax had 13 strikeouts, five in a row through the eighth and into the ninth innings when he faced Cubs pinch hitter Harvey Kuenn, the potential last batter. Scully's call: "You can't blame a man for pushing just a little bit now. Sandy backs off, mops his forehead, runs his left index finger along his forehead, dries it off on his left pants leg. All the while Kuenn just waiting. Now Sandy looks in. Into his windup and the two-one pitch to Kuenn: swung on and missed, strike two. It is 9:46 p.m. . . . Two and two to Harvey Kuenn, one strike away. Sandy into his windup, here's the pitch: swung on and missed, a perfect game." A perfect game, and with one meaningless hit, considered the greatest game of baseball ever pitched.

So I've seen a perfect game, but I think I have also hunted it. For millions of hunters, perfect game is none other than the white-tailed deer, for them the ideal fusion of intelligence, senses, and guile. Others, though, might choose the bighorn, or one of the other wild sheep, in deference to the grandeur of its habitat, the severe challenges of the hunt, and the magnificence of the trophy.

Ernest Hemingway talked about this, in a way, in comparing bonefish to striped marlin. He was addressing anglers who thought the bonefish, pound for pound, the perfect game. "Your bonefish is," he wrote to them in an article about Cuba and marlin, "a smart fish, very conservative, very strong too." The bonefish, though, would never be seen in 1,000-foot water or require the kind of extreme tackle needed for marlin. Most of all, though, it is too "smart by far to jump," and without jumping, Hemingway saw a fish that lacked a "patent of nobility." Similarly, I would have to look away from whitetail and sheep because neither has the capacity to injure seriously, or perhaps kill, me, except by the most bizarre sort of freak occurrence. To me the perfect big-game animal needs to be dangerous by nature, not merely by unanticipated circumstance.

Is it some exaggerated sense of machismo—and we know what that hides, don't we?—that makes me want my perfect game to embody the potential of risk? Or is there something, dare I say, existential about hunting an animal in which the odds may be drawn closer to a keen razor's edge?

We hunt game for food, and that can be enough. But we could also garden or raise tilapia without ever engaging in bloodsport. Today, outside the few subsistence cultures, and individuals, hunting is an option, not a true necessity for survival. So what could compel us to travel to distant lands to pursue the animals of our desire? A land like Africa?

Critics will call it "cultural arrogance," but there is the romantic (or is it maudlin or vainglorious?) philosophical belief that "the greatest and most moral homage we can pay to certain animals on certain occasions is to kill them with certain means and rituals," which is a notion so far out of the 21st century as to give the word "atavism" the ring of a neologism. And to those words, I would add, and certain places. Such as Africa.

You go there for exotic game to be found nowhere else. It is a matter, to a large extent, of esthetics. A sable, among the most exquisite game animals on earth, cannot be hunted under native conditions anywhere but in Africa, and not for the absolute intention of eating it, although it will be. Now add big game that has it in it to run both ways. Which brings us to buffalo.

I could offer the rationale for why the other dangerous game—from brown and grizzly bear to lion, leopard, elephant, and rhino—fall short of perfection; but it may be preferable to talk about what makes the buffalo perfect. Democracy is one very key factor. It is within reason for many if not most people to be able to hunt buffalo, if they really want to. In addition, and this is extremely important, they can usually hunt it again if they do it and like it. The simple economics of the day make it doubtful that anyone will hunt several lions or elephant or black rhino (especially at $350,000 for a permit) in a lifetime. Since taking my first buffalo at age 22, I have hunted them since. No, not in the scores or even the dozens, but enough to know how much it appeals to me. Not that buffalo didn't take some getting used to.

What you come to realize is that the buffalo is a creature of darkness—dense cover is its milieu. Elephant and lions, though they can be found in many habitats, seem to prefer ones that are relatively open. And for the leopard you almost always end up hanging a bait.

The thing about buffalo is having to go in after them, to where they live, not counting on them to come out and meet you on level ground. For buffalo, that is the 1,000-foot depth. Until you get used to that you carry the taste of brass in your mouth as you hunt, something that it takes more than one buffalo to cleanse away.

There is also the kind of weapon that seems called upon for dealing with a buffalo. Buffalo have been hunted, and killed, with any number of calibers (there is likely no calculating how many have been taken with the British 303); but there is never any sense that in carrying a 450 or 500, one is over-gunned, or that there is anything less than a buff that truly demands such inordinate calibers. It is the 15/0 reel of hunting rifles, and you are never unhappy to be carrying such a gun when you are stalking buffalo in cover that reaches above your head and that you have to shoulder your way through.

I won't pretend that hunting Cape buffalo is a "gamble with death" every time, or even most of the time, when you go out to do it; but somewhere in the back of your mind, as you are hunting buffalo, it remains an idea with a particular piquancy that is not likely to be found in hunting ducks in a heated blind. It may also be noted that you do not, or only under the rarest of circumstances, hunt purely solitary buffalo: There is almost always another set of eyes and ears, if not more, ready to detect an unwelcome approach. And that approach can be through the thickest of bush, making a big rifle all the more interesting to carry because a hunter could actually find it of some utility and not mere affectation. There is, in short, nothing like hunting Cape buffalo, short of knowing you are to be hanged in a fortnight, to concentrate the mind wonderfully.

Out of 300,000 major league baseball games played, 23 have been perfect, making the odds of my ever seeing another overwhelmingly against me. The thing about that other perfect game, at least my notion of it, that one in Africa, is that there is always a chance that I may still yet find a day when I will hunt it again.

Iodine

Before . . .

I T'S NOT CERTAIN if the true eccentrics of Africa are a vanishing breed, or already vanished. Described as a baggy-shorts-wearing cadaverous man with a large aristocratic nose, C. J. P. Ionides, nicknamed "Iodine"—game ranger, hunter of singular big game, poacher, a bachelor who valued ivory over marriage, fascinating conversationalist, and Africa's most renowned field herpetologist—may very well have been among the last, delighted to live in glorious seclusion in the bush in his own always peculiar way. Ionides was every inch an eccentric, but among the most consequential that Africa ever knew, even if a man not without the disfiguring pall of colonialism, and more than a touch of misanthropy, shrouding his spirit.

Constantine John Philip, called only "Bobby" for some inexplicable reason by his immediate family, was born, he tells us in his autobiography *Mambas and Man-Eaters,* in Manchester, England, in 1901 into a childhood he was not fond of recollecting. The fifth-generation of a prosperous English merchant family, his great-great grandfather having emigrated from Greece in 1817 saddled with the unpronounceable name of Ixplixis, which he changed to Ionides, meaning "son of the Greek," and which Bobby's

"tongue" found even more unutterable, Ionides was hunting butterflies by four.

In preparatory school, remembered primarily for famishment and floggings, his penchant for doing taxidermy on small creatures in his dormitory earned him the titles of "dirty little brute" and "awkward young swine" from his instructors. At Rugby he was a "sinister foreigner"; a search of his study after a false accusation of petty theft produced a startling display of contraband, including a "sawed-off shotgun [carried in the lining of his jacket for pheasant poaching], two pistols, ammunition, six rabbit nets, a cosh, a knuckle-duster, a tobacco pouch and a pipe"—though no stolen property.

Poaching money paid for his first alcoholic evening at Sandhurst, and to his swearing off whisky for life, sticking to a modest regime of gin and water thereafter. As he left for India with the South Wales Borderers to spend much of his time on *shikar,* his surgeon father gave him an uncommon piece of parental advice: "I'd be careful, if I were you. Remember, if you get VD it would interfere with your hunting." Food for thought for Ionides: By the time he made Tanganyika his permanent residence in 1926, coming to British East with the Kings African Rifles, "hunting was all [he] lived for" (which partially explains his decision to go on safari in Sudan, rather than attend the bedside of his dying father).

Ionides, anti-authoritarian to his Crown Bird–stained fingertips, though capable of the sternest sort of rigidity toward those serving beneath him, found an Africa as wide open as that Roosevelt saw more than a decade earlier, the Africa reminding T. R. of his time in the Dakotas. Settlers carried guns on their hips in town, and drunken shootouts were hardly uncommon. Which all met with Ionides's approbation.

Coming out of the army after two years in Africa, he went in for some minor ivory poaching in the Congo and elsewhere, which involved burning the carcasses so there were no large quantities of elephant meat showing up in the markets as evidence to give him away, which even for the day seems a rather unsavory, profligate practice, especially in the midst of hungry Africans. His ivory hunting amounted mostly to obtaining two official permits, then dropping additional bulls within the boundaries of assorted villages to make it appear that they were crop raiders killed legitimately by the villagers. The tusks he sold to an Irish black marketeer, with a percentage of the sale returned to the village chiefs. Elephant under 60 pounds a side were unprofitable, but 100 pounders were a regular take for him.

Unfortunately, the chiefs got "greedy," there was an outbreak of cannibal uprisings, the bottom fell out of the ivory market, the Belgian authorities levied a 50 percent tax on legal tusks, which were easier to trade, his rawhide boots disintegrated, and he went barefoot before finding the ideal hunting shoe in a pair of plimsolls, which were all he used for footwear for the rest of his life.

Withdrawing from ivory poaching, Ionides ran into a professional hunter in Dar es Salaam, who was pounding the bar and cursing his vanished servant for having impregnated his favorite African "bint," Ionides immediately attracted by his "diabolically criminal-looking face." Ken McDougall was a superb hunter, when sober, which was irregularly. Worse, he was a fighting drunk, making him one of the most "difficult and dangerous" men Ionides ever met. So of course, they went into partnership as "white hunters," with Ionides even giving McDougall his power of attorney to buy supplies, and whisky, in Arusha, the firm of McDougall & Ionides staggering from one brawling disaster to the next, Ionides learning that McDougall's stock phrase was, to all partially recollected dustups, "Never before in my life have I done such a thing."

Ending up £600 in the hole after a safari fell through, the American clients dissuaded by tales of McDougall's violent antics, Ionides dissolved the partnership and went on hunting on his own, returning to ivory poaching on the side to pay off his creditors. About this time he suffered a severe "beat-up" from an elephant cow wounded by a native muzzleloader, admitting his reckless behavior had been a major contributing factor, the attack leaving him with weeks of nightmares and with deafness in his left ear for the rest of his life.

Ill-suited to exchanging pleasantries with safari clients, Ionides sought a much less people-person occupation as a Ranger with the Tanganyika Game Department; and gaining it, in spite of his suspected past as a poacher, he went to work for the department on September 9, 1933, at £40 pounds a month, versus the £150 (over $10,000 today) he had raised his safari fee to. It was something of a Damascene moment for him, as he claimed never to have violated a wildlife regulation after that day.

Ionides listed the obligations of a Game Ranger of his time as conserve wildlife, protect human life, and control hunting. His instructions from the Game Warden of Tanganyika were, he said, "Go and be a Game Ranger," without further elaboration. With that for him congenially inexplicit charge, Ionides went down to Kilwa along the coast, opposite what one day became the Selous Game Reserve.

Ionides, more likely to be found safari-ing on foot through his vast precinct rather than seated behind his desk at headquarters, went about reordering and retraining his cadre of native game scouts, firing and replacing as needed. He undertook a reeducation program to convince the local villages and chieftains that cooperation with him and his scouts, and an end to poaching, was essential if they hoped to rely on the Game Department to come in when the elephant trampled their crops or lions ate their livestock, or people, accomplishing this by withholding aid when asked for, or getting the elephant "driven into the cotton," until the petitioners saw reason. With his scouts when they strayed and with villagers suspected of illegal hunting, his resort was often to the "traditional instrument of correction" in Africa, the rhinoceros hide strip known as the *kiboko,* until official policy outlawed its use, sometimes to the displeasure of his scouts who much preferred a half-dozen of the best to being discharged. At the same time, Ionides worked diligently to get his scouts better pay, refused to let them salute him, and deeply mourned the death of the multiple-wived, hard-drinking Issa Matundu who was his execrable cook for 20 years. As cringe-inducing as it may sound to our ears, he sincerely thought of them as his children and he their father.

In protecting human life, Ionides and his scouts gave chase to man-eating lions, child-eating leopards, and marauding elephant. For Ionides, there was poetic justice in the lions' taking of human beings because it was humans who were responsible for the dwindling of the great herds upon which the cats previously fed in contentment.

He felt most lions were capable of casual man eating; but it was the ones who got in the habit of it by realizing that humans were convenient prey—slow, thin skinned, light boned, ridiculously easy to kill once the trick of it was learned (go for the neck or head)—that were supremely dangerous. (In Ionides's time in Tanganyakia, the reported worst case of man-eating was carried out by the Njombe pride of lions that was believed to have killed between 1,500 and 2,000 people before the lions could be hunted down.)

The lions Ionides dealt with could rack up tallies of over 90 kills by themselves; and he killed 40 of them before retiring from the game department, eschewing traps and poison and developing a technique of tracking them on hands and knees in nearly impenetrable cover during the heat of the day when they laid up, often sleeping off a meal of "the whole of a fat woman," presenting him with only a swatch of tawny hide to shoot at pointblank through the undergrowth with his 470 double hammer rifle, admitting he was always afraid until the time came to fire. He never truly enjoyed the work, though, one reason being that he thought it unethical to shoot at some vaguely defined portion of a lion.

Leopards he found to be more ruthless killers, preying primarily on women and children and often attacking without real need of food. They were also far more difficult to hunt, causing him to resort to live traps and trap guns rigged along trails, and sometimes wounding natives passing by, in spite of his stern warnings. Leopards also seemed to bring out the worst anti-wildlife instincts in the colonial administrators, one who had previously seriously suggested machine gunning and depth charging hippos to reduce their numbers, and who had all leopards in the district classified as vermin in response to one particular child killer. Ionides succeeded, through subterfuge (he secretly convinced the local district commissioners to complain to the Provincial Commissioner about the damage wild hogs and baboons were causing without leopards around to curb their numbers), to have the vermin edict rescinded, noting that "intrigue," using the Swahili word *fitina,* was needed for a Ranger to protect wildlife successfully.

Ionides's celebrated snake catching career began during World War II as he returned from a patently Ionides-style military operation (hostages, threats of hanging, native retribution) carried out in Somalia when he rejoined the K. A. R. Shortly thereafter, it was concluded that he was of more (and possibly less savage) use to the war effort working for the Game Department in Tanganyika; and on his way back through Nairobi, he visited the Coryndon Museum where famed paleontologist L. S. B. Leakey asked him to help supply serpents for a new snake park attached to the museum.

Ionides's initial catching equipment was of the crudest sort: forked sticks and his hat, which became an icon. It was described, in *Snake Man* by Alan Wykes, as having begun life as a double terai, handed down in 1923 by a District Commissioner to a game scout, who passed it along to Ionides 17 years later. By the time Wykes saw it in 1959, it looked like something that had been in a "garbage tip" for a century, the outer crown torn away, the "brim worn into a mesh of felt and dirt," the inside "coated with a scabrous stiffening of grease." Serving as a nauseating water vessel and cooking pot, it was also what Ionides used to capture his first black mamba, eight feet, three inches, that crawled over his thighs as he sat in quiet contemplation in his unlit outhouse one night, shortly after coming back to Tanganyika. He managed to get away from the snake, get a light, and catch the serpent with a forked stick and his hat employed like a pot holder to hold the head, astounded at the strength of a mamba. Needless to say, his African assistants began thinking of the vile headwear as *dawa,* "medicine," an instrument of witchcraft. As for the mamba, like so many of the poisonous reptiles he shipped off to assorted museums worldwide, he punched some air holes in a box, packaged it up, and sent it through the mail, being sure to label the outside, "LIVE SNAKE."

Before his retirement from the game department in 1956, Ionides accumulated vast uninterrupted blocks of leave time, which enabled him to hunt throughout Africa for months and even years at a time, including almost the entirety of 1946 and '47 when he collected, his hunting then almost exclusively for museums, everything from mountain nyala to mountain gorilla. It had long been his ambition to take the rarities he discovered in H. C. Maydon's *Big Game Hunting in Africa,* devoting 20 years of his life to the pursuit. He hunted yellow-backed duiker; sitatunga; giant forest hog; bongo, "the blue riband of Africa, the giant eland"; barbary sheep; scimitar-horned oryx; addax; northern white rhino (five today, or less, known to inhabit the wild); that silverback who was shambling toward him with a puzzled expression when he shot it; and his proudest rarity, one not even known to science prior to the year of his birth, the primitive, deep-jungle giraffe, the okapi.

Ionides would have gone after more—the Somali beira, giant sable, pygmy hippopotamus—but he was a lifelong heavy smoker (that pipe and tobacco at public school, those untold Crown Bird cigarettes); and what he thought to be rheumatism proved, just before his retirement, to be popliteal thrombosis in his right leg. Having already experienced an appendectomy, amoebic dysentery, strongyolodiasis (roundworm infection), relapsing fever, dengue fever, typhoid, hemorrhoidectomy, and malignant and benign tertian malaria, he asked his physician when he would be recovered enough from this ailment to continue with his safaris. He was informed that he would never again be able to walk more than a quarter mile at a time.

A man who considered his life one of "perpetual safari," Ionides had to settle down, first in Liwale, just outside the Selous, decamping from there in high dudgeon when a neighbor felled all his trees and planted crops while he was away in the bush, making his final redoubt in Newala in (in the words of author Margaret Lane in her *Life with Ionides*) a "tin-roofed bungalow plastered like a swallow's nest" on the rim of an escarpment on the Makonde Plateau, overlooking the Ruvuma River and Mozambique beyond. With his servants, recordings of Wagner played on his Victrola, and history books, he subsisted on a hideous day-in-and-day-out diet of potatoes and goat meat boiled to the consistency of tire tread, remaining gaunt but muscled throughout life. The Makonde country possessed a unique appeal for Ionides, when, while on a recky back in his Game Department days, he happened on six "beautiful and dangerous" (Lane) green mambas in a single day. Discovering that the country was also thick with gaboon vipers, he thought, according to Lane, "'Well!'"

Collecting the most-venomous snakes in Africa became for Ionides a satisfyingly adventurous substitute for the big-game hunting now denied him. He acquired a light-aluminum unicycle bush cart—a sort of push-me-pull-you sedan chair—on which with knees drawn up against his chest, he rode as two of his servants careered him along the jungle trails. Yet he was still capable, despite a distinct fear of heights and a gammy leg and nearly aged 60, of climbing through the tangled limbs of a 100-foot mango tree to capture a mamba and to bring it down in one hand as he held on with the other to the tree. Or to catch his first water cobra by camping for 26 straight days with virtually no sleep on the edge of Lake Tanganyika, watching the surface for any slight disturbance made by a serpent.

There was no textbook to teach Ionides the art and science of snake catching, and in the course of his self-education he endured 13 poisoned bites. He survived, of course, capturing over 1,200 gaboon vipers by hand and thousands more snakes of all types, also by hand and with forked sticks, grab sticks, snares, even butterfly nets. And his hat. He developed techniques that sounded like something out of World Wrestling: the Boomslang Hold, the Night Adder Sideways Grip. Some of his catches went to museums, others to serpentariums, and many were milked for laboratories for antivenin production, Ionides operating a kind of dairy farm for venom—which suited him, because he was loath to kill a snake once he had it in captivity.

Among his herpetological finds were new species and subspecies of snakes, and lizards, some named for him (*Amblyodipsas katangensis ionidesi* Loveridge, for one), the list relegated to a footnote in his autobiography. Something else relegated to a footnote was his paramount achievement, the carving out of Selous Game Reserve.

When Ionides arrived, the reserve was a mere 1,000 square miles, which he set about deliberately to enlarge. His idea was to create a vast reserve (now, as noted, some 21,000 square miles) without any permanent habitation, supported by the fees paid by safari hunters. After years of ivory shooting and responsible for the culling of thousands of elephant during his term as a Ranger, Ionides wanted a place exclusively theirs, where they wouldn't be slaughtered for raiding crops and with enough thick, roadless country that they might be able to stay clear of systematic poaching. And into the 1970s, the Selous was the secure home of up to one-tenth of all the elephant in Africa.

Ionides's methods of shaping the Selous were no less harsh than his reliance upon the kiboko to discipline his scouts. When tsetse-borne trypanosomiasis and the infertile soils moved large numbers of people away from wide expanses surrounding the original sanctuary, Ionides incorporated that land into the reserve and worked to keep the people out, discouraging their resettlement by ignoring pleas to deal with marauding elephant. (An exception to the rule was his efforts to return the Wagindo to Liwale after they had been evacuated by the government under a contrived threat of sleeping sickness; as with the hole the death of his cook left in his heart, Ionides's personality was never less than contradictory, containing Whitmanesque multitudes.)

Ionides's policy of evicting Africans from their native lands and traditional hunting grounds to take them over is what was employed in the setting up of game reserves and parks throughout colonial Africa, and to Africans it was a complete inversion of their belief that human lives should take precedence over those of animals. They saw wildlife succeeding, because of Victorian-based sentimentality, to the lands traditionally theirs to hunt and till; and this was among the grievances that welled up into the volcanic crater of independence movements of the 1950s, though Ionides probably would not have been able to acknowledge that. ('Poacher' was merely the label placed on traditional hunters when their hunting rights were abrogated.)

For Ionides, the Selous was his work of art, as much as a classical poet's epic, and created with as little regard for humanity. Had he ever heard William Faulkner's indurate opinion that John Keats's "'Ode on a Grecian Urn' is worth any number of old ladies," he likely would have concurred. The sanctuary for elephant called the Selous seems as if it was worth any amount of African lives and suffering to Ionides.

In the Selous, which has always lain across customary trade routes for poachers (the label placed on traditional hunters when their hunting rights are abrogated), the elephant have been drastically, nearly tragically, depleted in recent years; the Tanzanian government is, while earning millions from sustainable safari hunting in the reserve, returning only a fraction to its conservation; and the Selous is being challenged by schemes for oil exploration, uranium mining, and dam building (opening it up with transects and access roads), chugging ahead at full mindless bore like a decapitated male mantis completing its assigned task as its mate devours it. (The developed world is hardly in a position to hurl stones at any of these misdoings, by the way.) With all that, it's hard not to see Ionides's dream threatened with dissolution.

Without Ionides, though—even with the dark arts practiced to assemble the reserve (that hat, perhaps?), with all his colonial arrogance and paternalistic attitudes, with the kiboko, and all that is supposed to appall us today—the dream, the wonder, the creation of the place called Selous never would have occurred to begin with, making it perhaps worth the unavoidable cost (was Yellowstone worth the exile of the Sheep Eater Shoshone?) of a few old Tanganyikan ladies.

Ionides's final dream, the one that would allow him to "die happy," was an expedition to Thailand, where he wished to collect specimens of the king cobra, the longest poisonous snake in the world, though he also wanted to capture in Central or South America a bushmaster, the largest known viper, Ionides always seeming to harbor one further extravagant desire.

I can find no record of either adventure. What can be known, though, is that the severe thrombosis worsened, leading to amputation; and his end came in 1968, lying legless in a hospital not in England, where he was born, but in Nairobi in Africa, where he lived and which he would not abandon, Africa's never abandoning him. There he died, anything but a saint, but in many ways a curious savior, all the same.

Sitting Around Campfires
with PHs

The 2000s . . .

AT THE HUNTING convention, Joe offered to stand me to a drink. A well-known outdoor writer and editor, Joe was also working as a professional hunter for a safari company; and he invited me to come by the "booth." It would have been just complete bad manners to refuse.

At 5:00 I swung by, and found a commissary-sized camp tent pitched in the middle of the convention-center floor, zebra skins spread out inside it. Joe was there, dressed in his going-to-town blue blazer and tie and elephant-hair bracelet, as were all the other professional hunters.

"Professional Hunter" is, as we've said, the official title, like labeling a cowboy a "livestock management specialist"; but professional hunters are still always "PHs," written in caps; and as a job description it carries the same panache as "PI," "DI," or "pirate."

One of the PHs, looking noticeably uncomfortable in a blue blazer, was a bear-like, bushy-eyebrowed old man. He seemed familiar;

and when Joe introduced us, I understood why. It was Søren. We shook hands, and he said he was pleased to meet me. I told him we had met.

"Really?" he asked, arching a thatch of eyebrow, searching his memory.

"Block 60 in Kenya, in September, 1974."

"Good God, no wonder I don't remember you," he said, the flicker of a smile almost disturbing his dour expression.

It was when I hunted with PH John Fletcher in Kenya's hunting Block 60, and Søren was camped several miles from us, guiding a Danish hunter. One night we drove over to Søren's camp for dinner; and the tension between Søren and his client, who did not speak English, was palpable. It turned out they had a leopard come into a bait late in the evening; and there was a bit of confusion, the client shooting before Søren could judge the leopard. Worse, the client had only wounded the cat; and it had gotten away, meaning that in the morning Søren had to crawl into the bush after it. On the drive back that night, influenced somewhat by alcoholic beverage, we had to brake for elephant as their eight-foot-tall backsides loomed up in the headlights.

The next morning we again crossed trails with Søren and his client, driving back to their camp. We asked how it was going, and Søren said fine, though he appeared particularly closed mouthed, and his client just stared straight ahead. There was no mention of the leopard, until one of our trackers got into a conversation in Kikuyu with one of Søren's. Oh yes, Søren's tracker said, they had gotten the leopard. It was right here. In a sack.

Fletcher overheard the conversation and shot a glance at Søren, who slumped visibly behind the wheel of his Land Cruiser. So we climbed out and went to look at Søren's hunter's leopard, which turned out to be an adult, a very, very small adult.

"As I recall," I said to Søren four decades later, "all Fletcher said was, 'Nice spots.'"

"No," Søren corrected me, pursing his lips, still chagrined almost 30 years after the fact. "I remember exactly what he said: 'Very pretty.'"

Later that night those many years ago, the client, crimson-faced in the gas-lantern light after a brandy too many, began poking Søren in the chest. Do not do that, Søren told him in plain Danish. But the client persisted until Søren, whose clenched fists were large blocky blunt instruments, had no further use for words.

Sitting in tents, or better by campfires, with PHs and listening to the old stories is at least part of the pleasure of going on safari. And the best stories are the ones in which something, sometimes most things (though never everything), goes wrong.

John Fletcher had his stories, all those years ago in Block 60. One was about hunting with the famous Mexican matador who wanted to kill a Cape buffalo with a sword. The first bull they faced, though, ended up running through the barrage of fire they put up. Fletcher had his 500 Nitro Express broken open, trying to stuff two more cartridges into it as the buffalo swept past the matador who pirouetted with practiced grace away from the bull's horns, and as the bull went by, swung the muzzle of his rifle up and shot the buffalo in the neck. The bull was dead on the wing; but momentum carried him on into Fletcher, knocking

Fletcher down. And there he sat, flat on the ground, a dead buffalo's head in his lap.

"And how is that," asked the matador, raising his hand in a flourish practiced in crowded bullrings, "for a client?"

"Do you still want to try to kill one of these with a sword?" Fletcher asked, looking up.

"Absolutamente no," replied the torero.

Another PH I sat around a campfire with, later in Zimbabwe, was Sten. Some years before, he had been taking a hunter into tall grass after buffalo when a flock of tick birds flared up ahead of them. Tick birds live on big mammals like buffalo, but something seemed wrong to Sten. And at that moment, with a sound like a tea kettle whistling, through the grass toward them charged not a buffalo but a black rhino. Sten stepped in front of his client and got off a shot from his 470 NE, but the rhino kept coming; and before Sten could fire the second barrel, he was on the ground, the rhino butting him with his muzzle.

At some point that prehistoric flesh tank was going to start stomping on Sten, so he threw his arms around the front horn, and wrapped his legs around the head as the rhino bucked up and down, trying to throw him off. Sten's hunter ran in and shoved his 340 Weatherby into the rhino's ear and pulled the trigger, the bullet nearly kneecapping Sten when it came out the other side. Except for a fractured pelvis, though, Sten was fine, and went on hunting for the remaining four weeks of the safari, hobbling around on a hand-whittled crutch.

"So what do you think about when you're being tossed up and down by a rhino?" I asked. "Does your life pass before your eyes?"

"You know," said Sten in his heavily accented English, "dat's a funny ting. All I could tink about when I was hanging onto dat horn was, 'By golly, dis one is long enough to make de record book.'"

Sometimes, the stories even have an odd confluence. Both Fletcher and Sten worked as technical advisers on the movie *Hatari!* back in the early 1960s. Fletcher remembered how John Wayne really was bigger than life, unfazed by anything. One shot, as Fletcher told it, called for Wayne to face a charging elephant. All morning Fletcher and the other PHs worked to haze a herd of wild elephant into camera range while Wayne sat in his canvas chair, smoking, reading, drinking coffee. Finally the elephant were rampaging properly toward the camera; and an assistant director went up to the Duke and said, "Mr. Wayne, your elephant is here."

Wayne put down his book, picked up his 458, walked out, turned back to ask if he was standing on the right mark, and then shot a bull elephant head on as it was bearing down on him (if you watch the movie, you can see the scene, and it looks as if Wayne was using some kind of non-lethal round, or shooting over the bull, to halt his charge). Wayne then coolly turned back to the director and asked, "That good?" and went back to his canvas chair.

Sten's job on the film included wrangling actors and crew for each day's shoot, which meant his having to knock on hut doors and lift tent flaps at dawn. According to Sten, "Dhere was never a morning when anybody was ever in de same place."

Sometimes, things going very right can also make for a good story for a PH to share around a campfire. As Sten told it . . . well, let him tell it.

"Tom," he said with a twinkling smile, thinking fondly of a time years before when he had been a young, unmarried PH, "do you remember de actress Elsa Martinelli in dat movie?" He paused, watching the flames, and with a sigh said, "Ja, dat was de finest tree months of my life." And like a true professional, said no more.

Dagga Boys & Monkey Oranges

~~~~~~~~

The 2000s . . .

SEEING IS BELIEVING, though not always as persuasive as not seeing. It cannot be, for instance, adequately appreciated how accomplished the Cape buffalo is at the art of concealment until you fail utterly at 25 feet to see 1,700 pounds of one, a body as gray-black and substantial as some massive canyon boulder, lying behind sparse branches of a bushwillow.

That's how it was with the first buffalo I didn't see on my first morning with professional hunter Rory Muil. Muil hunted in a 4,000 square-kilometer (a million acres, give or take) concession in the Binga Communal Lands of the Tonga people in northwestern Zimbabwe. It is 2,000-foot-high country above the Kariba Lake shore, densely brushed and timbered with mahogany, mopane, duiker berry, and grotesque pewter-barked baobab trees towering like Gogs and Magogs across the landscape. The Sengwa is the main river running through it. Among the other rivers is the Songo, where Rory and I hunted from a camp with green wall tents pitched on concrete pads and

covered by steep thatched roofs to hold in some of the night's cool during the day.

Kapinda is an area in the concession where stands of mopane trees grow to the bottoms of rocky ridges, scattering their bronze leaves like foliage fallen from oaks across rocky whitetail woods in northern Missouri. There were thickets of bushwillow (jess) still holding up their green-but-yellowing leaves, and long-yellow-grassed woodland parks rolling out on broad ridgelines. It was a hard drive at first light from the Songo to Kapinda—a kidney-bouncing ride in Rory's white Land Rover Defender, complete with stout brush guards wrapped around the front, a heavy rollbar with a rifle rack, steel ladders on the sides, and a high bench for the trackers to spot from in the back. The fabric covering the two front seats was bleached to the pallid blue of pool lounges, and there was not a door, mirror, or windshield to save your life. Rory figured it was worth the drive, because Kapinda was one of the best places in the concession for "dagga boys."

To understand both Kapinda and dagga boys (and maybe Rory, as well—and me?), you should consider the monkey orange. In Zimbabwe, the spiked-leaved monkey orange hangs from a small evergreen tree, its turquoise peel ripening to golden brown. Its pulpy flesh encapsulates numerous seeds, the way a pomegranate's does. The flesh is quite edible and by all accounts succulent. But the seeds of the poor monkey orange are in a paraphrase of Trini Lopez, impossible to eat, the Latin name for the plant, *Strychnos pungens,* denoting the genus from which strychnine is derived. Hidden in the seeds is nothing but poison.

Hidden in the wild and beautiful (to a hunter) Kapinda country was, if not quite poison, the distilled essence of *Syncerus caffer caffer* (the Cape buffalo): the dagga boy. *Dagga*[1] is a corruption of the word in Shona (Zimbabwe's native language) for "mud"; and a "dagga"—or mud—boy is an old bull who rules the wallows, coating himself in thick layers of cooling mire, metaling his hide against insects, and playing not at all well with others, as any cow, calf, or even lesser bull intemperate enough to wander into a mudhole with a dagga boy soon learns, to its regret. As many as half a dozen roguish dagga boys might run together, but it is more likely to find two to four at a time, or sometimes just one solitary, invariably truculent individual.

Tracking Cape buffalo on foot—as they should be hunted—was not a matter of going where the grass was trampled by the hooves of a 100-strong herd. It was, at its best, winding after a lone set of tracks, or two, the print half again as wide as a man's boot, the toes scuffed out where the dagga boy flicked his heavy hoof as he lifted it. A good track had a sheen, like a newly struck coin, before dust blew into it. Luckiest was to find fresh dung, not crusted yet or oxidized to brown inside, but green when pushed apart and maybe still warm to the touch. If the matter was coarse, it could even tell you that it was from a very old bull, his teeth worn so that he no longer chewed as he ought.

---

[1] Like the Inuit's supposed lexicon of 26 words for snow, Zimbabweans do have words in various dialects for different types of mud, such as *dope* for thin watery mud; *dhaka* for mud used as mortar; and *madhaka,* sticky mud created by rain-soaked earth; and although madhaka would seem to be the most accurate word for the type of mud frequented by Cape buffalo, dhaka looks to be the word from which dagga is derived. Dagga also carries the connotation of "crazy," the word synonymous with marijuana in many parts of Africa.

Tracking buffalo is much like ordering dance lessons by mail and having a stranger lay-out diagrams of the steps in only the vaguest order and across kilometers of ground, so that it can take hours to work out the routine (one, two, cha-cha-cha). You always have to maintain your poise, though, even when you get frustrated when the steps (the tracks) vanish and you then have to improvise by ranging out in widening gyres until you cut the tracks again—if you cut them again.

On the trail with me, or more correctly I with them, were three trackers—short dapper Tino, tall and slightly esotropic John who carried the water, and Mika with his shaved head and ragged hat, carrying a knobkerrie Tonga ax, made from a whittled mopane branch and hand-forged spring steel. And there was Rory, a tobacco farmer cum professional hunter, never without a Newbury Extra Mild smoldering between his fingers to repel mopane flies and to read the wind; a loaded .458 Model 70, the bluing polished away where he held it by the barrel, slung across his shoulder in a fashion that would induce a seizure in a hunter-education instructor; pale scars from the claws and teeth of a leopard, tattooing the precancerous skin of his forearms. He was a PH who really didn't care much for taking game himself ("Maybe a crocodile," he'd reckon, if pressed) but who took inordinate pleasure in guiding hunters to what they had come to Africa to find. I, of course, had come to find a dagga boy, or perhaps more so to see if I still remembered what a dagga boy was by hunting him on his own terms.

By 8:30 the first morning, after the drive to Kapinda, we left the tank-like Defender and set off on what looked to be the tracks of two dagga boys. Eventually we caught the tempo as the trail resolved itself into that of a single bull, leading us for an hour and a half below and around a grassy hill until we were going with the wind. We had to fall back to circle downwind, abandoning the concrete fact of the track, to get ahead of the bull, whom Rory thought had gone onto the hill above us, and—"slowly, slowly"—see if we could get onto his trail again.

We crested the level top of the hill and began a purposeful, searching meander through the tall grass and bushwillow. The August air was still cool and for a quarter hour we moved like a wary conga line, the five of us matching one another's footsteps. Then Tino, in the lead, walked past a small clump of low bushwillow, and next John did, then Rory, and I, and then Mika at the back hissed emphatically through his teeth. We froze midstride and looked to the right at the dagga boy, no more than two-dozen paces away, who had just gotten to his hooves behind the bushwillow. He had lain motionless as we approached and nearly walked past him, and only stood when we got upwind, our scents at last intolerable. Before I could get my scoped 450 Nitro Express 3¼-inch Ruger No. 1 to my shoulder (the single-shot rifle holding a cartridge loaded with a 500-grain Woodleigh soft-point), and the duplex reticle on the buffalo, he spun and ran downwind, off the hill, agile as a fighting bull entering the arena. The sun was behind him, making a silver-nitrate tracery around his deep-curled horns and heavy boss as he escaped.

"Pity, that," commented Rory, as dryly as a sip of brut.

Way cool, I thought, to my minor astonishment. This morning was the first time in 17 years that I had hunted Cape buffalo, and 28 since I first cut one of their tracks. Over time my memory of how large, fast, strong, and malicious they were had grown, magnifying them in my imagination to the point where I had been apprehensive about how I would react when I encountered one for real (i.e., would I dissolve into a puddle of ninnyhammer gibbering?). That was the anxiety hidden in me. Now all I felt was the parlous delight of simply being ticklishly close to buffalo again: I couldn't tell if that scared me even more than the thought of being genuinely scared.

It is not the Cape buffalo's manifest strength, ferocity, and tenacity during a charge (which are definite factors) that make it quite foreseeable that it might kill you as quickly as you it. More than anything else, what enables him to kill you is his bloody-damn genius for blending his great bulk in with a few leaves, twigs, and blades of grass and remaining as still and seemingly impassive as the faces on Rushmore—until he gets you to venture within a range where it is too close for him to miss, and where in a 4X scope he looks like a small patch of blurrily approaching bristly hair, which is why after we jumped that bull, I made sure that my scope was turned down to 1.75X.

A track (plus dung) is often the only empirical evidence of a dagga boy's existence in the material world, until you stumble onto, or over, him. Nothing else looks like his track, certainly not the sickle-padded four-toed splayed one of a hyena, the creased-pad pug mark of the leopard, or the lion's track, identical to the leopard's but super-sized. The print of an elephant is like a crazed porcelain platter. A kudu track is much smaller, more pointed and deceitfully delicate; a zebra has one that looks, not surprisingly, like a horse's; and though the track of a big eland may draw a second glance, it is quickly dismissed. Misidentifications, though, do occur.

Late in the afternoon of the first day, after we gave up tracking the runaway buffalo, Rory stamped on the Defender's brakes and leaned out, looking at the sandy dirt. He kept swiveling his head, uncertain about something. I looked to the left. Ten yards away, two bulls stood, gazing at us. One had a bell. Weeks before, we learned, cattle strayed from the herd of one of the trackers in camp. Now here they were, standing contentedly in the jess beside the dirt vehicle trail.

From his posture, Rory seemed on the verge of speaking, something he generally economized on, when I said, "Um . . ."

Rory sat up, staring at me from behind his wraparound sunglasses. I nodded tentatively toward the cattle.

"Oh hell!" he shouted in disgust. "Shoot the bloody things!" We didn't but roared off, leaving them to go on dodging lions, as they seemed to have been doing with some success, thus far.

Tea with milk was brought to my tent at 5:30 a.m. by one of the camp waiters. I heard him when he drew back the flap, before he said, "Good morning." I lifted the mosquito netting and sat up, taking the tea the waiter had poured milk into. We would be back in Kapinda early.

By 8:00 a.m. we were on another set of tracks, of a band of dagga boys. We stayed on the tracks for three hours, often losing the trail and having to range out until we picked it up again. The buffalo seemed as astray as young men in university jerseys and draped in ropes of multi-colored plastic beads, wandering the French Quarter on Fat Tuesday. Eventually they led us back in a wide inebriated circle to the road from which we had taken off after them, not far from where we had left the Defender.

We returned to the vehicle and ate chicken-and-mayonnaise sandwiches while Rory charted our course. The wind had freshened, gusting from the direction in which the buffalo tracks were going. That was good. We finished the sandwiches, checked that the magazines of the rifles were full, and went after them. We didn't need to go far.

For a kilometer we walked through head-high bushwillow and tall grass, Rory absently breaking off a dry stem to twirl in his ear. Then everything stopped.

At first it was just Tino who halted and pointed, crouching. Then Rory halted and leaned far back to see where Tino was pointing. Rory gestured to me to get low. My legs felt like cement when he motioned me toward a bare willowbush and to look—there.

Forty yards in the shade of thickly leaved mopane was a gray-black canyon boulder, with the gleam of a curved horn growing from it.

"Can you see them?" Rory asked in a whisper.

I saw the one horn, then a gray face with deep wrinkled rings around the eyes, the eyes turned toward us. I slipped the 450 through the branches and got down on the scope. More boulders lay near the first.

"I see the one looking."

"Not him. The best is the one on the farthest left, broadside."

Now I saw that farthest boulder had a rump and withers, and a head with a profile reminiscent of the portraits of certain stately medieval pontiffs, a tall helmet of horn instead of a miter covering it. The dagga boy had come out of hiding.

"I see him."

"He's lying down."

"Yes."

Rory paused, glassing him, then said, "In the middle of the shoulder."

I eased off the tang safety and lowered the crosshairs onto the bull's shoulder.

"Got him?"

"Yes."

"Sure?"

"Yes."

"All right."

I took a breath and let it flow out.

The big rifle boomed and in the scope l saw four buffalo (including the one I'd fired on) up and running, short-tailed broad rears vanishing. I had not heard the echoing impact of the bullet, but maybe we were too close. I levered out the empty case and slid in another 500-grain Woodleigh, this time a solid. There was no chance for a second shot, though.

Rory had run to the left behind me, craning to see where the buffalo went.

"Did you have a good picture?" he asked, looking at me sharply,

"Yes."

"All right," he said, relaxing. "Let's see."

We waited five minutes then went to the tree where the bulls had lain. There was no blood there. Rory and the trackers were studying the ground.

"I thought I had a good picture," I found myself weaseling, worried because there was no blood.

Rory looked at me.

"No," he said, reading my thought. "It won't have started here."

It started several yards away with one small spatter, already dried on the dirt. We moved forward, following more drops. They turned into bright red splatters of blood, big around as coffee saucers. Everyone was silent, looking at the trail, but looking up, too, watching ahead. Then Tino, John, and Mika all spoke out, in calm conversational tones. They pointed. I moved up and saw the gray-black shape on the ground ahead. Rory and I circled toward it, rifles up.

The bull had gone 250 yards, without a bellow, and was lying, legs folded, with his muzzle pushed forward on the ground, as if resting. Lung blood trickled from a disconcertingly small hole in his shoulder. We walked up to the buffalo, and I backed Rory as he extended the muzzle of his 458 to the bull's staring eye. When the muzzle touched it, the eye did not blink.

As we unloaded our rifles, Rory looked back at where the bull had come from and in his mind looked back on the tracking, the stalk, and my (for a change) decent shot.

"That's the way to hunt buffalo," he said with blunt satisfaction. And at least I hadn't been a ninnyhammer.

Tino, John, and Mika sharpened their spring-steel Tonga axes and knives on stones on the ground and working hard for most of an hour, cutting the bull in two. Rory drove the Defender in from the road and somehow we managed to wedge every edible—and some less than edible—scrap of the buffalo into it.

We made our way back to Songo Camp from Kapinda, the long trip lengthened by the heavy load. When we came in late that afternoon, we turned in a swirl of dust toward the skinning-and-butchering shed. The camp staff came out and saw the horns and hooves rising from the back of the white Land Rover, and offered a polite round of applause. Even that embarrassed me.

To cover the rush of feeling, I lifted my hand and gave a stage bow.

"Thank you, thank you!" I called. "You're too kind. I'll be appearing here all week. Don't forget your waitress. And try the veal!"

No, make that dagga boy.

Not Far to Africa

The 2000s . . .

Now since I have seen the ocean with my own eyes,
I feel completely how important it is for me to stay
in the south and to experience the color which must
be carried to the uttermost—it is not far to Africa.
—Vincent Van Gogh

IT IS NOT far to Africa across the ocean, particularly to Pointe des Almadies, the continent's farthest dusty western reach, stretching out into the Atlantic just northwest of central Dakar in Senegal. One who sailed past the Pointe was the Scots surgeon Mungo Park. For all his travails—imprisonment, hunger, thirst, tropical fever, routine stripping from him of his garments, robbery of his effects, a trio of "very large" lions that "came bounding over the long grass" toward him, and ultimately having "lances, pikes, arrows, stones, and missiles of every description" rained down upon his canoe by natives, resulting in his drowning in the Niger River—the youthful and ill-fated early 19th-century African explorer who wended his way through Senegal to satisfy "a passionate desire to examine into the productions of a

164

country so little known" never saw Dakar, the modern capital of the nation, which was not established by the French colonial governor Louis-Léon-César Faidherbe until a half century after Park's untimely death.

By dying—or rather, by failing to survive into the 21st century—Park was deprived of a life in full because he was denied the remarkable opportunity to encounter present-day Dakar with its sheep tethered to manhole covers on the city sidewalks, the towering red-hatted Republican Guard manning the wrought-iron gate of the presidential palace with a tarnished saber, or the echoing dawn calls to prayer of the muezzins from the minarets of the assorted mosques. What he especially missed, though, was browsing in the Village des Arts at Anse des Madeleines, "Madeleines Cove," where festively painted fishing pirogues are hauled out onto the yellow-sand shore and a raw torrent of gray nightsoil cascades down an open 20-foot-wide sewer into the surf.

Here in the tourist market, the urgent "take-a-look" shop merchants assail you from all quarters, pitilessly hounding you to purchase execrable faux-tribal ticky-tack, although some handsome—and doubtless poached— leopard and python skins are on offer, until you are compelled to declare categorically that you would not accept any of these souvenirs if they paid you, eliciting from them, then, hissed accented-English tirades of "You f*****. Don't come back. Don't come back to my country, you f*****!" Such incensed attitudes are no doubt come by naturally when it is considered that the bulk of these peddlers' tourist trade is composed of holiday-makers from France.

We didn't get out of the country, but we did get out of Dakar. As Jean Allard, *directeur* of Africa Safari's Campement de Mako, and I started east into the cool hazy January sunrise on the N1 bitumen highway, the road went to hell and the country went from coastal to urban to suburban to township to open low rolling savannah marked by the most African of prominences, massive baobabs whose bulk seemed to threaten to crack the crust of the earth. The trim iron-haired Allard, who had come to Senegal as a result of *le virus de l'Afrique*—the "African virus" that makes it impossible for its sufferers to stay away from the continent—got the Hi-Lux up to speed for 200 yards, then had to brake to weave around the potholes, resuming speed, then braking again, intermixed with brief slewings off the "pavement" onto the sandy shoulder for a journey of some 14 arduous hours. Broken- down lorries lay grounded on the side of the highway. Each village and town we passed through had its row of rough wooden stalls marketing peanuts in voluminous plastic bags; and if we halted for more than a moment, we would be mobbed by bands of rowdy little boys, palms thrust out, adamant that they be given "*cadeaux, cadeaux.*"

Late in the day we reached the large crossroads of Tambacounda, capital of eastern Senegal. Mungo Park passed through the "walled town called Tambacounda" a number of times during his two (one fatal) expeditions in search of the source of the Niger. Here we turned south toward the Guinea border and into the 3,500-square-mile Parc National du Niokolo Koba. The guide books wildly, if not deplorably, exaggerate the level of wildlife to be found in the park, with hollow claims of "hundreds of thousands" of animals including leopards, elephant, buffalo, wild dogs, hyenas, rare western Lord Derby eland, and Africa's largest lions, perhaps relicts of the great and vanished Barbary Coast subspecies, while in fact a good day of touring might produce random sightings of coffee-brown roan, waterbuck, kob, hartebeest, oribi, harnessed bushbuck, red duiker, rumbling hippos, big sun-struck crocs, outsized warthogs, plus a lone leopard in an enclosure, along with guinea fowl, blue rollers, rock hens, and vast troops of baboons. Perhaps because of the park traffic, the road onward from Tambacounda underwent a noted improvement, and we up-shifted past the tall forests and into the evening.

As we drove farther from Tambacounda, the people we passed— pedaling black-tired bicycles, riding on horse-drawn carts loaded with firewood, elegantly slender women balancing bundles on their heads— seemed conspicuously more friendly and less distraught. At the village of Mako, with its own merchandise stalls along the highway, including quarters of beef hanging in the open air, we drew smiling waves and no demands for gifts. We crossed the Gambia River bridge, the water running fast and clear over smooth stones and the women gathered in the shallows with their skirts tucked up, washing their laundry, and just at nightfall drove in under the strings of bare light bulbs and onto the raked gravel of the camp's parking area and found small neat bungalows with the names of animals on the doors— *Buffle, Guib* ("bushbuck"), Hippo—gathered around a tall anthill and under the large leaves of shade trees that rose into the dark and disappeared.

The concrete-floored thatched-roof dining area and bar lay toward the high bank of the Gambia and was decorated with batik paintings and the bleached skulls of hippos, warthogs, and crocodiles. Here we sat, road weary, sipping glasses of champagne and then having our first meal in the Senegalese bush, fresh francolin.

There were eight of us at dinner, plus the Senegalese driver of the rented van that had carried the rest of our group while I rode with Allard. Unlike in other parts of the continent I have hunted, where black Africans have, to my unease, displayed an almost obsequious (though doubtless affected) regard for white clients, the staff at Mako Camp and in the field demonstrated a distinct lack of disproportionate deference—which is not to say discourtesy.

So the highly skilled and well-mannered Senegalese driver of the van, who would be returning it to Dakar in the morning, unselfconsciously sat down at the table with us; and I was more than a little ashamed to realize I found this remarkable.

The other people at the table had come to hunt birds and warthogs, or to accompany those who had come to hunt them. Geoff and Debbie were from Colorado, and Geoff had just returned from hunting partridge in Mongolia. David was an elk hunter from Nebraska—though for reasons known entirely only to himself he prefers the label of "cartographer." Chip, Claire, and Elizabeth were from many places, most recently South Carolina. They had put the hunt together through their company, and in the last few weeks had traveled and hunted through Portugal, Italy, and Morocco with guns and falcons. With me was my legal counsel Carey—upon whom I relied to keep me from breaking out in severe cases of handcuffs. For more than 30 years Carey and I have traveled together throughout the world, since we went to the Central African Republic in 1984. Carey, who absolutely does not hunt, is often asked in camps what he's doing there. And he always answers that hunters go to the best places before anyone else. And here in Senegal we were, as far as anyone could recall, the very first American bird hunters.

What we had primarily come to hunt were francolin, the double-spurred francolin or *francolin à double éperon* in français; but there were also four-banded sandgrouse (*ganga quadribande*), African mourning dove (*tourterelle pleureuse*), African collared dove (*tourterelle rieuse*), and Bruce's green pigeon (*pigeon à épaulettes violettes*)[2]. Awaking under a mist of mosquito netting in the fresh pre-dawn the next morning, I had instant coffee and some baguette and butter for breakfast—the lone meal about which the French are utterly clueless—and we loaded the shells and guns into the Hi-Luxes and drove north back across the Gambia bridge.

For the first time after two days in Dakar I smelled the familiar sunrise odors of Africa, warming air, dew on dry grass, dust, cattle, wood smoke. In the village we picked up the *secretarios* and turned off the highway. There were fields of tall elephant grass, green-leaved bushes, and small cotton and peanut

---

[2]Latin names, in order: *Francolinus bicalcaratus, Pterocles quadricintus, Streptopelia decipiens, Streptopelia roseogrisea, Treron waalia.*

plots, lying fallow. Here and there a horned red cow pushed through the grass. The Africans beat the cover with long sticks, and almost immediately I heard the chuckling of francolin as they bobbed and weaved ahead, the bark of a baboon, and then a small cluster of the birds bursting upward with a record-scratching cackle, in tribute to their pheasant heritage.

I brought the Benelli SuperNova 12 gauge up and pushed off the safety. The first shot dropped one francolin, and I shucked in another shell and brought down a second. The Africans retrieved the chukar-sized brown birds. They had the chestnut heads with a "white supercilium" as the field guides described, and two spurs on each leg.

Geoff and David were ranged out from me as we swept through the grass and farm plots, flushing more francolin. The laments of doves were heard, and the occasional one winged within range. By midmorning the sun was starting to beat down and we had swung back around to the highway where the Hi-Luxes waited. As we gathered and compared game straps weighted with birds, we were all laughing and chattering—another lousy day in paradise.

Back at Mako, and after lunch, some napped, others swam in the camp's pool, while still others strolled down to the Gambia to catch a glimpse of the floating hippos. The first evening we went south and turned off the highway to follow a sandy track through small groups of round thatch-and-wattle houses and past wattle fences. We parked the trucks and walked down a sloping rocky bank to the slow-moving green Gambia. A pirogue adzed from a teak trunk with fishing nets in it was beached on the gravel. We took stands by the thorn bushes and within a quarter hour African mourning and the smaller rose-gray African collared doves were coming in. By then dozens of young village boys had jogged down the bank and sat around us. The doves flew, we shot, the doves (sometimes) fell; and for the boys who sprang up to retrieve them we were the greatest show on earth that evening. Two boys even ran fully clothed into the river to fetch a dove, which distressed me somewhat. I guessed they knew what their river held; and Park wrote that somewhere very near to here he had, in 1797, "bathed myself . . . as the natives had assured me there were no crocodiles in this stream." But I was not so sure, and it seemed a wiser course when one of the Africans from our camp launched the heavy pirogue and paddled out to bring back any birds that splashed into the Gambia. As the sun set, the gnats began to rise and shrouded the exposed backs of my hands. With the last hint of twilight, the sandgrouse came.

Of the four-banded sandgrouse, the guidebooks report that it is a "sturdy compact" and "gregarious" bird with long pointed wings that breeds in a belt from Mauritania through Cameroon and east into Sudan and Uganda. It is "yellowish-green" on the neck and breast, and heavily marked with brown on the back, the males decorated with black and white bars on their foreheads. Their call is described as "a loud *wulli wulli*"; and I believe I recall hearing a haunted something like that in the outer dark beside the Gambia, although that is about as far as my species recognition of the four-banded sandgrouse reached in the field, owing to the fact that I really never got to see one in daylight.

It is an understatement that the sandgrouse is "largely nocturnal." "Exclusively" might be more like it. By the time the wulli wulli was heard, the sun was well below the horizon and the birds were beneath a cloak of invisibility against the background of dim foliage across the river. The calm surface of the water reflected the lighter sky, though, and the sandgrouse hurtling through it. Somehow, it was almost possible to track the bird's vector and anticipate where it would be in relation to your shotgun muzzle and to fire a flaming blast out over the river. And if on every eighth or ninth shot a sandgrouse actually dropped, you could honestly say it was all done with mirrors.

After the evening shoot we headed back for generous chilled green bottles of Dakar-brewed Bière La Gazelle and dinner of more gamebirds. Then long sleeps in the West African winter nights and waking up again before dawn. That was the routine of our hunting days, if you want to call bird shooting in Senegal "routine." One morning we went out after warthog, I putting a Burris SpeedDot on the SuperNova and loading it with 300-grain sabot slugs. Geoff, David, and I split up; and I hunted around a large marshy meadow and except for a band of blithe chuckling francolin that marched around us while the tracker and I stood frozen beside a tree, didn't see a thing—and honestly was not upset in the least. David was the one of us to get a shot with a 375 he'd rented from the camp, but missed a smallish warthog, just as a monstrous one came into view, and then as quickly vanished. Fortunately, a Belgian hunter brought in a warthog a couple of days later, inducing something akin to mass hysteria in the camp (Robert Ruark said that "Africans get excited about two animals, and two animals only"—lions and elephant—but apparently in Senegal, the warthog is a third); and the next night, absolutely exquisite wild pork was served.

After the last evening's shoot, and the usual exasperation of trying to hit stealth-fighter sandgrouse, and dinner, a group of dancers and musicians came. The music was made with *shekere* gourd rattles, one-string *kora*-like basses, police whistles, and song. The barefoot dancers were women and girls dressed in yellow and pink T-shirts and long lime-colored skirts, and performed in pairs in a sort of dance-off to see who could outdo the other. Before the evening was over, Chip, who played electric bass for the '90s band The Cartoon Factory, had commandeered one of the gourd basses and joined in; and we were up dancing, too. I went to bed with the party still in full swing and Chip playing on.

We were supposed to fly out of Tambacounda at midday—no more driving on the wretched N1—but for once it was good news that the weekly flight to the capital was delayed until night, giving us a chance for one more crisp morning's francolin hunt. We hunted a new place around huts and small fields, "a woody but beautiful country, interspersed with a pleasing variety of hill and dale, and abounding with partridges," as Park had written about the vicinity. The powdery dust was stamped with braided lines of francolin tracks, and the birds could be heard in the brush. We pushed them ahead of us, shooting through the branches as they flushed, like hunting ruffed grouse in the New England brambles. It was a Saturday morning, and it is doubtful there was much in the way of kids shows on the television, or much in the way of televisions; so we were soon being trailed by another dozen young boys, some in their treasured soccer uniforms and shoes.

It was perhaps the best shoot of all; and after we handed out candy, took group photos, bought the last-minute gifts we had refused to purchase in the Village des Arts, settled our bar tabs, and with skin inflamed and itching from gnat bites shook hands all around, we loaded our luggage and climbed into the Hi-Luxes and set out for Tambacounda and onto Dakar, a city which, upon further reflection and in comparison with the genuine country and people of Senegal, is a place Mungo Park might have been fortunate never to have seen.

Blue Train

The 1990s . . .

IN SOUTH AFRICA'S Transvaal the bluffs of the Waterbergs are like the knuckles of a blue fist clenched on the long-dry land. In the Waterbergs, in a place called Kwalata, on the walls above stone ledges redolent of incontinent baboons, there are petroglyphs, the unmistakable, high-humped bison silhouettes of wildebeest rubbed with ocher; and beyond the rock walls are very much living red hartebeest (as in the drawing on the next page), waterbuck, gemsbok, bush pigs, warthogs, rhino, leopards, sable, kudu whose horns spiral out beyond 60 inches, the odd elephant or two, and marvelous, ghostly nyala that slip through the brush and away from sight like shadows sailing over the ground on a cloudy day.

Among the tall, coral-pink termite hills, red-bush willow and ironwood, the sand and bare rock, there are also the "blue trains." These blue trains are not the world-renowned railroad that traverses the country but the blue wildebeest: a three-letter crossword-puzzle solution ("gnu") to some, and to others the "mini buffalo" for its strength and hardiness, or maybe it's the "poor man's buffalo" for the lesser expense of hunting it.

The odd thing about the blue train is that there are so few hunting stories (so few of any stories) about it. If you search for a reason, what you find

is mostly a matter of appearances. Because—to some—the wildebeest looks so silly (half-ox, half antelope, with the tail of a horse is how it's described), or seems to behave so stupidly (with the black wildebeest it is lumped in as another old fool of the veldt) that it hardly merits attention. Wildebeest are certainly not among the glamorous "dangerous" game of Africa; and they are so ubiquitous that they can hardly be classed among the rare trophies. Perhaps there are so few stories about wildebeest because there seem few worth telling.

Appearances may be deceiving, though, and the wildebeest has more than enough of certain qualities (its durability, its distinctiveness, the way its absence turns the veldt as empty as the plains of North America are empty without bison) to make any number of stories about them truly worth telling.

I don't have any great number of wildebeest stories, but I have one, although it may be more about a rifle that didn't shoot right, about what a hunter owes his prey, and about a dog named . . . well, a dog named Jock. Or it may simply be about appearances, too.

The rifle was someone else's. When I reached Kwalata on a bright winter afternoon in August, my hosts had a 300 Magnum they wanted me to shoot. It's a good caliber, I thought, and it is. But then I let one of the professional hunters at Kwalata talk me into sighting in the rifle at 25 yards. It was, he said, the way he always did it; and even though it was the way I never did it, I went along. When the rifle shot a little low, the PH dialed the scope up the number of clicks he calculated to be the correct amount, and now the rifle hit just a hair above the bull's-eye: perfect.

In the morning on a tableland overlooking a wooded plain, when I had slunk through tall grass to the base of a willow and gotten a solid rest on a tree, putting the cross hairs just behind the shoulder of not a wildebeest but a hartebeest standing broadside 175 yards out and saw the bull drop at the shot, it did indeed appear perfect. Until the hartebeest staggered to its hooves and clattered off after the rest of its running herd, my hurried second shot missing.

We trailed the tracks across miles of plateau and down through canyons and back onto the plateau again. A splash of blood every 10 yards led us on, and five times we jumped the hartebeest, the bull each time keeping brush between us and him as he ran off. After three hours there were no more splashes of blood, and the ground turned too hard to find tracks. As we headed back to camp, I tried to determine what had gone wrong. I thought

I'd had a good hold on the heart and lungs, but I'd obviously shot high, above the spine, stunning the hartebeest to the ground. But was it me or the rifle?

Then in a narrow draw a klipspringer stood poised on the tips of its hooves in the rocks 60 yards away. One shot and the little antelope was dead; the problem, it appeared, was not the rifle. I decided I didn't need to check the scope; I needed only to aim more precisely.

The next morning we found a good bull in a herd of blue wildebeest. They were moving among some trees; and there was something about the gray and blue-black of their brindled hides, their shaggy beards and manes, the Pleistocene profile of their heads that made them look more African than almost any other animal I had ever seen. I found another tree and got another rest; and again, at about 175 yards, the bull crashed to the ground with a grunting bellow.

This time, though, as the wildebeest lay kicking on the ground, dust rising around it, I knew at once the shot was off. I was running at it to cut the distance; but it was back on its feet and running, too, and my next shot missed, like a slow-motion, bad-dream replay of the day before. I was hunting with the other PH at Kwalata, Derick, who had not helped me sight in the rifle, who with the three trackers and me had trailed the hartebeest the day before and who must have been wondering if I was ever going to kill anything cleanly—anything bigger than a 30-pound klipspringer, anyway. Now we were trailing a wounded wildebeest at a half-jog, until the bull turned and moved up into a steep kopje. Derick thought of the day before and decided we should draw back, head into camp, and return in an hour or so with a good dog to help us find the wildebeest. I agreed with a nod, not feeling like saying much at all.

The dog was a black-and-white bull terrier, named, of course, Jock. *Jock of the Bushveld*—the tale of a prospector and hunter and his bull terrier, Jock, and their adventures (including adventures with wildebeest) in the Transvaal of the 1880s—is South Africa's *Old Yeller*, and every "good" dog, particularly every good bull terrier, is automatically named Jock. I am not sure whose dog this was, maybe the entire camp's, but he was famed for his nose: If Jock could not trail the wildebeest, it was said, it could not be trailed.

With Jock to aid us, we returned to the base of the kopje and started to climb through the bald rocks. I was beginning to ask myself again if the rifle could be off, but then I had to think more about avoiding the thorn brush and cactus that grew between the bald rocks. Once, when I started to put my hand down for balance on a rock, a tracker warned me away with a hiss: A circle of lichen the size of a tarnished silver dollar was in fact a tiny coiled adder warming in the sun.

Derick was ahead of me when we topped out, and as I looked up he snapped his 318 Greener double to his shoulder. The wounded bull had been lying in the rocks at the crest of the kopje and got up and began to run before Derick had even seen it, giving Derick no shot. We scrambled across the top of the rocks to where we could look down on the green trees and bush below us; and by then a roostertail of dust was drifting above the trees a seeming ridiculous distance away—it looked like a mile—where the wounded wildebeest ran.

Derick shook his head. It was hopeless. We'd never catch the wildebeest today. Maybe in a week it would circle back through here with its herd, and we would pick it up then. Better to send one of the trackers back for the safari car while the rest of us hiked down the backside of the kopje. About a mile across the flat, the direction the wildebeest had run, was a dirt vehicle track where we could meet the car.

Derick sent the tracker back, then we started down through the rocks. I remembered Jock. Looking around, I saw him trotting along, his jaws opened in a permanent terrier smile. But why hadn't he found the wildebeest, I wondered, and why wasn't he trailing him now?

On the flat we cut good blood spoor already drying in the sandy soil, and there was still good sign when we reached the vehicle track. We looked at a splash of claret on the ground there, and I thought of one animal I had already wounded and lost and now another we were proposing to let walk around for a week with another of my bullets in him. Derick looked at me and asked what I wanted to do. Keep going.

The next vehicle track we would cross was more than a mile farther on, so Derick left a second tracker to wait for the car and to tell the driver where we had gone. Then we went.

The blood drops started to space out, but the trail remained good enough for even me to follow. I looked around again for Jock; and he was at our heels, trotting and smiling but not even attempting to put his nose in a track. Halfway to the second rendezvous the blood was playing out, and the hoof prints became difficult to distinguish in the soft sand. By the time we reached the dirt vehicle track there appeared to be no sign at all. It was past noon and hot even in the mountain winter. We were hungry and had brought no water. Derick found what shade there was beneath the bare branches of a tree, and Jock lay in Derick's shade. We would wait here for the car.

Halfheartedly looking for sign, I walked off the track 20 yards in the direction the wildebeest was traveling. And I found one large, shiny, dark-red drop of muscle blood. Derick saw me looking at the ground and asked if I'd found something. I nodded.

He said there was little chance of catching up with the wildebeest today, but what did I want to do?

Keep going.

All right, he sighed. He would wait here for the car. The last tracker, Poni, and I—and Jock—could go on. It was about two miles to the next vehicle track, and he would be there to pick us up. So we started off, having to whistle Jock up to get him to leave Derick's shade. The next blood drop was over 30 yards from the last, and as we walked the drops spread farther and farther apart. By now I was convinced that Jock's nose was some kind of myth: It seemed unlikely he could trail a line of Milk Bones across a kitchen floor. Every time Poni and I stopped to examine a track or cast around for blood, Jock found the least penumbra and lay in it, belly down and panting, until we walked on and he followed with reluctance. Perhaps, I thought, it would have been better to have left him with Derick.

We had been on the trail now for over two hours under the midday sun, and I was honestly no longer thinking about wildebeest. Mostly I was thinking about ice and water, or even water alone, and taking off my shoes and socks and then all my clothes and standing under a cool shower when Poni dropped to his haunches and pointed straight ahead.

Although it had brush to hide it, the wounded wildebeest, unlike yesterday's hartebeest, broke from cover into the open, angling in front of us. It was about 120 yards, moving at a gallop, when I brought up the 300 and thumbed the safety off. I put the crosshairs just ahead of its chest and swung, and at the last moment, as I was already squeezing off the shot, I lowered the sights to the line of its belly.

With another grunting bellow the wildebeest stumbled into a somersault, shrouding itself in dust. As I fired I caught something in the corner of my eye, a black-and-white streak. Now I saw Jock diving headlong into the cloud of dust. When the cloud of wildebeest regained its feet, Jock's jaws were locked on the bull's muzzle as tight as the bite of a badger. The wildebeest lowered its head, as though trying to swing the dog onto its upswept horns, then threw its head straight back, cartwheeling Jock into the air. Poni and I were running, and the wildebeest spun and started off again. I bolted another round, and thinking, *Low,* I hit the wildebeest again, staggering it long enough for Jock to get up and charge into the bull once more.

This time Jock caught the wildebeest by the ear and hung there, oscillating back and forth as the bull shook its head, trying to fling the dog off, I saw then that I had let appearances deceive me: It would not have been better to leave Jock behind; it was clear now that his true calling was not as a trailing dog but as a gaze hound and, above all, one of the African continent's great catch dogs. As violently as the wildebeest shook its head, Jock held on; I got to within 20 yards before I aimed at the very bottom of the wildebeest's chest. I waited for Jock to swing out of the line of fire; then I shot the bull through the heart, and it sank to the ground.

The wildebeest's wounds were, except for the finishing one, all high in the shoulder, leaving it glazed red like a bull speared by a picador's lance. (That afternoon, when I sighted it in properly—the way I knew I should—the scope proved to be over 6 inches high at 100 yards, and no doubt higher still at 200.) Jock, after sniffing the carcass and giving a satisfied growl, went to lie on his belly in the shade, sore but uninjured.

Poni came and shook my hand because we both knew we had done what we should by following this wounded animal all the way. Looking at the wildebeest again, I saw how wrong appearances could be, because this was in no way silly or foolish. It something very tough and very brave and in its own right magnificent, just like certain bull terriers, blue mountains, and so much of Africa that lay between the Vaal and the Limpopo. And there was a story about all this that appeared to be worth every bit of the telling.

But first we had to go back and look once more for that hartebeest.

Confluence of Memories

The 1970s . . .

I don't remember that there were any houses or roads or people anywhere, just treetops and water and distance and sky and birds and confluence. It may not be so rare but I thought so then and I do now—it's all so rarely the blessing falls.

—Eudora Welty

THERE WAS GUNPOWDER tea before dawn to erase sleep and an egg and a rasher of bacon for breakfast. Nareng and Kadatta took the over-and-under and the side-by-side from John's tent and placed them in the gun rack in the Land Cruiser—along with the 375s for any acts of God—and we headed south into the Rombo country and to the river, the dust in our nostrils even at this cool hour.

The sky bellied up to gray as we came to the manyatta, and we heard the dogs howling. The fly-blown yellow bitch leading the pack ran stiffly into the headlights, snarling, her teats dangling. She leapt and snapped at John's window; and he drew in his arm until we were past, on our way to sandgrouse.

John Fletcher had killed at least two charging rhino pointblank in his career, but he braked for small animals. Whenever hares ran in front of the Toyota, we slammed to a halt. Like that night we were coming in from a very long, very wet, and very unsuccessful stalk with the bed in the back filled with Maasai. Lightning stood out all around on top of the escarpment, and hares bounded everywhere. Every 100 yards John locked the brakes, peered anxiously through the glare of the headlights beyond the hood, and asked if the bunny had hopped out of the way yet. It looked as if it would take forever to reach camp, and the Maasai soon decided it was hopeless and set out on foot into the terrible night with their long, spade-bladed spears and ochered hair.

Or when a Maasai with an absurdly small dog appeared as we were skinning and quartering a waterbuck. After pro-forma praise of my one-shot kill, the Maasai got down to cases and asked for a hindquarter. John gave it to him, then threw the fresh liver to his dog. The liver was twice its size; but with a gulp of wonder and a tear of joy, the dog set earnestly to devouring a half of it on the spot, then dragged the remainder backward through the tall grass to a hollow beneath a bush, where it curled atop it and began to snore.

On the Simbair red-eye flight from London to Nairobi, my friend Bill and I bet on what Jacobean-named John Fletcher of Ker, Downey & Selby Safaris, Ltd., looked like. I took short and red-faced—like Wilson in Macomber (the story); Bill held out for tall and black-haired—like Wilson in Macomber (the movie). The hunter who negotiated us through Kenyan customs was red-faced and tall. He had high cheekbones and curly blond hair (one reason why he had been enticed to volunteer during the Emergency to blacken that hair with dye and darken his skin with walnut stain to join Mau Mau camps in the bush). Somewhere, I characterized him was a "blond Jack Palance."

We made camps throughout the safari concessions, the Lowe & Bonner tents going up and coming down. At least one night in each camp we asked Fletcher to point out the Southern Cross. Thinking a moment, he pushed himself out of his camp chair, got another drink of rum, then marched away from the glow of the campfire into Africa. When he could make out the stars, he exaggeratedly scanned the sky, pivoting from foot to foot. Then he stopped, braced his legs apart, took a short sip of his drink and returned the glass to high port, shot his free arm toward the horizon, and announced, "Behind that tree." Without another word he marched back to the campfire, leaving us in the dark to wonder how "that tree" always managed to obscure the astronomical observation.

The sun rose among the volcanic mounds of the national park on one side of us and glinted off snow on the tabletop of Kibo on the other. It was light enough by then to see without the headlights, and as my eye roamed the plain it was caught by the dark line of trees and water.

I knew the water, dull and inert now, would be sparkling like sapphire by eight o'clock. Then it would spring from the dry land around it and demand that you turn your head to look at it. But even in this gray dawn it attracted me by the impression it gave of being the most logical place on earth. Perhaps the eternal cycle of animals coming to drink (with the equally eternal cycle of predators lying in wait around it) was what gave it this sense of logic: the Reason of Waterholes, what the old philosophers had in mind when they talked about the Great Chain of Being.

The waterhole here was a wide ford of the Rambo River; and as we drew near, a majestically ugly warthog boar broke from cover in front of us, his mane of stiff copper bristles rattling against his neck. We saw a troop of black-and-white colobus monkeys scurrying from the water's edge and taking to the trees. And from the pug marks we cut, there was probably more than one leopard watching us. John parked the Land Cruiser behind some wait-a-bit bush; and taking our shotguns and shells, we took our stands behind tall acacias with the other predators, around the waterhole.

Being good is terrifically demanding—except for those who are born to it—therefore, we settle for being correct and sometimes for just remembering what it was like to be correct. I think that I behaved with John Fletcher very nearly as I ought to and learned a thing or two in the bargain. The things I learned from John, however, are probably not what most people would classify as significant. I know for a fact that moving silently through brush, keeping downwind of elephant cows with calves, winching a lorry out of the mud, and shooting Cape buffalo absolutely dead, are not lessons that those who handled my helter-skelter higher education would consider vital. Yet these lessons had more profound effect on me than the ones learned from humanities class. And ironically, these were lessons learned from a man who didn't purchase a book unless its garishly illustrated paper cover promised at least a dozen episodes of gratuitous violence. And a little sex.

Sandgrouse are columbiformes of rare adaptation—pigeons built like grouse. The female of the ground nesting species has learned to wait for the pink leaves of particular deciduous trees to fall before laying her matching pink eggs in their camouflage. Male and female will fly 40 miles to collect water in their crops and alimentary canals and hollow abdominal feathers, and transport it back to their nestlings. They have also learned to drink up in five to 10 seconds to prevent being consumed by predators who have learned their daily watering schedule (but even so, a Nile crocodile once in a while manages to shag a sandgrouse out of the blue if it sails too low over the water, a falling blessing). This centrality of water to their existence makes sandgrouse seem more a variety of waterfowl in the desert lands they inhabit than any greenhead or honker along the Pacific Flyway in a wet year.

Now the sandgrouse would be on time for John and me today. They had shown up every day between 7:00 and 9:00 a.m. for some 25 million years, and today would be no exception. We slipped no. 6 high-brass shells into our 12 gauges and locked them up.

They arrived in small clusters. We crouched behind the trees until they set their wings, then we stood and shot. They came so fast it was something of a surprise to see them die—like burning lights suddenly winking out. Then the sandgrouse came in for real. It was shooting into a plague of locust or standing on a stream bed underneath a run of salmon. It was too intense to last for very long, but for many minutes black men were dancing around to gather birds as guns discharged high over their heads. Then it ended.

I stood there blinking, maybe trembling a little. *Damn* about summed it up. I broke my over-and-under and walked unsteadily over to John. He was blinking some too. He grinned. I grinned. Everyone in Africa grinned.

Once in Mexico for no lofty motive, I took in a *mixta* bullfight featuring the rejoneador who had hunted with John for three full months; so before his fight I went out to the corrals to pay him John's respects. The rejoneador was wearing the breeder's traditional *traje corto* and was mounted on a tall, excitedly pawing white parade horse caparisoned in leopard and jaguar skins. He instantly offered me a courteous but rather chill smile when I mentioned John's name, his mind, perhaps, on the bulls he would soon have to kill.

"A dear friend of mine," he said. His plumed horse's shod hooves cracked on the cobblestones. "He must be getting a bit *mzee* by now, though," he added abstractly, gentling the stallion with his knees and reins.

I mumbled reflexively about Fletcher's being young enough (he was fortysomething at the time, 20 years younger than I am now), accepted another of those practiced smiles, and went to find a beer.

The mention of John getting old disturbed me—raising the very real possibility of his quitting the game before I amassed the outlandish sum required to hunt with him again (having had the money, once, at the right time, to hunt in Africa the way it should be hunted); and I was disturbed enough by the rejoneador's words to wish I could say that he did not give a particularly grand showing of his talents that Sunday afternoon. And lo! he did not.

It's been over now in Kenya for generations, of course—no, Kenya and Kenyans carry on; but without safari something not unimportant is missing. And the last I heard, John after the closure had packed up for Sudan and within a few years retired to grow avocados, or maybe onions, on a farm, quite possibly at the foot of the Ngong Hills, a line Fletcher was not likely to have been intimately familiar with. And I would be happy to know he was still alive. Luckily for me, he left behind my good memories of him and the country that once was.

As we passed the manyatta on the way back to camp, the bitch came rushing after us again with the pack at her heels. John braked and dropped a sandgrouse at her paws. She stopped barking and showing her teeth and nuzzled the bird suspiciously. Then with John and the pack watching, she soft-mouthed it like a well-bred retriever and took it off a little way to eat it. She did not bark at us again.

There was sandgrouse for dinner. The flesh was coarse and dark, somehow wilder and more authentic than the fat, grain-fed meat of some North American game. We ate epically. And after the epical John Fletcher poured the last of the burgundy into our glasses, we bade goodnight while bushbabies cried in the trees above us.

In my tent I kept the pressure lamp on to update my journal, ending the entry of September 22nd with, "Big fun on the Rombo!"

Extinguishing the lantern, I wandered toward the tall woodland of sleep, not realizing, yet, how "big fun" could imprint a life to be lived in ineffable longing—of a kind for which I would never want to discover the right, and certainly not the last, words.

The Most Expensive Safari
in the World

Before . . .

ABOUT HIMSELF DIRECTOR John Ford once said, "My name is John Ford, and I make Westerns." Another director with the stature of Ford and Hitchcock might have said, "My name is Howard Hawks, and I make movies." And over 50 years ago the movie he made was *Hatari!*.

Even if you are not old enough to have seen *Hatari!* during its initial run in theaters in 1962, you certainly saw it on television. However or wherever you first saw it, if you were young and impressionable enough and had not yet been to Africa, and you did not decide right then that you were someday going to go, you were watching a far different movie than I.

On the unlikely chance that you never have seen *Hatari!*, it is about a multinational team, such as found only in the movies, of game catchers at work in Tanganyika. They operate out of a ranch owned by an orphaned young woman who is the object of both paternal and romantic attention. After one of the veterans is gored, a "new guy" has to pass initiation to join the team. Then a beautiful wildlife photographer, who was expected to be a

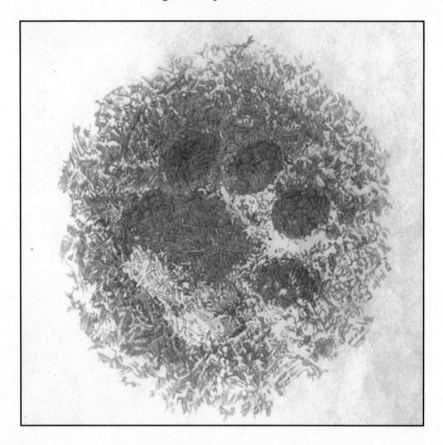

man, arrives to plague and captivate the hero. In between the chase goes on, or rather in between the chases goes on the rest of the business. Finally, baby elephant wreak havoc on Arusha's commercial district to a Henry Mancini score. None of which really matters because what *Hatari!* is all about is East African vistas, wild animals, action, and attitude. Whatever "plot" there may be is strictly in the service of portraying the movie's characters as a band of professionals who revel in their own competency and both admire, depend upon, and are challenged by the competency of their teammates. In that way, what the movie's all about is Howard Hawks.

An upper-class Midwesterner raised in Southern California, Hawks was an eclectic sportsman with a taste for hunting, fishing, yachting, tennis, golf, skiing, gambling, airplanes, fast horses, fast cars, and fast women.

He flew with Howard Hughes; hunted, fished, and drank with his close friend and regular screenwriter William Faulkner; and hunted, fished, and drank some more with not-so-close friend Ernest Hemingway. (When Hemingway declined to write screenplays for him, Hawks claimed, according to Todd McCarthy's biography, *Howard Hawks, The Grey Fox of Hollywood*, that he told Hemingway, "I'll get Faulkner to do it; he can write better than you anyway." On the other hand, Shelby Foote, author of *The Civil War: A Narrative* and a Faulkner friend, said, "One time Faulkner asked Howard Hawks, Am I a better bird-shot than Hemingway? Hawks said, No, you're not, but my wife Slim's better than either of you.")

From the 1920s to 1970 Howard Hawks directed almost 50 movies in virtually every genre: Western, war, gangster, prison, detective, biography, musical, inspirational, aviation, motor racing, boxing, science fiction, and comedy, comedy, comedy—even Hawks's darkest movies contained humor. His stars were never less than A-list and included Humphrey Bogart, John Wayne, Gary Cooper, James Cagney, Cary Grant, and Kirk Douglas. Hawks was hardly thought of as a "women's" director; but his female stars from Joan Crawford to Barbara Stanwyck, Rosalind Russell, Katherine Hepburn, Marilyn Monroe, and Angie Dickinson usually gave as good as they got in jousting with the male leads in his pictures. Even Hawks's character actors, such as Edward G. Robinson, Boris Karloff, and Walter Brennan, were unsurpassable. And his body of work includes certifiable classics such as *Scarface*, *Bringing Up Baby*, *His Girl Friday*, *Red River*, and *Rio Bravo*.

During a fallow period in the mid-1950s when for assorted reasons Hawks was unable to make a picture for four years, he had the idea of a film about big-game catchers in Africa, starring Gary Cooper. The inspirations for this movie were likely several.

One might have come out of the prominence at the time of the work of Ian Player, older brother of South African golfer Gary Player. When Ian Player joined the Natal Parks Board as a ranger in 1952, South Africa was disastrously embarked on an effort to eliminate almost all its species of large wild animals to protect livestock from disease; and by the time he got to the Umfolozi Game Reserve, 200,000 head of game had been killed off in the preceding six years. Only 300 white rhino survived, and Player understood that these animals needed to be dispersed to protect them from mass infection such as anthrax and from poaching. He started a famed translocation program labeled "Operation Rhino" which became the subject of documentaries and films, and Hawks watched 16mm footage of the capture routines for hours as he envisioned his movie project.

Another source was the death of the African-animal photographer Ylla. Born Camilla Koffler in Vienna to Hungarian parents, she took "Ylla" as her professional name and was widely regarded as the best wildlife photographer in the world when in 1955, while photographing the annual bullock-cart races in Bharatpur, India, she was thrown from the hood of the moving Jeep she was perched on and killed. This incident illustrated the inherent risk the game catchers faced as they sped after wild animals across the Tanganyikan plains, one warthog hole away from calamity; and Ylla is the acknowledged model for the female photographer in the movie. It would have to be assumed, though, that the primary inspiration for Hawks's story idea was the pioneering wild-animal capturing work of the Kenyan Carr Hartley.

In the wake of World War II when the animals from so many European and Japanese zoos had been destroyed (and often consumed), Hartley became one of the most important providers of wildlife for restocking. This was all before such niceties as helicopters and darting; and Hartley's hands-on approach, according to Brian Herne's book, *White Hunters*, resulted in numerous lion maulings, rhino tossings, buffalo tramplings, and an oryx horn through his knee.

Hartley's technique, described in a 1949 article in *Sudan Wild Life and Sport* about the capture of rare Northern white rhino, was to "put his foot on the accelerator" of his four-by-four Dodge Power Wagon and try to avoid the "tree stumps left by the wood-cutters collecting steamer fuel" as his "boys" stood in the back of the truck, "ready with nooses of three-quarter-inch hemp rope fixed into a notch on the end of a stout bamboo pole." After "swerving precariously alongside" a galloping rhino cow and calf for several hundred yards, Hartley's crew lassoed the calf and the seven men in the back of the truck held onto it as its mother spun around and threatened the truck with her 40-inch horn. Shouts and horn honking got the cow to jog off, and then everybody jumped onto the calf, and with "special shackles" tied up its hind legs, forelegs, and snout. A "stout pole was cut," and the calf "was hoisted after some trouble onto the back of the lorry and driven back to Shambe" on the White Nile. And there you have the action sequences of *Hatari!* virtually shot for shot.

With the story idea for what was being called the "Africa project" in his head Hawks turned to one of his favorite screenwriters, Leigh Brackett, to come up with a script, or as near to one as Hawks ever shot, though in this case maybe less so. A prolific science-fiction writer, Brackett, who worked for Hawks on *The Big Sleep* and *Rio Bravo*, would contribute to all of Hawks's remaining films from *Hatari!* on and later wrote *The Empire Strikes Back* for George Lucas. Hawks, having discovered Brackett through the hard-boiled mystery novel *No Good from a Corpse*, appreciated the fact that Brackett wrote "like a man," especially because Leigh was a woman.

At various stages the Africa project would be about two guys and a gal; two guys, one a drunk (à la *Rio Bravo*); two guys sharing an "ironic rivalry," according to Brackett's notes, quoted by McCarthy, over whom would outlive the other in their hazardous calling; a veteran hunter now reduced to camp stooge due to injuries; a penniless "sexy cherub" (Brackett's description) who washes up in camp to the initial disgust of the love-singed tough-guy hero; a hard-drinking, hard-working deaf-mute woman (seriously); and a one-tusked rogue elephant that has to be hunted down by the hero, *Moby Dick* redux, after it kills a friend. (The sex-confusion angle of the photographer must have been informed by Brackett's own experiences during her screenwriting career.) Ultimately Hawks realized that because of the unpredictable nature of what nature might do, there could be no predetermined plot, other than the basic idea of tracking a crew of game catchers through a hunting season; and by the time Hawks actually left for Africa all he really had on paper was some snappy patter.

Interviewed by Peter Bogdonavich in 1962, the year *Hatari!* premiered, Hawks explained the improvisational aspects of the movie by saying:

> Well, you can't sit in an office and write what a rhino or other animal is going to do [at least not in the days ante-CGI; but what would be the possible point of making a move like *Hatari!* in a computer?—*note mine*]. From the time we saw one of them to the time we either caught it or failed to, it wouldn't be more than four minutes. So we had to make up scenes in an awful hurry; we couldn't write them . . . We were lucky enough to catch every kind of animal in Africa—everything we'd hoped for—usually if you get one-third you're lucky.

As a title for what was nothing more than a sheaf of pages, some 30 possibilities were considered with *Untamed, Africa Roars, Bring 'Em Back Alive,* and Hawks's favorite, *Tanganyika,* among them. It was the studio, Paramount, that anointed *Hatari!,* Swahili for "danger" or "peril," feeling it would appeal to the youth market (much in the news at the time, the national-independence movements in East Africa were identified by the Swahili word for "freedom" or "independence," *uhuru,* which *hatari* vaguely echoed). Then there was the location. Kenya was the first pick, but the British colony had passed new laws that prohibited the kind of high-speed motorized Hartley-esque animal capture Hawks wanted to depict in the film, so *Hatari!*'s setting was transferred to Tanganyika.

For the cast, Hawks's initial choice, Cooper, bowed out over the issue of script approval (Script? We don't need no estinkin' script!). In retrospect, the choice of John Wayne for the role of the head game catcher Sean Mercer (with its ring of a soldier of fortune) seems foreordained (although it took $750,000 and a promise of 10 percent of the grosses after the first $7 million in revenues to get the Duke to ink a deal—Hawks, of course, had given Wayne at age 40 his first genuine job of acting as "Thomas Dunson" in 1948's *Red River,* a performance that surprised even Wayne's mentor John Ford). Hawks then wanted Clark Gable to star opposite Wayne, but Gable died before shooting could begin.

After that the French star Yves Montand, Peter Ustinov, Peter Sellers, Leo McKern (Australian-British actor later famous as "Rumpole of the Bailey" who turned down a part because he reportedly "abhorred" the Nixon-backing Wayne's politics), Art Carney ("Hey, Ralphie-boy!"), Patrick McGoohan (*The Prisoner*), Stella Stevens, and Claudia Cardinale (Italian actress who starred in Sergio Leone's *Once Upon a Time in the West*) were all looked at. Those making the final cut were German actor Hardy Krüger (unforgettable afterward as the "airplane" designer in *Flight of the Phoenix*) who played Mercer's umlauted lieutenant "Kurt Müller"; the "much-perfumed," according to one professional hunter on the set, Italian actress Elsa Martinelli as the Ylla-esque photographer "Anna Maria 'Dallas' D'Allesandro"; comedian and Academy Award winner Red Buttons as the ex-pat New York cab driver "Pockets" (Buttons/Pockets's real name, Aaron Chwatt); Gérard Blain as "Charles 'Chips' Maurey" (touted as the "French James Dean," Blain was so short he made the five-foot-eight *Rebel Without a*

Cause look like an NBA center; to give him the gravitas of an actual big-game hunter, Hawks dressed him in black "to cut a stronger profile" [McCarthy]; when he showed up for his first scene, Martinelli's impression was that "he looked like he stepped out of a Fritz Lang movie"); Bruce Cabot as "Little Wolf" or 'the Indian'" (born, it seems, one Etienne Pelissier Jacques de Bujac, no less, his star power peaked early on in *King Kong*; and he made do in later years on the strength of being a Wayne crony); Michèle Giradon as the ingenue "Brandy de la Court" (the French actress deflected the aggressive advances of Hawks, more than twice her age, and had her part sliced wafer thin; she achieved little subsequent success and would die at 36 of an overdose of sleeping pills); and Valentin de Vargas (née Albert C. Schubert) as "Luis Francisco Garcia Lopez" (previously one of "Calvera's" pistoleros in *The Magnificent Seven*). And so to Africa.

The main camp and set was established 75 miles west of Arusha on a property called Momella Farm near Lake Manyara in northern Tanganyika with a motor pool of 40 Willys Jeeps (provided, like the Nikon camera equipment, by the company for "promotional consideration"), a garageful of mechanics, and a menagerie of trained animals under the supervision of South African game catcher Willy de Beer. The cast stayed in the Lake Manyara Lodge while the crew remained under canvas at Momella, the area illuminated at night by generator-powered floodlights to discourage animals from venturing in. Nonetheless, as Buttons and Wayne played cards outside one evening, a leopard came out of the bush and was stalking toward them. "See what he wants," is all Wayne said when Buttons mentioned the advancing predator. Wayne apparently remained equally nonplussed when called upon to shoot a charging elephant, driven to him like a grouse on a moor.

While the other actors were asking, Where the hell's the script?, Wayne after the ordeal of producing, directing, and starring in the great patriotic gas balloon *The Alamo,* was approaching the entire film as a holiday. And so was Hawks, who slipped out early every morning for a spot of hunting—hoping, but failing, to take a leopard (should have gotten into that card game)—and returning in time for each day's scheduled shoot with his shoes improbably shined.

From October through December 1960 before the rains, the crew got footage of the animal chases and captures; and the wildlife called the shots on what kind of footage they got: Of 16 rhino pursued, according to Hawks, only four were caught. Buffalo, giraffe, wildebeest, hartebeest, and elephant were chased, depending on what the game spotters located. Zebras proved the toughest, knowing instinctively to head for the broken rock where the Jeeps could not follow. In fact, the wild animals seldom did anything the film company wanted, when the film company wanted them to do it, if ever. (When elephant and hyenas wouldn't "speak" on cue, a PH who could imitate the sounds was brought in to dub them.)

Acting doubles were seldom used for the cast during the chase scenes, despite the fact that even Wayne was scared silly (in the best of ways) as he careened across the dusty corrugated plains, strapped into the catcher's seat on the truck fender by a single belt. Yet Wayne lassoed game himself ("there was no doubling at all"—Hawks), although Hawks refused to let him rope rhino despite the Duke's entreaties. Wayne said he never had as much fun on any other movie, and all the other actors agreed. And the professional hunters, behind the scenes, and sometimes in them, were having fun and excitement of their own.

On what Hawks called the most expensive safari in the world (the movie cost a for-then steep $6.5 million to make, and grossed $14 million), he had an A-list of professional hunters to compliment his list of actors. The venerable Ker & Downey was the principal outfitter, and the veteran PHs included Eric Rundgren (who was cast in the movie), John Kingsley-Heath, Bill Ryan, John Fletcher, Sten Cedergren, and many others needed to keep film rolling and stars happy. And they all have memories.

In his memoir, *The Adventurous Life of a Vagabond Hunter*, the late Cedergren remembered sharing "three fingers"—three Duke-sized fingers—of whisky with Wayne, which knocked him on his butt; and he also cherished some rather discreet recollections of Elsa Martinelli, perfume and all.

The also-late John Kingsley-Heath may have had the most adventures to remember. In his book *Hunting the Dangerous Game of Africa*, Kingsley-Heath, with whom Wayne hunted privately during the shoot, recalled how the payment of many thousands of pounds to various parks officials allowed the production team to get away with some rather dubious activities with regard to wildlife.

To get a shot of lions under a tree, Kingsley-Heath, et al., dragged a dead zebra through Serengeti National Park behind a car to draw a pride to its "mark." In Lake Manyara National Park, hunters, gunbearers, and trackers used small explosives to try to herd elephant through a safari camp for a shot of them trampling the tents. But the elephant always balked at the sight of the tents, and so Kingsley-Heath hit upon the expedient of fabricating shrunken tents and camp equipment and using 11 small tame elephant technical-advisor de Beer had on hand. Kept from food for a day, the elephant, as the cameras turned, stampeded enthusiastically through the mock camp as de Beer stood on the far side, rattling a pail of cabbage.

There was tragedy surrounding *Hatari!* Carr Hartley's one-time sister-in-law Diana, who went into competition with him as an animal catcher, delivered two cheetah to the set and learned that a "tame" lion she was familiar with was in one of the enclosures. She went in to greet it; and the lion almost immediately reared up and bit her chin, throat, and chest, mauling her to death (so much for heartwarming "animal reunions," to use the title of a reputedly legitimate nature documentary). Three native Africans were also killed during the shooting, and de Beer got chewed on by a juvenile leopard in his care.

The five months spent in Africa filming *Hatari!* could not help but have a profound impact on the cast. For Wayne it was the "savage sounds" of the animals in the dawn. For Red Buttons, the sight of Kilimanjaro made him understand why the Maasai believed that God must dwell on its summit. Hardy Krüger ended up buying both John Kingsley-Heath's hunting car and Momella Farm, building a lodge, and living there with his family for over a dozen years. Valentin de Vargas felt that at the end they were no longer actors. "We were," he said "animal catchers."

As for Howard Hawks, without an actual script, without even a coherent plot, he took magnificent real-life African footage and the mostly improvised performances of actors thrust into a wild unfamiliar world of fierce beauty, big game, and thrilling pursuit and crafted a picture that for 157 minutes transported a young moviegoer to a place he knew he had to see, one day, for himself. And then what Hawks wanted was to do it all over again with the same cast, this time in India on a movie to be called *Bengal Tiger*. When he told the studio executives the story, they told him that was the movie he'd just made.

As quoted by McCarthy, Hawks replied, "No, not at all. That's the film we were supposed to make." Yet never did.

POSTSCRIPT: Of the cast and crew, both human and animal, who assembled half-a-century ago in Tanganyika to make *Hatari!*, only a few are, at the time of this writing, still here. The star John Wayne, director Howard Hawks, and screenwriter Leigh Brackett all died more than 30 years ago, and actors Red Buttons, Bruce Cabot, Gérard Bain, Valentin de Vargas, and Michèle Girardon have joined them. And most of the professional hunters who worked as technical advisors, guides, doubles, security, wildlife wranglers and capturers, have also passed on. The principal game handler for the movie was the legendary Willie de Beer, owner of Tanganyika Game Limited, licensed for capturing wildlife; and working for him was a young Jan Oelofse. Oelofse went on to own Jan Oelofse Hunting Safaris in Namibia and to publish his memoir *Capture to Be Free*, authored by his wife, Annette Oelofse. In a phone interview with Oelofse, I asked him about his career and his memories of having worked on *Hatari!*

I began the interview by asking Oelofse if he minded giving out his age.

Jan Oelofse: Yah, no problem. I am not so vain. My age is 77. I'll be 78 this year [2012].

How had he come to be a part of *Hatari!*?

I was working for an old gentleman in Tanzania (it was Tanganyika at the time), Mr. de Beer, and Paramount wanted to do a movie, an African movie, and they came out and visited our camp. And the movie was more or less based on our lives there at the time. And since I was working for him [Willie de Beer], I was a participant in helping to work on the movie. He got the contract and, you know, I was a young man at the time, 50 years younger than I am now, and that's how it happened.

What could he tell me about Willie de Beer?

His parents left South Africa. You know, a lot of the Afrikaans-speaking people left South Africa after the Boer War. And then early in the 1900s, his parents went up to Tanganyika when he was a small boy. And there they settled, and he started in his young days to capture game. And it was always a dream for me to go and work with animals, and Tanganyika was the mecca of wildlife at that time. And then eventually I ended up with him. He was like a father to me, actually, you know?

How did he, Oelofse, get to Tanganyika?

Yah, well I came up from Namibia, which was Southwest Africa at the time [in the mid-1950s]. And I worked a while in Zambia—I ran out of money by the time I got there. So I worked there for a few months, and then I continued up to Tanganyika.

Before we talked about *Hatari!*, could he tell me about his career after the movie?

Well, I left East Africa in 1964. You know, after independence, it was very difficult for us to get work permits there if you were of Western descent. So then I went back to South Africa; and I joined the fish-and-wildlife for Natal, the Natal Parks Board. And I worked for them for eight years; and then during that time I discovered and designed a technique to capture animals in the thousands, you know, and that really was the forerunner of the whole game industry in South Africa today. Previously, they couldn't farm with game because it was difficult to obtain some, because it was very hard to capture them. With my technique, I could capture hundreds and hundreds in a day; and then it made it possible for people to buy game and stock their ranches and turn large areas over to conservation areas that were previously used for [cattle and sheep]. I [also] did a lot of movies for Mutual of Omaha, Marlin Perkins. I did a whole lot, about 20 series for him. I was quite a bit involved in movie making etc., you know in my younger days until about 20 years ago or so.

[From Oelofse's memoir, he went into the private game-capturing business in 1973, using the now well-known "Oelofse Method" to capture wildlife and supply it all over southern Africa. Eventually he purchased a ranch in Namibia for surplus wildlife, turning it into the 60,000 acre Okonjati Game Sanctuary and Mount Etjo Safari Lodge. In 1982 Oelofse was named the Safari Club International's "Most Outstanding Hunter."]

When did Oelofse first start work on Hatari!?

Yah, I was already working for him [de Beer] for quite a while before the movie started. And the animals were all entrusted to my care at that time, all captive animals, you know? About a year before they came or longer, I prepared already. I captured them [the animals] myself, most of them. I started training the elephant for the movie for any parts they had to play and some of the other animals, so I was involved actually quite a while with it. They [the young elephant] accepted me as a matriarch and they were like . . . they accepted me as a mother figure or a father, and they followed me everywhere where I'd go and you know I actually slept a lot of nights with them in the cages, initially, to make them get used to me and so on.

What were some of his jobs on the movie?

I worked with leopards and all sorts of things and you know in some of the scenes we were capturing animals and so forth. We were doubling and standing in for some of the actors. But my main thing was to let the elephant do what they [the film crew] wanted them to do, and I also had a cheetah there that I brought from Namibia. Her name was Sonia. She also appeared prominently in the movie.

Was Sonia the cheetah that came in while Elsa Martinelli was in the bath?

Right. I was lying behind the bath, and I could see . . . I think I am one of the few guys that saw Martinelli's buttocks. [laughter] I lay behind the bath, and I called the cheetah in. She would only respond to me, you know; and then she walked up to Martinelli; and we put egg yolk and stuff and blood on her legs that smelled like blood to attract her, and it was supposed to be soap that she was licking off.

What other animals did you work with?

Yah, I had about 42 animals, you know, which included cheetahs, hyenas, lions, leopards, elephant, and some bird species, etc., etc.

But your main duty was the elephant?

Yah, I was involved in all the scenes. The elephant wouldn't respond to anybody but me. And wherever you see the elephant, I was somewhere in the background or somewhere just out of screen, to control them. And when they ran down the street [in Arusha in the final scene], they were running after me in fact. And the camera was just, you know, I was just out of view for the cameras.

What was John Wayne like?

He was a very nice gentleman, and I spent a lot of time with him. And, uh, you know, off set sometimes I took him out into the veldt and we went hunting and so on and game viewing. I had good impressions of most of the stars. I can't say bad about any of them. They were all nice people. And my only sad moment was when I had to leave all my elephant behind after we finished the shooting in Hollywood.

How did the animals get to Hollywood?

We did the movie in a couple of months in East Africa and then we moved across. I came in a plane across from Africa to Burbank Airport in Los Angeles. It took us five days with a DC 6 at that time. I was a couple of months in Hollywood. I can't remember exactly how long now.

Did you consider staying in Hollywood?

Yah, you know, it was a whole new world to me. But I was always yearning to go back to Africa. After I finished, I went on a tour through America and then Europe; and then I went back to East Africa again.

And the animals?

Paramount bought them from Mr. de Beer, and at that time I was just working for him. Once they finished the movie, I delivered them all to San Diego [the San Diego Zoo].

How did you feel about that?

You know it was all in day's work to me. It is the kind of work I did and I liked to do, and it was a wonderful experience for me. It was just sad to leave them behind in the States.

[We talked about the elephant. Oelofse remembered there were five young ones he brought to Hollywood and then delivered to the San Diego Zoo; and he had long wondered what had become of them. By going on the internet, I learned that at least four, the only four recorded to have been donated by Paramount, were now all dead, and had died at relatively young ages, for elephant, none having gotten out of their 30s.]

I am actually sad to know that they died. I thought I might, you know, since elephant normally grow quite old—there was probably something wrong with their diet or whatever that they died so early. I would have loved to have made acquaintance with them again after 50 years, but now it's too late. My God, they probably missed me. Yah, what a shame.

I mentioned that the oldest female, Hatari, had a calf, which could still be alive.

She certainly wouldn't know me [laughing].

I thanked Jan Oelofse for having taken the time to let me interview him.

Yah, nice talking to you; and I'm looking forward to seeing you next year again.

Jan Oelofse died a few months after this interview, one of the last links to Hatari!.

Old No. 7

The 2000s . . .

THE MERITS OF mefloquine as a recreational drug go sorely uncommented upon. As I lay tucked asleep, the malaria prophylactic produced phantasmagoric, labyrinthine, radioactive scenarios—Salvador Dali directed by David Cronenberg—without my having to be surrounded by an auditorium full of Dead Heads. As safe and sound as my hallucinatory sleep might be, it was often disturbed (in a physical sense) by roars, or rumbles and screams. That wasn't the mefloquine's fault.

Remembering where I was, I sat in the dark under the mosquito netting and swung my legs out of the bed—pausing, if it occurred to me, to peer around for the silhouettes of scorpions before setting my feet down. Lifting the net, I crossed to the tent flap and stepped into the cool August night air where bats swooped past my face.

Sometimes, I heard the distant roar of the lion that ended the dream. More frequently, though, from the Songo River flats below camp, the scream came again, and under the Southern Cross I saw the moon-washed elephant bumping one another as they all tried to crowd around the salt lick. These cows and calves, the "Songo Bitches," expressing their extreme displeasure at

being jostled by one another, were not park or wildlife-preserve elephant. They were members of a healthy wild population of legally hunted elephant—a thing far different from the semi-narcoleptic attractions found at Africa's finer game lodges. These elephant were much too wide awake ever to permit one of those zebra vans to drive up to them. Either they would vanish into the brush, like ectoplasm dissolving at the end of a séance, before the van ever got anywhere near; or they would let it get near, then "stuffing try to kill" the van and all its occupants, as Zimbabwean PH Rory Muil put it.

Where my tent was pitched, and where I hunted with Rory, was in a million-acre hunting concession spread across the Tonga tribe's Binga Communal Lands up from the Kariba Lake shore in northwestern Zimbabwe. The place was called Songo Camp, and the elephant were the almost-nightly entertainment. Some nights they might be accompanied by the bellowing of Cape buffalo; but by morning they, and the buff, would be gone from sight; and I would have to go looking for them, the buffalo in particular.

If mefloquine gave me bizarre but relatively harmless dreams, it was nyati, the buffalo, who produced another sort of delirium—one that carried a serious threat of addiction, as I knew too well. Not everyone necessarily gets hooked on nyati. In terms of side effects, the first hit is usually free. A hunter may get "lucky" and stumble onto a bull in open terrain and make a practically anticlimactic one-shot kill, and wonder what all the fuss is about. Another hunter, after chasing snorting, stampeding buffalo around in the bush for days, may be so unnerved by the experience that he will happily make his first buffalo hunt his only buffalo hunt, and from then on stick to less distressing game, like grizzly bear. It is only after a person deliberately hunts Cape buffalo a second time, or a third, that he makes a crossing to being something, and someone, distinctly different from whatever he was before.

Once over the line, it is a fact that such people will hunt buffalo whenever they are in Africa and there are buffalo to hunt. Robert Ruark quoted his (then) youthful PH Harry Selby: "You will always hunt buff. It's a disease. You've killed a lion and you don't care whether you take another. But you will hunt buff until you are dead, because there is something about them that makes intelligent people into complete idiots. Like me."

Even as I watched those elephant like white hills in the moonlight below the camp, I was thinking about the six Cape buffalo I had killed in 28 years—because that was how many buffalo there had been for me to hunt in 28 years. (One, a Nile buffalo up in the Central African Republic, had been more a matter of my counting coup after a PH and his hunter had wounded the bull and we tracked it and found it waiting for us, gathering itself for a charge; but I counted it all the same.) I was back again in Zimbabwe after many years, in the hardly best of times for the country, for the sole purpose of hunting buffalo some more. I had, in short, a buffalo on my back; and after six of them, served neat, the only possible cure for my jones was a shot of Old No. 7.

I don't know if it requires a special darkness or a heart of clear radiance to be drawn to the hunting of Cape buffalo. The only thing I do know is that it is unlike all the other hunting of all the other game I have given chase to in Africa. The glamour species such as sable, kudu, and nyala can regularly be spotted from a vehicle and stalked. Lion and leopard are almost invariably baited into rifle range. The pursuit of giant eland, or bongo, can be grueling to the point of heartbreak; but only the bongo, reportedly, has even a slight tendency toward aggressive behavior if confronted. Black rhino, though no longer hunted (except at astronomical expense and the most complicated permitting process), are belligerent by disposition, but are also intractable innocents. White rhino are similarly heedless and exceedingly docile. Elephant are five times the size of buffalo, arguably smarter, and hunting them is never anything less than a long, hard, throat-tightened slog. Their charge is nearly always bluff, though, and a bullet through a flared ear—no more to an elephant than a piercing to a teenaged girl—can turn them.

Buffalo seldom charge unless made to, but they never bluff. Their sight and hearing, while not acute, are far from poor (having few "natural" enemies, they haven't had to evolve those senses to the level of the smaller prey species); their sense of smell is astounding; and all their senses are wired into a large brain and a redoubtable, decidedly uncowlike intellect. You have to hunt them on foot, you have to get close, you have to use a heavy rifle, and you have to shoot straight the first time.

Among Cape buffalo, the dagga boys are the most unadulterated form of the buffalo drug. Dagga boys behave as if they belong to the Skull & Bones society of the wallows. Either bullies or grandees, they lay claim to the mudholes by seeming divine right; and their attitude toward much of the rest of the world, including humans, is about on par. That, and all of the above, is what makes them so interesting.

If you hunt dagga boys, you want a PH you can rely on, first, not to take you (too) unnecessarily into harm's way, but, second, to be there to lend an assist if a "situation" needs sorting out. Until you really learn how a PH will react during a buffalo incident, you look to external signs for a clue. It might be his eyes—if he meets yours directly—or his posture or how much rubbish he may or may not talk. Or you can look at his wrists.

There are PHs who collect all variety of native good-luck string, copper, elephant-hair, ivory, or rhino-cartilage bracelets (the last only on an old-timer, a *mzee*, these days—one PH who hunted into his eighties affected such a hoop for a time as a young man, till he found that it rubbed uncomfortably on the backs of others in intimate liaisons). The suspicion arises that bedizened PHs may just fancy themselves Maasai morani (who tend to wear wooden bracelets that look an awful lot like the black-rubber drive belts off vacuum cleaners), bent on proving, or hiding, something. As a rule: The cheaper the crook, the gaudier the patter; and likewise, the more rattly the bangles, the more dubious the competence of the PH. Rory, who resembled a shopworn version of the actor Patrick Stewart, wore a Timex, with a cloth strap.

This seemed to matter when we found ourselves trailing a dagga boy whose track showed he was dragging a right hind hoof. He had likely been caught in a poacher's wire snare and pulled free—no mean feat, considering that the snares were generally constructed from double strands of 12½-gauge high-tensile fence wire. (Three days prior to my arrival in camp, a poacher and several of his associates went down to the Sengwa, the area's main river, in order to spear a buffalo who had tangled a snare around his head and horns and had the poor manners not to strangle himself to death. As the spearmen approached what they took to be a harmless, neck-roped buffalo, the bull was filled with a surge of adrenaline and snapped the snare—with a breaking strength twice his bodyweight—and proceeded to butt, gore, and stamp the poacher into the ground while the poacher's cohort fled. Then the buffalo walked off, still wearing his crown of wire.)

We trailed the skidding track through the open jess down to a dry creek bottom where the tracks played out. A mopane tree grew out of a dense clump of bushwillow; and we spread out around and above it, hoping to pick up the trail again. One of the trackers, Tino, was down in the creek bottom when a pair of oxpeckers flew out of the bushwillow. Everyone, and everything, froze.

Rory and I were on the creekbank above the brush. Rory slid to my side when the birds flew.

"If he charges," he whispered, his eyes on the bush, "he's coming, and we'll have to grab him." As he said this, he held up his free hand (the one not wrapped around the barrel of the 458 Model 70 with iron sights and the bluing worn off) and closed it on the air.

"Do you know where he is?" I asked, so I would know where to swing my 450 Nitro Express 3¼-inch Ruger No. 1.

He shrugged.

"Haven't a clue."

As it turned out, the buffalo was 20 yards away, lying in the bushwillow under the mopane, watching. It took us a quarter hour to verify that, as we moved side to side and in and out to try to get a look at him. The best that could be seen, with a binocular, was an eye and a segment of horn.

"This buffalo should have been gone by now," Rory said, unease and excitement rising in his hushed voice.

Do you think there's fear to be seen in a handful of dust? Imagine a bush, yards away, where a dagga boy waits, having decided not to run.

As long as we stayed downwind of the buffalo, he was not going to show himself, so we crossed (rapidly) the rocks and sand of the creek bottom and circled upwind of where the buffalo lay on the opposite bank. As our wind drifted into the bushwillow, and we waited with our rifles, we heard the buffalo getting to his hooves. Then we saw his gray-blackness moving. Then he walked into the open.

He was a young dagga boy, packing his hind hoof. His hipbones showed, and he'd been fortunate not to have been taken by lion. He moved lamely under the slanting afternoon sun, looking at us levelly as he drew off from us. We watched him go. He could still survive and in time mend—maturing into a bull who did not run. Rory calmly consulted his Timex and said we should head for the Land Rover.

In the days after that the buffalo hunting was a matter of old tracks, no tracks, blown stalks, wrong buffalo. In the middle of the bush, another tracker, John, found a 1961 Rhodesia and Nyassaland penny, with a hole in the center and elephant rampant on the obverse. I bought it off him and strung it through the band of my hat, hoping it would change our luck; but we went on hunting without any noticeable improvement in our fortunes.

We were not without buffalo meat in camp, though. Whenever a buffalo was killed, the trackers cut it in two with their tribal axes and knives and took everything from the body cavity—even stabbing handholds in the bulging white wall of the stomach to roll it out onto the ground and cut it up into tripe. When they were done, all of the buffalo, except the 200-pound bale of grazed grass from the stomach and the contents of the lower intestines (what Lewis and Clark's "wrighthand" cook Charbonneau would have described as "not good to eat"), was loaded into the Land Rover and transported back to camp. There was abundant, virtually fat-free meat in camp from buffalo killed by previous hunters, and we ate it as rolled fillet; braised oxtail; steaks; biltong; cold in sandwiches; the liver, fried; testicles, likewise (Buffalo McNuggets); in traditional muriro stew with onions and rape greens, scooped from the pot with stiff cornmeal *sadza* (the main staple of Zimbabwe) rolled into a ball in the hand; and once for lunch as a poignant, handcrafted cheeseburger—the cheese Zimbabwean cheddar, the onion and tomato from the camp's small vegetable garden behind the wattle-and-daub cook hut, the homemade bun baked in the hut's woodstove, the mustard stirred up from dry powder—as artisinal and rustic as if someone were placing a call to you on a telephone he had carved from wood. But eating yesterday's buffalo only made me want to find tomorrow's even more.

The routine of the hunt was to check waterholes for a track that was not *neruro* (yesterday). Today's track, if not up-to-the-minute, could still be used to judge what the bull would be doing in an hour, in the afternoon, tomorrow. If shiny and crisply outlined, we would be on it on foot.

We were indifferent to a great deal as we tracked, whether the bounding escape of a big kudu or the gray apparition of a rare roan bull galloping off. We weren't blind to our surroundings, though. Once, Rory picked up a small tortoise, fast asleep under the grass, showed it to me, then placed it back carefully into the cover. Snowy flashes caught our eyes, and looking we saw *marangwonda*, scattered bones, the immense broken skeletons of elephant, too heavy to have been dragged off by scavengers. We would also find wide sandy elephant beds where the giants lay on their sides, a lesser indent up at the head where a tusk furrowed a resting spot. (In marula season, the fruit fermented in the elephant's stomachs and they flopped down, snoring, sleeping one off.)

The buffalo knew too well, though, where to lead us to make the tracking of them, if not impossible, then at least dubious: unbroken dry shoals of quartz pebbles, tall thick grass, shelves of flat bare rock, and across noisy acres of fallen leaves.

"Like walking around in a crisp factory," Rory would say, taking a fatalistic drag on his Newbury cigarette.

Mentally translating "crisp" into "potato chip," I thought of "a dangerous man," Floyd Thursby, in *The Maltese Falcon* who "never went to sleep without covering the floor around his bed with crumpled newspaper." Cape buffalo were nothing if not the Floyd Thursbys of the African bush. With thoughts like that—especially at moments when the trackers halted in voiceless unison, like a synchronized swim team practicing out of the pool, all of them staring at the same (for me) unidentifiable object in the bush—I had to remind myself that I was coming for the buffalo, not he for me (except for that unpredictable, but statistically significant, instance when he actually could be coming for me).

For six days we hunted like that. Far from frustrating, it was six days of valuable practice—I even began to find tracks myself when we had lost them. As the days went by, I also began to develop a premonitory awareness. At the end of a long fifth day, I told Rory my secret prediction: We would find the dagga boy, Old No. 7, on the seventh day. Rory did not argue.

On the seventh morning we looked for buffalo on a high grassy flat where we had seen tracks heading the evening before, klipspringer bounding out of the kopjes ahead of us. The buffalo had already moved on, though. I didn't have to ask Rory where we were going next: We would go to his favorite area for buffalo, Kapinda, a distant part of the concession where stands of mopane grew up to the bottoms of rock ridges, the jess could be thick, and long-yellow-grassed woodland parks rolled out over broad ridgelines.

The morning grew warm as we drove the more-than-20 kilometers to Kapinda. Reaching the area, we rolled slowly down the indistinct dirt roads, looking for tracks, and at midmorning found large round ones—those of two dagga boys together.

We parked the white Land Rover in the shade of a tree. I took my soft case down from the rifle rack welded to the rollbar behind the front seats, unzipped it, and slipped out the 450. Sliding in a snap cap, I levered the action closed and dry-fired offhand at 50, 30, 15 yards, keeping my eye on the unripened turquoise monkey orange or yellow leaf I held in the crosshairs of the 1.75-6x32mm scope, keeping it steady through the shot, the power ring turned down to 1.75X. I ejected the snap cap and chambered a 500-grain soft-nosed bullet, loaded to 2,100 feet-per-second velocity, and set the safety. I took a long drink of water (but not enough to slosh in my belly) from one of the canteens John carried in his day pack. It was time to go.

The track led across all the usual dubious terrain. We lost, and found, the dagga boys' trail time and again until we tracked them into a keep of tall crenulated rocks on a high ridge. We knew they had to be just ahead; and they were, bedded.

What gets buffalo killed, above all else, is the wind; but it is also what keeps them from getting killed. This time the wind swirled in their favor.

We heard thunderous crashing, like three-quarter-ton mule deer busting from cover, unseen. Hunkering in silence in the rocks, we waited to see if the buffalo would tell us what to do next.

Fifteen minutes later, Samuel, Rory's head tracker, spotted the two good, old dagga boys feeding among the mopane out on the flat ground below the rocks, as if all had been forgiven. They had not been irreparably spooked and drifted back toward the rocks.

"How far can that rifle shoot?" Rory asked. It was not a question I liked. "Not that far."

"Two hundred yards?"

"To shoot well? One hundred. Less."

Rory was calculating. We had the wind up here and could see the buffalo clearly. If we went down, we would lose sight of them and did not know how the wind was, there. A low ridge ran near the buffalo with large rocks piled on it. If we went down in a wide circle, using the rocks as landmarks, we could get within 100 yards or less of the bulls—if it all went right. Rory knew I didn't want to do this at sniping ranges: Oddly, I felt better the closer I got to buffalo, even glint-of-the-eye distance—as long as I was seeing more of a buffalo than just that glint. There was also something fundamentally unseemly about trying to "fell" Cape buffalo "at a venture." Hunting buffalo was, at least for me, ultimately a highly personal matter, and therefore ought to be carried out up close. There wasn't really a choice, now, though.

Rory decided and we crawled out of the rocks and when we were away from the buffalo's line of sight stood and worked our way off the ridge. I stumbled more than once on the way down (either from simple clumsiness or excited tension), and I was certain I had started the bulls. We couldn't know, so we went on with the stalk. On the flat ground, moving toward the low ridge and the landmarks, Rory asked me what I had chambered. I told him soft.

"Solid," he whispered, and I reloaded the single-shot quietly. Reaching the low ridge, we left the other trackers behind; and Samuel, Rory, and I climbed it and moved along the crest. The rock we had singled out to navigate by (black and wind-carved) was just ahead. I could see off the other side of the ridge, and I saw a black shape standing beneath the low branches of a mopane. I reached out and touched Rory; and he whistled softly to Samuel, and we all stopped.

We lined up three trees and used them for concealment as we worked closer, until the dagga boy was 60 yards away, slightly downhill. There was no cover or any place to get a rest, and I slid out alone from behind the last tree and set the fore-end of the 450 in a leather-covered cradle on the top of the hiking staff I used. I found the buffalo in the scope. I turned the power ring up to 4X. The bull had his head in the branches and leaves, but I could see a blocky rump, slightly swayed back, and heavy belly, his real weight carried in the bulked hump of his shoulder. He was quartering toward me, and as I looked among the branches and leaves of the tree, I saw a boss and the curve of a horn and a glint: He saw something where I stood, but he waited for the wind to tell him what it was.

The buffalo's left ear drooped and below its tattered fringe I could see his chest and the base of his neck. I stage whispered to Rory that there were twigs in the way, and he whispered back, "Not enough to bother that bullet; all quite thin stuff."

I looked back through the crosshairs and saw that he was right. I found a place on the bull's chest that looked open.

"I'm going to shoot him in the chest, just below his left ear."

"That's a good place."

I held a little longer, making sure that what I was seeing in the blackness in the scope really was the bull's chest. I slid the tang safety forward.

"Don't shoot unless you're absolutely happy," Rory warned.

I was tense, concentrated, and yes, happy—nearly euphoric in a semi-terrified way. My finger pressed the trigger and the rifle fired.

The bull spun out from beneath the tree in a splintering of branches. He ran counterclockwise in a half circle, placing himself 15 yards farther out along the line of fire, but partially covered by the mopane's trunk. His head was up, domed by the heavy boss, his Roman nose scenting for the source of the bullet that had struck him. Out of nowhere the second dagga boy pounded past and turned into the wind, drawing along the wounded bull with him. They went straight away, making for a second, lower ridge.

I had another solid in the chamber and threw the scope on the wounded bull (the rear one of the two), 100 yards away now. I scarcely felt the powerful thunderroll of the gun as it fired and the second 500-grain solid broke the buffalo's left hip. It didn't seem to slow him, but the first solid was finishing its work as he ran.

As I reloaded once more, the two bulls went out of sight over the second ridge. Then the first reappeared, going away from sight; and I saw the horns and boss of the second, lit from above by the harsh noon sun. I mused about whether I would have to try an even farther, unseemly shot, when the second bull lurched to his right. His head twisted down, and his body dropped, dust rising from where he fell from view, 200 yards from where I stood.

We hurried down off the first ridge, heading for the second. Before we were halfway there, we heard a mourning bellow from the other side.

"He is dead," announced John with a solemn nod. Not quite. Coming over the second low ridge, we found the buffalo lying on his right side, his back to us, his bellow faint and his head wobbling feebly on the ground. As a grace I walked up close behind him and gave him a third solid in the back of his deeply creased neck.

It almost seems a requirement of hunting stories, especially ones about "dangerous game," to offer a ballistics formula. There is the one describing kinetic energy or "Pondoro" Taylor's (sadly, rather questionable) "Knockout Value" for large calibers. Looking at this old dagga boy, the formula I came up with was:

$$\text{Ruger No. 1} \times [(.458+500 \text{ grs.}) \times 2100 \text{ fps} \times \{(1 @ 60m) + (1 @ 100m) + (1 @ 2m)\}] + 1700 \text{ lbs} = \text{Old No.7}$$

It would take more than a formula, though, to define this buffalo's wide boss, embedded with pale green cambium from his butting and rubbing his way through tree bark. Or horns that were worn back to where the thickness carried all the way out to the blunted tips. (The most elderly bulls could batter their horns back to stumps, so they looked as if they wore Wehrmacht helmets; this bull's horns were an honest badge of at least 15 years in good standing as a dagga boy.) Or define why, even as "he lay in death," as Theodore Roosevelt wrote in *African Game Trails,* he still "looked what he was, a formidable beast."

By the time a road had been hacked through the bush so that Tino could bring the Land Rover up to retrieve the carcass, the buffalo had exacted his own final revenge by dying in a spot remarkable for its infestation by mopane flies, a small stingless bee that sups on sweat and tears and other human and animal liquid excreta and is said for all that to produce exquisite honey.

They soon had Rory beside himself (though a native Zimbabwean, he'd never acquired an indifference to the tiny insect). He gathered up cabbage-sized lumps of dry elephant dung and set them alight to smolder in an almost incense-scented cloud of smoke, in the vain hope that the flies would be driven off by it. They weren't, and they became so annoying to him that he resorted to stopping up his ear canals with his old cigarette butts to keep them out—or maybe just so he could keep from hearing them.

Meanwhile, the trackers, working away with axes and knives, had opened the buffalo and let run out a rivulet of blood, drained into his body cavity by the first solid through the veins and arteries at the top of the heart—which nonetheless had not stopped him from running as far as he did. Trying to step around the blood and other fluids, they laughed and horsed with one another, nobody showing so much as a hint that "in the depths of his conscience" he felt the unease that José Ortega y Gasset claimed all hunters experienced (and these men were nothing if not among the truest hunters I had ever known). The killing of other animals might very well bring unease and regret; but no one was ever really unhappy after finding a big Cape buffalo, dead.

Paying the mopane flies no mind, I opened a warm beer from the cooler in the Land Rover, to propose a silent toast here among the trees and brush. The beer wasn't bad, but I realized that my drug of choice was neither it nor mefloquine, but the object of my salute: dagga boys. To find the pure dagga boy you had to get as far away as you could from the Africa of a million UPF-rated sun hats and photographic opportunities during game drives across clean, well-lighted plains. That was the kind of Africa the last decent parts were swiftly turning into; and there was nothing genuinely wrong with that, if you were satisfied with "Africa Lite."

Where I wanted to be, though, as long as it continued to exist, was an older place, where things worked out harsher, even crueler—though no more so than the continent's natural background radiation of cruelty. At this moment, that place was located approximately 28-degrees east of Greenwich and 17-degrees south of the equator. It was located with these men and mopane flies, heavy rifles, smoldering dung, bright fresh blood, and always, a dagga boy. It was where I had come for my ancient, savage fix, my shot of Old No. 7, neat as always. If it meant troubled sleep, that was all right because it also meant that it was not Africa Lite out there, not yet. It was still Africa Dark. Let there be dark.

Dreaming the Lion

The 1980s . . .

I sat up in the dark, listening. Moving blind hands, I searched for my rifle; but it wasn't beside me. I had to find it and to hear the roaring once more so I would know in what direction the lion, *bamara*, was moving. Waiting and listening, I heard that silence, with a lion walking in it, build to almost intolerable volume. There were nights when it would be an endless minute or more before I would be awake enough to realize that I was away from the lion now, that I was not in Africa anymore.

Along the River

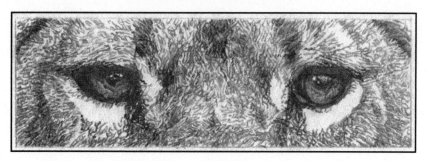

Such are the hardships to be endured when discovering new lands in the manner we set about it!
—Bernal Diaz,
History of the Conquest of New Spain

211

AS WATERHOLES WENT, it wasn't much. Bright-green reeds grew jaggedly around it, and the standing water was a less bright, oily green. Still, we could dip our canteens into it and purify its water with iodine pills or draw out a bucketful of it to wash with; and if you dropped a bottle of beer into it, it would eventually turn the beer coolish and soak off the bottle's label that showed an elephant's head printed on a red oval. Though it was only eight miles from our starting point in Ouanda Djallé, we had made a tardy beginning on this our first day's walking (the caravaners' "little start"), so we decided to pitch our camp beneath a large banyan tree near this waterhole called Mie Mai.

The ground was black with ashes in late January, the height of the dry burning season. As we all drifted across the bare earth under the midday sun to where we would make camp in the shade, it was impossible to calculate with any degree of certainty, counting professional or "white" hunters (one white, one very much black), trackers, gunbearers, water bearers, a cook, the cook's helpers, porters carrying crates and bundles on their heads with long-accustomed ease, camel drivers leading four camels and four horses, and bewildered hunters on safari, what our exact number might be.

That morning back in Djallé—the phrase "back in Jolly" acquired the cachet of a punch line among us as we marched on, describing all manner of equipage, from extra shoes to spare eyeglasses to additional ammunition to laxatives, that to save weight we jettisoned, only to discover a crying need for farther on in the country—back in Jolly, at any rate, it had been entirely too confounding to take anything like an accurate tally. It had been hard enough, among the lime-washed headquarters buildings of the French safari company we were hunting with, just to organize the gear, animals, and hired men into the semblance of a unit a tad more cohesive than, say, a Chinese fire drill. Thirty souls, give or take, would not have been far off the mark.

Here in the northeast of the Central African Republic, the safari had initially called for a dozen camels, half-a-dozen horses, and two donkeys to transport our burdens. We were to strike off east into an unexplored portion of the safari company's vast concession toward the border with Sudan, going afoot because motor vehicles had never been there and roads were nonexistent. No one knew if there was even any game to be found there, but it would nonetheless be the rarest of opportunities to be the first hunting party into an area where only Africans had been before and to conduct a safari along the antique principle of putting one foot deliberately in front of the other. It seemed, simply and anachronistically, the right thing to be doing even, or maybe especially, at the latter days of the shocking 20th century.

What we had not bargained for was a band of very important Saudi sportsmen sweeping in ahead of us and making off, to a well-appointed hunting camp on the small Koubo River 60 kilometers to the north, with most of the safari company's stock of camels (for no better reason, I assume, than a certain *maladie du pays,* since they did all their traveling exclusively in vehicles). Claims of miscommunication were made, but obviously the fix had been put in somewhere. So because "money talks and all the rest walks," we had to recruit porters, many of them at first refusing the offer of employment when the harebrained nature of our excursion became clear to them, then accepting with the utmost reluctance when it became equally clear that the manager of the safari company meant to take names and to remember them when future job opportunities arose. As we straggled in a quarter-mile file out of the village, past the adobe houses and fields of maize, porters running off to bid goodbye to their families, the first of numerous loads spilling from the humped backs of the green-mouthed, braying, balking, sad camels the Arabs had seen fit to bequeath us, and wound our way around the base of the tall naked rock, the djebel called Kaga Moumo that marked Ouanda Djallé's position in the tropical geography, "plans" were jettisoned as readily as gear and we began to learn the invaluable art of living ad hoc.

The Central African Republic is in the language of the travel guides a lightly populated, landlocked, Texas-sized nation lying just above the equator. It is encased, beginning clockwise from the north, by the countries of Chad, Sudan, Zaire, the Republic of the Congo, and Cameroon. When it was part of French Equatorial Africa it was called Oubangi-Chari. It is bled by those two great river systems: the Oubangui in the south, draining on into the Congo of Stanley and Mr. Kurtz; and the Chad which is nourished by the many smaller rivers of the north before flowing on into Lake Chad.

Transitional in climate between the sub-Saharan and the equatorial, the C. A. R. is for the most part a 2,000-foot high rolling plateau, a "Guinea" savannah of tall grass and trees. It is the country, particularly in the northeast area known as Ouandjia-Vakaga, of the giant eland, equinoxial buffalo, the Western roan antelope, and the lion.

The riparian folk of the country's south, the Ubangi, were once noted for their platter-lipped women who would purposely disfigure themselves by slitting their lips and inserting large wooden disks into them as an expedient against being selected for the harems of the Arab slaving sultans who raged unchecked across the territory for generations. In Ouandjia Vakaga the slavers exterminated many tribes, from the Bingas to the Challas to the Bongos to the Melas, in the conduct of their enterprise. Various sultans based in Ouanda Djallé carried on their grim commerce until by main force the French military put an end to it, though not until 1912. Independence was achieved on December 1, 1958, and with it came immediate native military rule. In the late 1970s the republic briefly attained imperial status when the infamous Colonel Jean-Bedel Bokassa had himself crowned emperor in what eyewitnesses categorized as a profoundly bizarre and fantastic ceremony. The emperor's excesses escalated rapidly to legendary and deranged proportions, including a reported taste for human flesh, and he was relieved of his duties and permitted to scuttle off into comfortable exile in lieu of the firing squad. (Unaccountably, Bokassa chose to return some years later and now resides in prison, serving a sentence of life at hard labor [update: Mr. Bokassa—he dead, a good many years now, though not before declaring himself the 13th Apostle].)

The inhabitants of the C. A. R. who were working around us now, laying out our beds on the ground under the banyan tree and putting the white mosquito nets over them, cutting sticks to tie together into a crafty dining table with benches, rolling out their own sleeping mats, and building cooking fires, were for the most part of the Goula and Youlou peoples, while the camel drivers were Sudanese. Except for the Sudanese, they all shared the Sango trading language, the C. A. R.'s lingua franca. As I sat in the shade, one of the trackers, a suspected reprobate and retired poacher, approached the professional hunters and presented his bona fides—letters of recommendation from hunters in whose employ he had previously been. He was bare headed and had removed his shirt, and the stump of his left arm hung limp. He had lost the arm, it seemed, when his black-powder musket exploded on him a decade earlier, when he may or may not have been up to something. The truth, as is so often the case, varied with the teller.

Flopped in exhaustion in the dirt, one of the paying hunters, a largish American gentleman from parts unknown, let's leave it at that, was already complaining bitterly and loudly about the pace we had set and the sorry state in which the new boots, that he hadn't had the sense to break in before the safari, had left his feet. The professional hunters, the white one and the black one, tried to ignore him as they nodded cautiously over the tracker's yellowed letters.

Contrary to rumor, the letters said the tracker was perfectly reliable, and for some reason I took to him at once. Impulsively I located a spare camouflaged cap I still had in my duffel and gave it to him. Putting it on at once, he smiled dazzlingly. Taking back his letters with a nod and tucking them under his stump, he shook hands all around. Bidding us "Hello" in English, he retired to his place among the other trackers. He was called Djouma, and his was the first tracker's name I learned. The annoyed white hunter, wrapping himself in his Colonel Blimp persona, informed me then that one never gave a gift to the trackers until after the safari, for fear of its leading to insubordination.

The black white hunter, François, was of the Banda tribe and had hunted in Ouandjia-Vakaga for several years. Yet even he had never been in this neck of the bush before. A track star while in high school, known as *la souconpe volante* ("the flying saucer"), he had lit out one day, during one of the C. A. R.'s not infrequent periods of political upheaval [that have not abated, even now, over 30 years later, as this book goes to print], for the territories from the capital city of Bangui, where his father was then *chef de police* and he was a college philosophy major, to become a PH. He spoke English with effort (far better, of course, than I spoke either French or Sango), was a giggler, and showed no fear of any kind in the face of dangerous animals. He was also found to have an insatiable appetite for reggae.

The white white hunter, the W. W. H., was a short, round, bearded, blustery, British colonial whom, though I never came truly to dislike, I cannot say that I ever came to understand. My first guess was that he was in it only for the money, but there may have been a less cynical explanation for it, and him. I just never discovered it. He had arranged for the foot safari with the French company, even though he had never before hunted the C. A. R. after living and hunting most of his life in many other parts of Africa. At times he grew downright martial and would speak fondly of his war years in Rhodesia, now Zimbabwe, spent killing "gooks."

The paying hunters included the Gentleman-from-Parts-Unknown and an Old Boy in the company of his wife. The Old Boy and his wife were in their late-50s but still unmistakably preppie, Ivy League, and Old Money. In their Willis & Geiger safari-wear and with their copy of *Rowland Ward's Records of Big Game, 18th Edition* (Africa), tucked under the Old Boy's arm, they cut the perfect figure of the Sporting Rich, though of the most unspoiled variety. The Old Boy's wife, although an indefatigable walker, had lost her interest in hunting; but the Old Boy hadn't and had seen more of it at the best of times than I knew I ever would, from Kodiak bear in the '50s to polar bear off Kotzebue and shikars in the Madhya Pradesh in the '60s to the big game of Tanzania, Namibia, and South Africa. The Old Boy's family built steam cars, one of which Theodore Roosevelt got behind the wheel of, to become the first President to drive a car, and later heavy trucks. One night he mentioned to us in passing that his grandfather had died of blood poisoning after reaching out to shake his jockey's hand in the winner's circle and receiving a severe nip on the wrist from his own thoroughbred, while his father, notorious for driving too fast, was killed in an automobile crash in 1929.

Unlike the Old Boy's, the Gentleman-from-Parts-Unknown's grandfather, the Gent told us, had not died from the bite of his racehorse. And he, himself, had made his money in the coarsest of ways, and meant for no one ever to forget it. He had been to Zimbabwe to shoot once, for a week or two, but had no sense of Africa or of hunting either, at least as I comprehended them. I didn't know what his reasons for being here were, and I don't think he actually did either, except that to him the word "unexplored" held the promise of being able to kill bigger and less wary wild animals with which to populate his living room.

That left three others: my non-hunting friend—a Beverly Hills attorney—a Missionary-Photographer, and me.

My attorney friend had come with no romantic preconceptions about Africa. His only wish was to see someplace wild, someplace that was not a city; and the C. A. R. sounded as likely a choice as any. Thinking he needed to justify his presence, he concocted an outlandish story about being a cinematographer and went so far as to haul along an elaborate 16mm movie camera and hundreds of feet of film. But after exactly 30 seconds of trying to film the loading of the camels back in Jolly, he took one hard look at the device and packed it sensibly away in its padded aluminum carrying case, never to remove it again. He owned the only L.A. Dodgers cap in Ouandjia-Vakaga (until he presented it to our young camp helper Idris), dragged continually on a Marlboro, never complained, and was the all-around class clown. The Africans titled him *Patron Sans Souci,* the "carefree boss."

The Missionary-Photographer came from missionary stock. He was a bilingual shooting parson, had been involved with the W. W. H. in organizing the foot safari, and had been invited by the French safari company to come along to act as the W. W. H.'s interpreter, take photos, and try for a giant eland. The blunt and brazen W. W. H. soon proved an arduous trial to him: After the hunt, both would behave extraordinarily unpleasantly toward each other, and for months afterward I would receive tedious letters from one attacking the character and behavior of the other, and vice versa. So the M. P. attached himself at once to François, engaging him in interminable conversations in the French language to the exclusion of the rest of us, and later describing him in a written encomium with the word "willowy." He was far from unfriendly, though, during the safari and would never hunt on Sunday.

I, I fear, would hunt on Sunday or Christmas or the Fourth of July; and when I had heard that someone was going to walk across African savannah in a place where there was a chance of seeing giant eland, I made shameless inquiries and wrangled myself an invitation from the French safari company to come along. I outfitted myself with a 375 with a 1.5-6X scope, Dorst & Dandelot's *Collins Field Guide to the Larger Mammals of Africa* that I'd picked up in Nairobi years before, Serle & Morel's *Les oiseaux de l'Ouest africain* that I'd bought in Paris on the way over, Bernal Diaz del Castillo's 400-year-old firsthand account of Hernan Cortes's adventuring in Mexico, a Webster's pocket dictionary, notebooks, pens, cameras, film, tins of Copenhagen snuff, a binocular, and a sturdy pair of well broken-in boots. Nevertheless, by the second day my feet went south, I let the gunbearer bear my gun, I drank enough water for three people each day, ate salt tablets by the fistful, and still sweat so much that I would never need to urinate on the trail and would often break out shivering in the sun from heat exhaustion. Yet after too many years of being out of Africa I was happier to be back than I could possibly explain to nearly anyone else's satisfaction.

Our first night in Africa, following an afternoon of sighting in the rifles when the Gentleman-from-Parts-Unknown demonstrated an unsettling inability to make his shots find the target, ended with the W. W. H. sitting at the stick table in the blue light of the battery lanterns, drinking whiskey, and defaming (I now think primarily for our benefit) the French, both individually and as a race, for having only four sorry camels to grant us. The rest of us had already crawled into our beds when he at last got up and arranged himself in his with his 460 Magnum at his side. The air was startlingly cold and the full moon at zenith immense and round as a dollar. The W. W. H. lay with his head toward the lighted clearing of our camp. Never lie with your head toward the brush, he advised aloud, because that was where, in the "lion hour" between midnight and dawn, the lion came. Let him take you by the feet and you had at least the ghost of a chance of blowing his brains out before he dragged you off. I changed position.

No lions came that night. Leaving the other Africans behind to strike camp and pack the animals, we (with our weekly antimalarial chloroquine phosphate pills for Saturday breakfast) set off with our trackers, gunbearers, and waterbearers at dawn. We made 12½ miles that day to the Ouandjia River, seeing on the way only the fresh dung of small elephant (the size of the dung corresponding to body size, the coarseness of the dropping the elephant's age—finer texture meaning better teeth and so a younger animal) and a troop of baboons lumbering away from us, displaying red rumps. The Ouandjia is one of the rivers which, flowing north into the Bahr Aouk, goes on to feed the Chari in Chad. When I hobbled down to it, I tugged off my boots and socks and stood in the cool water and decided never to move. It was clear and running, and after seeing the W. W. H. dip up a tin cup and drink it, with the water spilling silvery over his beard and onto his chest, I took the cup from him and, disregarding the dire predictions of Boy Scout manuals the world over, drank the sweetest drink of my life ("For thirst," said Bernal Diaz, "knows no laws"). And nothing befell me, mystifyingly enough.

As we lay on the sandy riverbank, the Africans went downstream to burn the tall grass to clear our campsite, and we could see swallows looping in the smoke of the wide fire, plucking insects rising out of the grass. Our food stocks were already so low that we were reduced to sardines for lunch. That afternoon, though, the Old Boy and François went out to look for game.

While they were gone, the W. W. H., the Gent, the Patron Sans Souci, and I found two square rock pools the size of small swimming pools in the river just above camp and went there to bathe. As we were all undressing beside one of them, the Gent started in on one of his reactionary political commentaries, which I had not yet learned to ignore; and I thought I might enjoy soaking in the other pool alone. As I was about to slip into the neck-deep water 100 feet from them, the W. W. H. made sure he called out to me,

"Mind the crocs!" I remembered with some disquiet a photo I had once seen of the legs of a white man who had gone swimming in an African river he was convinced could not contain any crocodiles, a photo of just his legs in a cardboard box. I peered into the pool intently, then climbed in, staying in the water a long, somewhat uneasy time while a hadada ibis harangued us from the branches of a nearby ironwood tree.

As we limped back into camp in the evening, our feet still stinging from the New-Skin we had painted over our blisters, François and the Old Boy returned, packing an excellent Lelwel hartebeest on one of the gaunt horses. At dinner we were fiends for meat, eating long into the dark as the fire, which had jumped the other side of the river, continued to flare up. The camels lay placidly below us in the sand in full view of the flames. A few of the Africans crossed the river, and we could see one of them, backlit, climbing into a tree with a bundle of burning grass, directing the smoke at something. In a while they all crossed back, carrying combs heavy with wild honey.

I went hunting the next day with an assistant guide, while the W. W. H. and the Gent, mounted now on a rickety but remarkably resilient stallion led by a water bearer in a ragged shirt, went one way, and the Old Boy, his wife, and François another. On my walk I saw oribi, hartebeest, western bush duiker, a sounder of warthogs, an unforgettably blue *rollier d' Abyssinie* (as it said in Serle & Morel), ground hornbills resembling grazing antelope in the distance among the trees, and killed my first game in the C. A. R., shooting a dove and a rock hen with a 22 rifle, the Africans desiring them for the pot.

Back in camp the Old Boy came in with a nice duiker, a very small antelope whose Afrikaans name means "diver" for the way it plunges into the underbrush, which we would eat in its entirety for lunch. Then the W. W. H. returned to tell us that he and the Gent had heard poachers' gunfire and even their voices, and seen no game. It would be wise for us to move on tomorrow. That night I heard hyenas crying for the first time in 10 years.

As we were about to leave camp the next morning, the M. P. asked me how old I was. Thirty-two, I told him. Thirty-two that day.

We made almost 20 game-less, hallucinatory miles to the south that day, getting lost for several thirsty hours until we back trailed and relocated the upper Ouandjia in an utterly exquisite grove of cool green trees. I spent the rest of my birthday sitting fully clothed in the river, that fell across large smooth rocks, drinking red wine from a foil pouch.

"How's the water?" the shirtless Patron Sans Souci inquired, a wet bandanna strapped around his head.

"The marvelous thing is that it's painless," I said, taking one more sip of wine. For dinner we ate some small fish François trapped out of the river.

On the trail the next day we found Arabic runes carved into the bark of a tree. It was the poachers' newsletter and apparently warned of our presence in the country. The poachers, on camelback, had at first come over from Sudan for ivory; then after shooting out the elephant, they turned to poaching just for meat to sell back in Sudan. Because professional hunters, who are the de facto game wardens in most of Africa, never ventured into this area, the poachers considered it their private preserve. I did not know what it would take to dislodge them, but it would be a force superior to ours.

Farther along, the Gent dismounted from his weary horse long enough to gut-shoot a big dog baboon in hopes of expanding his collection. He was well pleased with the full-body-mount one he already had on display at home, dressed in one of his young son's old suits, seated at an old-fashioned school desk in the kitchen. The M. P. acted as Samaritan and finished the baboon off for him.

We left the carcass beside the trail for the porters to pick up. They were supposed to skin it out but instead burned all the hair off it, then butchered it up and cooked it in the camp we made that day at noon after 13 miles of walking. We made that camp in a dense thicket of trees at the Ouandjia's source, a deep hole in volcanic rock where the chthonian water sprang up cold and clear and reasonably pure. The Old Boy's bowels, we now learned, had been malfunctioning for some days by, implausibly for the place and circumstances, refusing to function. He could see no alternative now but to walk all the way back to Jolly for the laxatives he had seen absolutely no need for and so had left behind. A bicycle trail used by diamond prospectors, that we had circled away from on our exploration, ran 30 miles from here back to the headquarters. Tomorrow morning he, his wife, and François, with the M. P. tagging along, would set out on it.

The Patron Sans Souci and I were faced with the grim prospect of at least days alone with the W. W. H. and the Gent and their considered opinions of Africans, the Red menace, and the very end of the world as we knew it, or, rather, as they perceived it to be. Worse was the very real possibility that the Old Boy and his wife, who to the Patron and me had become nothing less than Ward and June to our Wallace and the Beav', were fed up with the whole affair and would not come back at all. (Perhaps that's why the M. P. went with them, so he, too, could go out if they left.) In the Old Boy and his wife we had found two people we could form an alliance with out here in Africa, while with the W. W. H., and even more so with the Gent, the most that could be hoped for were ugly recriminations. We were not happy.

That afternoon I listened to the Africans making their camp in the open outside our thicket, singing lilting falsetto songs that I wished I understood, and felt this prefatory lonesomeness. That night at dinner, deciding there was no dishonor in eating it even if the Gent had shot it, I requested some of the baboon, to the perplexity of the *chef de cuisine;* and tasting primate for the first time, I found it delicious. I was put in mind of a story a famous Mexican big-game hunter told of the time he tried baboon on safari. He enjoyed it immensely too, so much so that he asked for seconds. To his dismay, he was brought on a platter a curled, charred, child-sized hand—considered the most succulent cut—and instantly expressed a loss of appetite.

"Listen," the Gent, grinning rather primate-like himself, still incensed over the loss of his trophy but with a belly full of its rich meat, was boasting now, from the corner of his mouth, to the W. W. H., "I hate them as much as you." François happened to be conveniently away from our newest table of sticks.

"You don't understand," the W. W. H. explained with chilling, patronizing mildness. "Hate has nothing whatsoever to do with it. The simple fact is, they're 20,000 years behind us." I stared away from the lantern into the night, turning my back to the table.

The next dawn, when the Patron Sans Souci and I walked with the Old Boy and his wife from our cove of leaves to say farewell, we found the Africans clustered around one of the sad camels. Branded with three scars on its flank, bent-necked on the ground, it remained where it had lain down to sleep in the night.

"The camel," said one of the Africans in French-accented English, "eez died."

We looked upon it, then at one another. Come back, Shane, I wanted to say to the Old Boy and his wife. Come back.

Over the Divide

Without knowing our way, we found some good
meadows—which they call savannahs—on which
deer were grazing.

—Bernal Diaz

THE NAMELESS WATERHOLE was all that remained of the river our map had no name for. It stood shaded in a hollow of leafy trees, looking brown and pestilential and smelling like an old bar towel.

One of the trackers sank into it a round terra-cotta pot we had found that morning on the trail at the site of a poacher's deserted camp and drew out some water. After letting the water settle awhile in the pot, he presented it to the white white hunter who, after drinking deeply, pronounced it "ice cold." Then the Gentleman-from-Parts-Unknown partook, followed by the Patron Sans Souci. When my turn came, I asked the Patron how it had been. If you strained it a little through your teeth, he allowed, it was not completely foul. Though I had long ago abandoned all pretense of drinking only totally purified water on this safari, the thought of schistosomes performing vigorous wee scissors kicks and synchronized backstrokes in my intestines was too much for me. I tapped the plastic container of warm filtered water (our last) set beside me, and finding it still half full, drank sparingly from it instead.

We were now some 10 miles west of the last camp at the source of the Ouandjia River. After our dawn parting yesterday with the Old Boy and his wife beside the deceased camel, I lay down and slept through to dinner, arising only long enough to go off into some tall grass and, setting fire to my toilet paper afterward to help keep Africa beautiful, accidentally burned over not more than an acre or two of tall grass, the fire swift and cool, doing no visible harm to any of the trees. The Gent occupied his day with an unprofitable horseback hunt around the country, failing to slay a thing (though a duiker he wounded with his 375 did, heaven only knows how, manage to escape). Today, at least, his feet felt sufficiently healed for him to walk and spare the pony further abuse. We would lie here under the trees by this waterhole now until the sun passed its zenith and then, with our trackers, gunbearers, porters, horses, and the remaining camels, move on to the next water that the Africans indicated, by snapping their fingers in the air to count off increments of distance, miles and miles farther on. It would take several hours, they showed us by pointing to where the sun would have lowered to in the western sky when we reached our destination.

As I rested on a bed of fallen leaves and roaming ants, I recalled the lurid misfortunes, from arrow wounds to fevers to witnessing his comrades sacrificed by the Aztecs, that Bernal Diaz had described in his history. What we were enduring here, I realized, was in comparison a very rich slice of cake, with frosting. Then, almost before I knew it, it was time to go on again.

The heat of the afternoon was baking and windless. The country, though, was beginning to be not so scorched and blasted looking as it had been before, showing green trees now and shady park lands. And when I became lost in the unbroken rhythm of my walking, there would also be animals to wheel me out of my daze: bounding triplets of oribi; herds of hartebeest; dark elk-looking sing-sing waterbuck; and equinoxial, or Nile, buffalo. These are an intermediary between the Southern, or Cape, buffalo and the dwarf buffalo of West Africa's jungles. Though smaller horned than the Cape, the Nile buffalo is of about equal body size. We saw a large herd late in the day, and I got to watch the W. W. H. and the Gent put a sneak on the big-muscled animals who were every color from sleek black to bright red. As I watched from a crouching position, dreaming of oxtail soup and sincerely wishing the Gent all the luck in the world, it was as bracing as iced bourbon to see the wild cattle of Africa once more. None of these creatures seemed to measure up to the Gent's trophy requirements, though, while I could only keep thinking over and over, my God, they're meat. When he and the W. W. H. stood to break off the stalk, a lioness, who from the opposite side of the herd had been hunting the now stampeding buffalo as well, could be seen running away.

The long day went on until at sunset, my sore-footed hobbling come to resemble the pirouetting of a trained bear, we crossed the Galénguélé Ridge, the divide between the Oubangui and the Chari watersheds, and made a camp on the flowing Poto Poto River at the foot of a grassy hillside. This time, with the Old Boy's wife gone, I stripped off not only my boots and socks, but all my clothes and lay down in the shallow stream.

A delegation of the Africans, who had been subsisting for some days solely on cooked manioc, confronted the W. W. H. after setting up camp, and holding their stomachs for dramatic effect, implored him to make the Gent shoot something fleshy first-thing "Yesterday," by which they meant "Tomorrow" or maybe they actually did mean yesterday, never mind about bloody horns! It appeared that I had not been alone in my carnivorous lusts.

At dinner, while the Gent treated us to a tirade of appalling political and racial inanities as we sat in beerless paralysis, we four were served a single, very small can of cooked chicken, the absolute last of our iron rations. We sat before that chicken like Bugs and Elmer isolated in a cabin in the snow, contemplating the single boiled bean that will comprise their last supper. Above us on the hill one or two campfires flickered.

A strong wind and a huge light awakened me at midnight from my hunger-filled sleep; and I saw the entire hillside no longer flickering but entirely engulfed, the tall flames whipping down onto us. The Sudanese poachers, to emphasize what was the Central African equivalent of "my beach, my wave," had sent us a grassfire as an invitation for us to move on. As I stood in my slippers and underwear outside my mosquito net, feeling the heat on my face and unsure in which direction to bolt, the Africans lying near us at the foot of the hill arose and, yawning, adroitly ignited backfires. They then went back to sleep, leaving the three surviving camels tied down five yards from me to growl their outrage at this disturbance and the fire to consume itself. *Les chiens aboient, la caravane passe,* in more than a manner of speaking.

The next morning was sheer bathos when after only an hour's walk we discovered a maintained road, then a quarter-mile along it a hunting camp of round thatched-grass huts, called *boukarous* in Sango, with real beds inside. This camp was Pipi, and here I truly hoped the Old Boy and his entourage would rejoin us, driving down on the Ouadda Road from Jolly in a safari company vehicle. If they did, it would once again be time on this safari to adapt.

The small staff at Pipi greeted us and offered us startlingly cold filtered water from a kerosene refrigerator and rank buffalo jerky that shimmered like verdigris. For luncheon they would prepare some tasty fillets of male lion the previous hunter left behind. ("We were pleased enough in camp with the very little food they brought us, for evils and hardships vanish when there is enough to eat," wrote Bernal Diaz, all too rightly.)

Still, the Patron and I waited in glum silence. Then around noon, just as the Gent was launching into a paean to gold and other "hard currencies" which he had gleaned from his reading of some deranged survivalist manifesto, we heard the unbelievable sound of a vehicle engine. The Patron Sans Souci and I fled from the Gent's jeremiad in mid-screed to greet loudly the Old Boy, now purged and looking fabulously jaunty in a pair of motorcycle goggles, his wife, François, and the Missionary Photographer as they arrived in a total wreck of a windscreen-less Land Rover piled with trackers and food and fuel and beer and multicolored bottles of flavored syrups for soft drinks. It seemed as if everything might be all right for a time.

Fixed as my mind is on the archaic, when walking across Africa made far more sense than it appears to today, I could not leave the camel-and-foot aspect of our safari so quickly behind. Now that there was a vehicle, a couple of hartebeest got taken in short order. The next day the camp staff cut the meat into thin eight-foot strips and draped it out like laundry on lines to dry. In the afternoon I found myself wandering up behind camp, past the lines of meat, to where the three Sudanese camel drivers sat around the ashes of their fire. The youngest was patiently dissolving some yellow lumps in a bucket of water, to medicate the camels with the minerals. The middle-aged one had a callous on his forehead from his five-daily bowed prayers in the direction of Mecca. And the eldest one was splitting a hartebeest shank with his steel dirk to free the raw marrow-for "power" as he explained through explicit pantomime.

"*As-salaamu alaykum*," he greeted me, raising both hands into the air in a gesture of peace, still holding the greasy knife. He was tall and desiccated, and the sparse hair around his taut black scalp was white. His eyes were lidless slits that had stared at desert suns much too long. He wore leather sandals, a long white cotton djellaba, a white-and-red sheath for his dirk tied to his upper left arm, and a string of leather phylacteries containing bits of paper inscribed with Koranic passages bound around his upper right. I salaamed him in return and made a note to ask with him later, somehow, about caravans, bandits, and the crossing of burning sands, armed primarily with a faith in the Prophet's words. In short, Real Life.

That evening, still on foot after roughly 120 miles of walking in eight days, I shot my first antelope. It was a western bush duiker the Missionary and trackers and I spotted in a woody place five miles from camp. The Missionary whispered that the antelope looked exceptional. Remembering our duiker lunch on the Ouandjia, I crept up to a dead tree 50 yards from where he was feeding on fallen leaves, got a rest, and put a 300-grain solid through him. And watched him run.

We took off after him, and the trackers soon found blood, then I found another dull dusty splash of it ahead, and another, until there the 30-pound animal lay 150 yards from where he was hit, dead. His orange-brown coat was graying and the ridges of his straight black horns had been smoothed with age. The Missionary enthused that these horns are real big, enormous in fact, rivaling the top-listed in the Old Boy's Rowland Ward, now our camp bible. Later, various professional hunters from the safari company declared that after literally years in the Central African Republic they never encountered bigger. With all that, though, what we were talking about was an awesome 4⅝ inches of horned fury, and the praise was strikingly like being congratulated on having just bagged the world's-record cocker spaniel. My main concern was, How'll he eat?

What I had walked all this way for was a chance to hunt giant eland, *Taurotragus derbianus gigas*, the grander Central African version of the already grand-enough Lord Derby's eland found in far-western Africa. The "largest and handsomest, and one of the least known, of African antelope," according to Theodore Roosevelt, it is in a league with the bongo, the greater kudu, and mountain nyala as not only one of the continent's most beautiful spiral-horned antelope, but most beautiful large wild animals, full stop, ranking alongside the royal elk, argali sheep, even the markhor.

Called *bosobo* in Sango, its sandy coat is slashed by a dozen white stripes, a curly black ruff of hair surrounds its thick, dewlapped neck. Standing six feet at the shoulder and weighing nearly a ton with its heavy horns scrolling out to beyond four feet, it is acutely wary and virtually incapable of remaining still so that it will move all night and right through the heat of the day, browsing at a brisk walk on the large green leaves of young *Isoberlinia doka* (a short, faintly purplish-red vuba hardwood tree). I had yet to see a photo of a live giant eland when it was not on its feet, usually in midstride, nor heard of anyone who knew precisely when it was that the animal slept.

Nonetheless, when I strode back into camp at dusk I was fully prepared to brag on the duiker one of the trackers now carried on a stick laid over his shoulder like a bindle. The Old Boy and his wife, François, the W. W. H., the Gent, and their trackers had all succeeded in wedging into the clunking Land Rover that morning and had seen, against all known odds, a truly fine giant-eland bull lying in the shade beneath a tree. The Gent was, by a previous cutting of cards, the one with the right of first shot ("I won the damned thing drawing lots. You can't go against lots. That's the only way the luck has a chance to even up, ever."); but as he fumbled with his radically customized 375 (a "bells-and-whistles" gun the Patron, who didn't know a Mauser from a muzzle-loader, had accurately characterized it), the Old Boy had sighted in on the animal with his own rifle. Matters became confused, then heated, and the eland managed to get up and lope off without a shot being fired at it. The Gent had then gone off on foot in a rage with François for many hours, never laying eyes on the eland again. The day ended with them running all the oil out of the Rover, scavenging the quarters of a young eland freshly killed and abandoned by a lion, and the Gent firmly convinced that everyone was out to screw him. They were all sitting around the oil-cloth-covered dining table now, powdered with red dust like gingerbread people sprinkled with cinnamon, drinking gin, and not speaking. No one seemed overly interested in hearing about my Colossus of Duiker.

A long safari, removed from any outlet to the rest of the world, can be like a mail-order marriage for the strangers thrust together on it, and for at least the duration of the hunt there is only the most radical possibility of divorce. Our marriage had now obviously become a rocky one. I picked up a bottle of flavored syrup and attempted some cleverness to lighten the mood.

"'Will you have lime juice or lemon squash?'" I inquired of the Patron Sans Souci, who had wisely spent his day alone in camp reading some of the not-yet-terrible Le Carré. He went on reading in silence.

Later, in the dark, the Gent demanded belligerently of the W. W. H., "Can't you get one of these chimpanzees to go back to Jolly and get us some oil?"

"You son of a bitch," the Old Boy snarled at the Gent, throwing down his napkin and leaving the table.

I was here to write about the hunt, and as much as possible to stay out of the way of the paying hunters. I knew my place. Even though I despise stupidity. But I exceeded my authority now, went even beyond-cleverness, as I folded my hands and leaned across the table to get close to the Gent's face. I wanted to ask him the question that had been on my mind from the very moment I met him, though I was almost certain he could not answer it: Why, I wondered out loud, my eyes unblinking, did someone like him ever come to Africa?

Leaning far back away from me, hugging his arms tightly around his chest, and blinking his eyes rapidly, he sneered, "Don't waste any of your sympathy on me." I wasn't aware that I had. But that answer was no stranger than almost anything else he said.

The next morning at the Missionary's urging, "for the sake of the safari," the Old Boy apologized to the Gent. But the Gent, after a quite audible private argument in the middle of camp with the W. W. H., resolved, it seemed, to punish us all by refusing to hunt. So the W. W. H. and I went off with Djouma and some other trackers on a long hot walk through a grassy valley that produced only more sore feet. We sighted a small roan antelope, who snorted at us before galloping away, and a lone giraffe who ran off the way one imagines a startled television-transmission tower might. (Nobody, of course, has yet explained the existence of the giraffe to my personal satisfaction. Like those aircraft engineers who contend that by all the known laws of aerodynamics the humble bee cannot fly, I can imagine no known law of nature which adequately accounts for an animal who has much greater difficulty bowing to drink than it has in stripping from a tree with its blue tongue a leaf-fluttering 20 feet above the ground.)

Back in camp that afternoon, we found that the safari company had sent us an extra vehicle, a working four-wheel-drive diesel Toyota, and the Gent, relieved to have some decent equipment under him at last, agreed once more to go shoot at animals. And returned at sunset with a buffalo, probably from the same herd he had turned down on the trail when we had all wanted meat so desperately.

The very next noon, *mirabile dictu*, he and the W. W. H. pulled in with a superb giant eland. How it had happened no one who knew, I think, ever really said; but everyone else was flatly shocked. Suddenly the Gent was downright expansive. He even invited me to go out with him that afternoon in the Toyota so I could look for a buff, or whatever else he had already killed. I knew that to see more game I was going to have to travel farther from the area around camp than I could reasonably walk to and back before dark, so I sighed and thought, What the hell. I made sure I rode in the open back, while the Gent sat inside the cab.

It was passing strange to be bouncing across the country in a vehicle after so long on foot. I let the wind flow over me and kept my eyes moving all around as we traveled. We drove back past the camp where we had very nearly become midnight barbecue and found an old bull buff with nubby horns all by himself. I passed, deciding that we had enough meat for now and that I might find something bigger later. And I did.

As we drove in I was standing up, holding onto the roll bar, when I saw a flash of tawny-golden color a quarter-mile ahead of us through a stand of tall teak trees. I leaned down and whispered sharply through the driver's window for the W. W. H. to stop and back up. I sighted the tawny thing once more. Putting my 7X binocular on it, I saw in the late afternoon sun the folded, heavy skin of a huge walking animal's rump, something so big my first reaction was, rhino. My immediate second reaction was that there were probably no rhino in the C. A. R. anymore outside a parc national. I knew then what it must be: a giant-eland bull, solitary as Bugs and Elmer's bean.

I jumped down from the Toyota and grabbed my 375.

"What is it?" the W. W. H. whispered.

"Eland."

From the ground I had lost sight of the bull, and I slipped forward to try to find him again, the W. W. H. and Djouma following closely behind. Then I saw him, walking easily, undisturbed. Djouma could not yet see him, so I took him by the shoulders and pointed him at the big mature eland bull.

"Yes," he said excitedly, "yes. Thank you, Tom," pronouncing it Tome. Now the W. W. H. saw him too and commanded me to shoot him from this very spot. The eland was well over 300 yards away.

"Out of the question," I said.

Djouma understood our argument, if not our words, and hissed, "Yes," going off at once in a swift Chuck Berry duck-walk, flitting from tree to tree. I went after him, leaving the W. W. H. frozen and speechless where he stood. We moved to where the trees ended at a wide bare field of black volcanic rock. The eland was on the other side where another stand of the big trees began, turned sideways to us. The distance had been cut to under 200 yards, and Djouma gestured for me to shoot. I rested the rifle against a tree and let off the safety, putting the crosshairs into the middle of the eland's shoulder hump, trying not to let his wonderfully long horns distract me. As my finger lay on the trigger, the eland turned and wandered into the tall timber and a thicket of Isoberlinia doka within it.

"No," Djouma whispered. I lowered the gun and slipped the safety back on. Djouma caught hold of my sleeve and, bent double, we crossed the open ground like some single, rare specimen of trotting mammal.

Inside the timber, Djouma circled downwind in wide arcs around the dense patch of short green-leaved trees the eland must have been feeding his way through. The African moved in a deft half-run, his plastic-sandaled feet never touching a twig. Jogging heavily behind him, I crunched down on a dry leaf, and Djouma wheeled on me, *tsk*-ing in reproach. We proceeded this way for many minutes, Djouma biting his lip as he searched through the trees for a glimpse of the eland.

Djouma suddenly halted, taking my arm and whispering rapidly to me in the French language. He pointed to the solid wall of trees, then held his thumb and forefinger a small distance apart. Too small? Wait a moment? What is it, Djouma?

Impatient, I started to raise my rifle, but he pushed it down. "No. No. No," he insisted in a whisper.

The bull eland glided out of the cover 80 yards away. He was quartering toward us with his ears up and the light through the trees behind him. He stood looking, unable to define us, and Djouma whispered, "Yes. Yes. Yes."

I brought the 375 up slowly, putting the duplex reticle of the scope on the point of the bull's left shoulder and let the safety off.

Dust lifted off the eland's shoulder where the 300-grain soft-nosed bullet struck him. The eland bucked and spun, disappearing into the cover. We ran full out through the trees after the wounded bull, then Djouma snatched my arm, and there was the enormous animal staggering ahead of us, his shoulder broken and the bullet deep in his chest.

I was going to shoot him again, but I saw that he was about to fall. He dropped his heavy-horned head as if its weight suddenly became too much for him and began to sway, then lay down. He had his legs folded under him, and now he lifted his head and looked straight ahead, silent. I walked up to 20 yards from him, trying to control my panting from the run. Working the rifle's bolt, I angled another round in back of his ribs and into his chest. He rolled over, dead.

He was sandy golden and half again as big as a horse. The clean white vertical stripes, black neck ruff, and heavy hump were just as I had always heard them described. He had a powerful warm sweet smell that I would be unable to put out of my mind as long as I lived, and his black spiraled horns were nearly 40 inches long on a straight line from the bases to the tips, and over 48 inches around the spiral. One-armed Djouma threw off his cap and his shirt and bounced into the air ecstatically, proclaiming himself a "grand tracker" again and again. He daubed his finger in the eland's shoulder wound and blooded himself. Then he came over to where I sat on an old termite hill, staring stunned at this perfect creature, my unloaded rifle laid across my knees. As he reached, grinning wildly, to mark my forehead too, a distant lion began to roar.

It had been a better, more "successful" stalk than any I had ever known. The sole bad part was that in the middle of the lion hour two nights earlier, the night of the lost eland, amid the brays and protestations of the camels, the old Sudanese had arisen and with the two younger ones packed the animals in the darkness and gone back to Jolly. Now I could not show the old man this fine, astonishing eland or salaam him or discuss the finer points of caravan life and the art of putting one foot in front of another.

After the Game

As for the horrible noise when the lions . . . roared
. . . it was so appalling that one seemed to be in hell.
—Bernal Diaz

I FLOATED IN the waterhole that was chill and sparkling. Tini Falls fell in a 200-foot veil into it, and I did my level best not to consider the five-foot crocodile that had slid into its den at the water's edge when we had arrived. It was a sanctuary, of sorts here, and nothing, no matter how possibly red in tooth and claw, was about to make me let go of it until I was perfectly ready to.

Djouma, to whom I had given all my Copenhagen after the eland hunt, lay sleeping sweetly on a large black rock above the pool, while the Old Boy's wife paddled in the water in her Willis & Geiger clothes. The Patron Sans Souci and François had come swimming too. The W. W. H., though, refused to enter the water on grounds of the croc, and the Old Boy just wanted to sit, smoking his pipe. The Gentleman-from-Parts-Unknown stood apart from us again, diligently fishing for perch with bloody hunks of wormy reedbuck liver, unwilling to waste one minute of his vacation on leisure.

Our safari was now nearly done. Begun on foot, it was ending in Toyotas. Four weeks, through the cycle of the moon, and it was almost time to leave.

We were now based in the Chari watershed 100 kilometers north of Pipi in the large Koubo camp previously occupied by the infamous Saudis. It was mid-February and this was country of wild palms and grassy plains—by the map the flats of the Koumbal, Yata, Mbongo, and even the Ouandjia (that had wound its way through our journey) rivers, all gathering strength for Chad. In places there were pockets of volcanic-red and green-forested hills where the Old Boy had hunted for giant eland, as hard as I had ever seen a human hunt. And across it all were good numbers and varying types of wildlife.

Two week earlier at Pipi, when I had come in at dark with my giant eland, I found that the Missionary-Photographer had stumbled across and killed an excellent full-ginger-maned lion that he really didn't want, giving us two record-book eland and a lion on the same day. That is the way Africa can work, sometimes: windfall on the heels of famine. And now meat no long represented a problem for us, eland proving to be the best wild fare I ever tasted.

So a day later we decided all to hunt one more morning, then break camp and drive back to Jolly. The Patron and the Old Boy's wife, who were not here to hunt anyway, announced that they would set out ahead of us and walk the 25 miles back to Jolly on the one-lane dirt road that the rest us would be driving up late in the day.

At dawn of that day, the Old Boy handed his wife the over-and-under 12 gauge he had brought, loaded with double-aught buckshot, and kissed her goodbye, as she, the Patron, and young Idriss set off on foot. We hunted till noon, then returned to Pipi and gathered our gear and headed for Jolly. As we drove in during the late afternoon and evening, we expected to see the marchers at any time, waiting exhausted for us along the road. But when we reached Jolly, they were already there—beaming, sunburned, and freshly bathed, the Patron in a tweed sports jacket and wrinkled shorts sitting at the open thatched-roof bar, drinking an ice-cold beer from a bottle with an elephant head on a red oval label. Later the Patron would tell me that as soon as they were out of sight of Pipi, the Old Boy's wife had broken open the 12 gauge and removed the cartridges. Whenever they reached an infrequent village along the old colonial road with whitewashed stones lining the sides, the villagers came out to welcome them and bring tea to drink and straw mats to lie on while they rested in the shade.

From Ouanda Djallé, trading the rattletrap Land Rover in on another Toyota, we headed farther north to Koubo, held to be among the finest areas in the French safari company's concession. At Koubo the Patron and I selected a boukarou at the farthest reach of camp on the margin of the narrow Koubo River, and the very first night there I was awakened by hyenas trotting around the flimsy grass walls.

I found a penlight and flashed it into the night, catching a pair of yellow eyes of a hyena, that most peculiar distant relation of the cat—not dog, as one might suspect—are noted, according to Dorst & Dandelot, for occasionally attacking sleeping humans and "causing serious mutilation by *biting off the face* [italics definitely mine]." Their jaws are some of the strongest in Africa and are ideal for crushing. They are very far from the cowardly slinkers of legend. Yet they are fastidiously clean creatures, essential scavengers, and to love Africa in all its stark relief is to love, or at least appreciate, the hyena, Peter Lorre laugh and all. Killing one could not for me be hunting, merely shooting. (The Gent, to be sure, later shot one—badly.)

All the same, as this one *ooooooooUP*-ed merrily in the darkness and ran away from my feeble light in his sloping uphill lope, I resolved then and there never to be without my rifle in my boukarou at night.

The next day I hunted a handsome Buffon's kob, a reddish-orange antelope the size of a black-tailed deer and related to the waterbuck, lechwe, and reedbuck. The buck was running in a herd of 20 or 30 other kob out on one of the big grassy flats, trying to cover a doe. Then he stopped, winded by the pursuit, and I crept up to about 150 yards from him and rested the fore-end of my 375 in the crook of the German shooting stick the Old Boy had given me. The kob looked farther than he was, and I made the amateur's mistake of holding high and shot over his back with the first bullet. He sprinted off in a wide circle and stopped again.

There were three tall trees growing together on the flat, and I kept them between us until I got just a little over 100 yards from the kob. His ringed horns had a deep S-curve to them; and in the late-afternoon light the look of his muscles under his hide had a sculpted, austere, somehow ancient quality. It felt as if this whole affair of stalking an animal across the clean, well-lighted heart of Africa was without time. It seemed so familiar—not so much a matter of my having been here before, but that in our own fashions the kob and I were in this together, and always had been. My bullet took him behind his shoulder and off he went once more, dying in midstride.

For the most part, the Gent and the Old Boy were doing the bulk of the hunting, it being their safari after all. The Gent got to shoot things on a fairly regular basis and this, presumably, was what pleased him. Djouma, spotting vultures circling one day, even led him into the tall grass after a beautifully maned, large lion, who proceeded to sit up directly in front of them, then flee before the Gent could manage to fire.

There were lions most everywhere (we counted 32—young and old, male and female, one for every year of my life—before the safari was done), and on another day I watched the Gent, Djouma, and the W. W. H. cross a small creek and stalk a pair of them feeding on a buffalo that the lions had battered to the ground. I was 30 yards away and could see that the lions had just started to feed, having gotten to the favored first parts by chewing out a large hole around the buffalo's anus and then pulling his intestines out through a tear in his lower abdomen (often a buffalo is not yet dead while all this is taking place). Now one of the powerfully built lions was worrying the big red buff's head the way a dog worries a rag. I could also see the three men advancing slowly on them, the Gent raising his rifle two or three times, always when he was beside a tree, but never thinking to use it as a rest to steady his aim. During all this I had a round in the chamber, my scope turned down to

1.5X, and my thumb on the safety, fully expecting that any second now I would be dealing with a wounded lion coming at me in a full-roaring charge. Luckily there were no manes on these lions and the Gent held his fire, letting the big cats crash off into the brush once they sighted the creeping humans.

On our way back to the Toyota I made what I thought to be a rather modest and reasonable proposal, that in the future the Gent might consider taking advantage of a rest when one was available.

"Let me tell you, *scribe*," he began, as he now always began in his prevailing snarl, going on to explain how he did not much care for my offering him advice. The W. W. H. sniffed, "He'll probably be writing about some bloody theory of rests when he gets back."

So when we spotted the decent Nigerian bohor reedbuck, with his forward-hooking Panic horns, a quarter-mile farther on, and I slipped down with Djouma from the Toyota and we snuck behind cover to where there was 150 yards of open grass flat between us and the animal standing quartered away, and knowing that the two back at the vehicle were studying me closely with their binoculars, I very pointedly rested the fore-end of my rifle in the fork of the shooting stick. I broke the reedbuck's neck—even though I was aiming for his left shoulder—and Djouma, who had been subjected for weeks now to the Gent's haphazard shooting, erupted in delight, pounding my back, giving me a thumbs-up salute, and pumping my hand as we walked to the buck. I heard the Toyota grinding up behind us (and the W. W. H. saying drily, "Nice shot; not quite as big a reedbuck as I had thought, though"), and knew I had shot for every wrong reason imaginable, for the worst of all reasons for killing any animal: to prove something. And hoped I would never do it for that reason again.

All this while, the Old Boy was dogging eland. He was pursuing herds of them around the rocky hills, sometimes 15 miles a day on foot, never able to overtake them. When he would return in the afternoon, he'd be so tired he would let me go hunting for roan antelope and buffalo with François while he rested in camp.

One long, exciting stalk François and I had after a very good hull buffalo was botched by one of his trackers, Alamine. We had dubbed him "The Torch" for the wooden match he carried at all times between his white teeth, ready to ignite every last blade of dry grass he encountered to clear the soil for new growth. Part way through our buffalo stalk, we told Alamine to wait behind, since fewer people had a better chance of closing with the buff. But as we crept up on the small group of bulls, here came Alamine looking for us, strolling right into them, scattering them like a busted covey of three-quarter-ton quail. C'est la vie was about the best light I could put on the incident, remembering the sight of a meter or so of sweeping buffalo horn.

The winter trade wind, the *harmattan*, had begun to blow down out of the Sahara, yellowing the sky with the fine dust it bore and tarting up the sunsets like carnival goldfish. Some call this dry breeze "the doctor" for the way it remedies the summer's dampness, but harmattan has roots similar to harem in Arabic and describes something forbidden, the wind known to bear with it such diseases as meningitis. On one of these hazy dust-blown afternoons, François spotted a long file of grazing buffalo, and we went after them on foot to see if the herd held any good bulls.

We arced around the buffalo for a mile or two, trying to position ourselves where we could best see them without spooking them. With François's chief tracker Tchekel in the lead, and François, me, my gunbearer Alamine, and the water bearer Amath behind, we climbed up onto a bare spine of rocks. We were beneath a large dead snag, craning for a view of the buff, when Alamine pushed past me, spit out his match, and began hissing Sango words at François. Which sent them all flying off for dear life, leaving me standing by myself, gaping, watching Alamine running away with my 375. For one second, as I snapped my head around, I could not discover what it was that was surely about to kill me—buffalo stampede? lion attack? tribal uprising? Then the furious swarm of African bees pouring out of the hollow honey tree engulfed my face.

I overtook and passed François and the team at about the 100-yard marker. At 200 yards a small band of hartebeest looked up with a start as one white man and four black ones were bearing down, howling and flailing their arms around their heads: a sight they hadn't seen for at least several millennia, sending them racing off in half-a-dozen different trajectories. At 300 yards the bees gave up the chase and I could halt, miraculously unstung, while the others tallied their wounds.

I assumed that would pretty much be that for the buff hunting today. *Au contraire*, said François, rubbing a sting on his neck, they have paid no heed to our capering. So we sneaked back toward them—this time I bore my own rifle—and finally closed to within dirt-kicking distance of the whole grunting, feeding herd. Hunkered down, we watched them for several minutes at this exceptionally unsettling range, seeing tickbirds pecking on them and the huge red and black animals tossing their heads and flicking their ears at the annoyance. They paid us no mind; but the herd held only one young bull, which was looking our way and slowly approaching.

When I pointed out to François that the bull was on a course to us, he dismissed it with a flick of his wrist.

"Too small," he said.

"'Too small?'" I asked with what might charitably be described as incredulity. "He's going to walk over the top of us!"

In the end François merely stood and shooed all 50 of the wild oxen away, their running hooves making the earth vibrate like a drumhead.

As we made our way back to the Toyota in the dusk, François, the trackers, and I all began to giggle at the same time as we remembered the bees. I could not resist teasing François, noting that for a fellow with so little apparent fear of big, potentially obstreperous mammals, he certainly did let a few insects get the better of him.

"Well, Tome," a teary-eyed François explained, "you can shoot ze buffalo; you cannot shoot ze bee!"

The Missionary, who through his command of the French language had monopolized François in conversation every night at dinner, each day on the trail, and in the Toyota until the Old Boy's wife coolly but firmly asked him please to speak with François in English when we were all together so the whole class could share in the conversation, had to leave a week early to return to his ecclesiastic duties at his office in Europe. And after his departure, François's English underwent a marked improvement. One night at dinner, while we were discussing wildlife conservation in his country, he mentioned a European "game expert" who was continually criticizing the Central Africans' own honest efforts in this area. The expert was noted for his very vocal opinions that Africans were in general many years "behind" certain other, unnamed races.

Smiling in a private way as he carefully turned down Bob Marley on the Patron's cassette player, François asked, in a precise, rhetorical voice that everyone could hear clearly, "Why does he come to Africa if he believes this?" The W. W. H. and the Gentleman-from-Parts-Unknown spooned oxtail soup to their lips in silence, not lifting their eyes from their bowls, while François went on smiling.

The next morning I was out with the Old Boy when one of François's trackers spotted a trotting herd of giant eland in the trees ahead. The Old Boy had been chasing eland for weeks now; and when he took off with the Africans, his wife and I waited behind, hoping that this would be one herd he overtook. We waited half-an-hour before we heard the distant shot. Then a minute or two later there was a second. It was an hour before the Old Boy returned.

I had walked off a few hundred yards into the cool trees, unable to bear the tension of sitting. When I looked back, I saw the Old Boy standing there with his wife. There was no reaction from either for a moment as he spoke beyond my hearing. Then the Old Boy's wife put her arms around him, rising on her toes as he bent forward; and they kissed; and I knew he had his eland, the trackers now back in the trees skinning and quartering it. I jogged up to him and employed my last line from American Lit. on the safari.

"'You god damned bull fighter,'" I said, shaking his hand.

Now all the hunters wanted roan. These horsy antelope (*Hippotragus equinus*) are the largest in Africa next to the eland, weighing over 600 pounds on the hoof. Their bodies are gray and with their long (more mulish than horsy, actually) tufted ears and their faces painted in black and white, they resemble circus clowns nearly as much as they do their jet-black relative the sable. Their scimitar-curved horns give them a sturdy handsomeness, though, and they are among the most challenging antelope to hunt. They inhabit the same country as the eland, and if you start trailing them they can lead you on for hours. If wounded they have also been known, like the buffalo, to charge or to lie in ambush for the hunter.

There was an excellent bull in a large herd of roan very near camp, so near, in fact, that the roan had grown used to vehicles and hunters driving past them and would move off in the easiest of fashions when approached. At Koubo there was an unwritten rule (the most important kind for a hunter to adhere to) that these antelope were to be left alone. Even the Saudis, who had received a special dispensation to shoot an eland cow and who had all craved roan as much as we (and who all did not kill one) had not tried to shoot this bull. Then one afternoon the Old Boy went out with the W. W. H. and the

Gent in their Toyota, and minutes later the sound of a shot came from just around the bend in the dirt road. Several minutes later the Old Boy came marching back down the road alone, his rifle laid across his shoulder and his face flushed with anger.

"What?" I asked, knowing.

"They shot the camp roan," he said matter-of-factly, placing his rifle with exaggerated care in the rack in the thatched-roof dining area and looking around for the Scotch bottle.

(Strangely, in spite of everything else, it was at this moment that the Gentleman-from-Parts-Unknown and I ceased to be on speaking terms. I, for my part, was no doubt just being childish.)

The Old Boy finally found his roan far out on the bright river flats a few days later. He had missed a very good herd bull earlier in the day in the timbered hills, missed twice with his 375 at close range, and was disgusted with his shooting. As we came down out of the hills, he wanted to head directly in to lunch and forget about roan all together.

François and I were standing together in the back of the Toyota when we saw a large brown marsh mongoose rippling across the ground by the edge of a waterhole.

"Rikki-tikki-tavi, eh?" I said, acting insufferable.

"Ah yes," François replied, savoring the thought. "Keepling."

Then François sighted a good bull standing alone in the shade of a tree out in the open. The Old Boy slid out, with his 7mm this time, and slipped low across the open to a tree to get a rest. He killed the roan at well over 200 yards with a single 160-grain bullet, distant baboons barking in the heat of the day as the antelope collapsed.

"Shook one in," the Old Boy said as he stood beside the roan.

Several toasts were proposed for the Old Boy that night, and I recall the Patron Sans Souci making mention as he toddled off to our boukarou about how red wine always made him so sleepy.

Those who have heard one will assure you that a tornado roaring toward you sounds like an approaching express train, and that is the way the lion sounded when his roar crashed through my sleep at one-thirty the next morning. Actually, trains and tornadoes probably sound much more like a lion roaring than the other way around. I sat up and found my 375 beside me, leaning against the aluminum carrying-case housing the Patron's redundant movie camera. The lion was across the shallow stream of the Koubo, maybe 50 yards off, just seconds away if he charged all out. His chest-deep roar would come full, then trail off in a series of grunting coughs, but as long as he roared I knew where he was. Often there would be interludes of a quarter hour when he was silent except for the sound of his walking in the now-moonless dark of the lion hour.

Everyone else in camp, with the infuriating exception of the Patron, had been awakened, too, and from the boukarous spread out around the clearing I could hear rifle bolts being run home. The camp staff, sleeping around the campfire, piled more wood on it to send the flames high into the sky and illuminate the area around them. No one spoke.

Sitting in the blackness of a wispy grass hut, meditating on the possibly parallel fates of myself and Three Little Pigs, I was something more than apprehensive.

"For Christ's sake wake up," I whispered loudly to the Patron. I figured he would rather I woke him than have the lion do it by leaping onto his bed. Also, I'd be damned if I was going to sit here being scared witless all by myself. But the Patron, true to his name, just went on snoring, as free of worry as a newborn.

For an hour-and-a-half the lion roared, walking up and down beside the stream, meaning no harm, I suppose, merely being a lion. Then he unceremoniously wandered off, and I put down my rifle and fell asleep again. I woke past dawn, just as the Patron Sans Souci was opening his little eyes, rubbing his knuckles in them. He announced with a wide yawn that his uninterrupted night's sleep had left him thoroughly refreshed. Right as rain. He was somewhat confounded, however, when I, bags big as Dopp kits under my eyes and my hair standing out in spikes, began shrieking at him, wholeheartedly.

The Old Boy and his wife and I drove off with François that late morning, planning to meet up with the others at Tini Falls at noon for a picnic and our swim in the waterhole. The falls was a famous, if remote, sight in Ouandjia-Vakaga, and we all wanted to visit it. Hunting our way there, we spotted an excellent roan bull by himself in the timber, and François and his trackers and I set off after him.

We chased him through the green Isoberlinia trees for two hours on foot, getting up on him once and having him stare us down, then snort, like a steam locomotive getting under way, and gallop off before I could get a shot. The trackers and François were able to follow the trail in the volcanic dirt, over rocky lava ground, across every terrain until we saw him again and once more he snorted, running away through a stand of timber with his neck-mane erect, like the knight's on a chess board. I followed him in my scope but would not risk a shot through the trees. We went on tracking him, the Africans always locating his track until he entered a large grove of trees whose fallen leaves blanketed the ground deeply for an acre all around so he could no longer be trailed. He was gone now, and we went out and found the road again.

Alamine, perhaps just nostalgic for flame, immediately built a small fire and sat in its smoke. The rest of us simply sat covered in sweat bees while Amath ran back to bring up the Toyota. As I waited for the vehicle, I believed I could be content if this long safari were to end on this spot, after that last fine chase.

It went on, though, up the road to where we crossed the Oumyawa River, the route posted with an old eland skull-and-horns hung in the fork of a tree, to the Tini River branch and its falls and waterhole where I floated. For our picnic we had cold roan meat, bread, and beer. Then I floated some more until I was ready to leave, seeing at last that you have to let go of it all sometime.

The final days slipped by impossibly fast. The others were ready for home; I was mostly ready to be away from the Gent's unique brand of "sport." Back at Koubo after the picnic, the Old Boy, his wife, François, his trackers, and I decided to go out on foot, to make a long circle around the country and once again put one foot, astonishingly, in front of the other. I took a spiral-horned harnessed bushbuck on the walk, giving the camp workers more meat for them to dry and take home.

There was a lion kill in a burnt-over piece of ground; and François, the Old Boy, the trackers, and I went there one morning, to see if the cat was on it. As he climbed out of the vehicle to head in, the Old Boy handed me his over-and-under and the double-aught cartridges his wife never used on the road.

"Back me up if we get into a charge," he said, the words leaving me impossibly pleased. When we went in, and there was no lion, I was seriously disappointed.

A day or two later the Gent, of course, killed the de rigueur, almost maneless, young male lion while standing in the back of a Toyota. Then on the next to last day, I got to chase with the Old Boy and François after a buffalo the Old Boy had wounded, and to put in the last round when the old bull, who had been waiting for us in the shade of a bush, refused to go down from an assortment of 375s and 458s from the other two's rifles, and was gathering himself for a charge. ("Uh," I asked, "may I shoot?" absurdly standing on etiquette as they struggled with the bolts on their rifles and the standing fierce buffalo rocked from side to side 30 yards from us; please do, they replied, please do. I did and the buffalo lurched forward with a bellow, lying still and black on the ground.)

The very last day, after circling the country with François all afternoon without seeing any game, we were on our way in when at one minute to six in the African evening we spotted a very decent roan bull in a herd. I stalked toward him in the twilight, then raised my rifle and squeezed the trigger, harder and harder—the way you do when hunting the animals who migrate through your dreams—until I realized I hadn't taken off the safety. The roan bull started to drift off with the herd, and I followed in a slink until I came to a big tree with the roan standing out at 70 yards in the dimming light. This time I remembered the safety but crept up on my scope. When I shot the rear of the eyepiece ringed my forehead and the herd ran. I saw through the blood running into my eyes the bull walking very slowly, then lying down. And at the very last minute, as I stood marked with my own blood, the hunting was done.

The next morning, the lion roaring off a ways from camp, we began to make our way back to Jolly. Along the way I watched all the running herds of ancient game and could feel the sun on their hides and the air in their lungs as if their hides and lungs were my own, just as I could feel within me the motion of their strides. It felt like a promise, and I hoped not a false one. I was going on, but the running animals would remain, with luck and care, for a long time. There were even to be seen round shallow tracks and broken trees along the road, fresh signs of elephant. Then we saw the naked stone of Kaga Moumo rising above the village of Ouanda Djalle.

I had followed the moon and rivers in a cycle through Africa, and now I was back among adobe and daub-and-wattle houses, with cities and the world just beyond the horizon. And the only thing I really wanted to do, I knew, was turn right around and take the long way back again.

I had to fly out, though, in the DC-3 that had brought us in, village hopping back to Bangui. When we made a landing in Ouadda, the pilot in his crisp white epaulet shirt, his tightly cut hair steel gray, on his wrist a Rolex as a symbol of his office, came past me where I sat in the rear by the door, and climbed out. Mechanics came and took out two rows of seats across from me, then a Land Cruiser ambulance with a red cross painted on the canvas top backed up to the door of the plane. Two men from the ambulance carried a stretcher onto the plane and lay it in the empty space across from me. On the stretcher under a thin blanket lay someone very, very old, or brutally aged by disease, making semi-conscious rattling sounds. I studied the person for several minutes. Then the pilot came back onto the plane. Holding a folded handkerchief over his nose and mouth. Seeing me, he waved his Rolexed hand emphatically at me, motioning me to go forward, up the slanting deck of the airplane cabin. And I did, as far as I could get. That came later, though. For now, I had to say goodbye to Jolly.

Bernal Diaz, writing (as a cranky yet obviously still noble old man in pinched circumstances, having ended up an insignificant magistrate and the owner of worthless estates in Guatemala) of his days half-a-century earlier, tells us that he and a number of his comrades after gaining the wild lands of Mexico, mostly because they had seen no better prospects in their lives, callowly abandoned them for someplace they thought would be much better. But, he says, "we were thoroughly deceived." It might very well be that these wild lands of Africa, which I felt shamelessly were somehow more than ever "mine" alone, were for all the hard and hungry and thirsty parts—and in spite of the apparently failed attempt to relive the past of foot safaris; the certainly the failed brotherhood of all hunters—as good as it got for me. Yet now I was leaving it all.

Then as we drove into the dusty yard among the whitewashed buildings of the safari company's headquarters in Jolly, I saw the Sudanese camel drivers sitting around the cold ashes of their last night's fire, and everything seemed all right. I remembered something that I had known for 10 years, since I last laid eyes on Africa, that it was a land that was always with you no matter how far from it you thought you had gotten. You never let it all go, not even in your wildest dreams.

"As-salaamu alaykum!" the old Sudanese shouted to me above the accumulated clatterings of the motor vehicles, raising his bony arms toward me, the dirk bound to his upper arm.

I raised my arms back to him, recalling that the soul travels at the pace of a camel.

"Wa-alaykum-as-salaam!"

Welcome to the wild.

In Burnt Lands

The 2010s . . .

VICTOR IN BLUE vinyl shoes and a navy-blue sport jacket, and Theodore, the younger tracker, wearing a *Breaking Bad* knit cap, pushed through the tall brush as I followed, without benefit of a professional hunter. It was shaded and cool in the leaved tunnels, the foliage the leather-green of armchairs in dark club rooms, as we wound our way through, glimpses of round-bodied helmeted guinea fowl in their festive dotted plumage scurrying across the leaf cover. We came out at an arbored opening above the sandy bed of the Mayo Rey, the light in its last hour across the dry river, and sat on the bank to watch.

I glassed with the 8X Zeiss Terra, looking under the canopy on the other bank. In a few minutes a sing-sing waterbuck walked out, making its way down to the small pool of water remaining in the far channel. I put my right hand on the camp rifle across my knees, holding the binocular in the left. The young waterbuck had small horns and was lame, moving with painful care down the bank to splay its legs, lowering its muzzle to the water. After it drank, it limped back up the bank and slipped from view into the leaves, awaiting the mercy of a leopard or hyena. Downriver a doe and fawn

harnessed bushbuck, picking their way like deer, crossed the yellow sand to
get to water of their own.

We sat until the sun went down behind the filigree of treetops across
from us, the light the so-well-remembered-over-so-many-years impatient
twilight of Africa, then stood and started back through the bush. We wanted
to be back in camp before night fell.

After the *chasse libre*, His Highness granted us an audience.

Sa Majesté Bouba Abdoulaye Aboubakary, Lamido de Rey Bouba,
six-foot-three—a former volleyball middle blocker—with a basso voice and
booming laugh like that of the late actor-dancer-choreographer Geoffrey

Holder ("crisp and clean, and no caffeine"), dressed in his traditional gold djellaba and kufi, was in residence in his compound in the capital city while the country's National Assembly was in session. In the warm Cameroon January, he invited us to visit him in his home, begging that we not trouble ourselves with removing our shoes when we entered.

We were back in Yaoundé, 600 train and truck miles south by southwest of His Highness's *lamidat* (the Fulani sultanate of Rey Bouba, transected by the Mayo Rey, or the River Rey), where we had hunted for nearly two weeks in the lamido's more than 100,000 acres of wildlife reserve.

Lamidats or *boubas* such as Rey Bouba are scattered across the California-sized west-central African country of Cameroon, shaped like a dragon and named for the shrimp found by the Portuguese in rich abundance in the coastal rivers in the 15th century. Rey Bouba, coming into being 200 years ago with the Jihad of Usman dan Fodio, is, though seldom visited by travelers, one of the largest and most well-preserved lamidats, with crenulated dried-mud walls two-stories tall and—reminders of the kinder, gentler jihadists of days past when lands were taken by the blade and not the Kalashnikov: steel-and-brass shocks of curved cavalry sabers in their leather scabbards, stacked discreetly against the entrance gate. Rey Bouba is a small nation, or kingdom, within a nation, with the lamido its hereditary ruler.

"So, Tom," His Highness asked, sipping fruit soda as a breeze billowed the sheer white curtains through the open sliding door, "how did you find the hunting in my country?"

This early in the year the grass stood more than head high; and the places to hunt were in the select patches that had been burned over, the tussocks, like stray fright wigs nesting on the ground, made black and the ashen blades still long and intact, not yet blown apart or broken down under a hoof. In the wet season millions of worms cast up mounds the size of golf balls that dry hard as golf balls and cover the ground so that walking on them is like stumbling across a field of so many . . . golf balls. The name for this ground is *kiibi;* and risking twisted ankles, I tried to keep up with Daniel, the head tracker, and the other trackers, who floated over the jagged ground. A gray scale of ash that fluttered upward from the ground when we stepped on it was the perfect medium for preserving tracks and for betraying when they had been imprinted.

We hunted for three or four hours in a circuit leading back to the truck, going on foot in the first hours of the morning, feeling the heat of the day expanding exponentially around us, unbraiding lines of tracks and assigning them identities: Western kob, waterbuck, bushbuck, warthog, Western roan, Lelwel hartebeest; and ages: yesterday, last night, an hour before, minutes ago. Like a round cloven track the size of a coffee saucer, coined in the ash, heading toward rocks and long grass, a bull savannah buffalo.

At the Gare Voyageur in Yaoundé—across from the row of shanties and stalls from which beer and soft drinks, broiled fish on sticks, flip-flops, and large woven-poly bags are retailed, and where men walk up and down, selling cigarettes by the one—to reach the country of the lamido I boarded the *couchette* on the overnight train to N'Gaoundéré ("Navel Mountain"—it's an "outie," goes the feeble joke among Lutheran missionaries). The equatorial days and insect-chirping nights in Cameroon, reside in perennial equinox, each span 12 hours with virtually no twilight between. So the railroad journey north-by-northeast through the bush, departing at sunset, was nearly all in darkness, stopping at every milk-run station, but also in the hours when the cool air flowed in through the opened window of the *wagon lits*, making the trip without air conditioning tolerable. I rode the train with two other hunters, my friends Pam Cooper and her nephew Lance Crook. The fourth person with us was Daniel Sodea.

Daniel was a Gbaya, the foremost hunting tribe in Cameroon. How great? Another of the Gbaya I met in the lamido's area was one of the trackers, Adamou Davide. In his 60s, more youthful looking and rangy, Davide was the last of the python hunters. No young men, anymore, desired to take up his occupation of hiking four days from his village to reach python country. There Davide sought out aardvark burrows that female rock pythons had taken over. Binding one arm in antelope hide, and carrying a bundle of burning grass in the other hand, Davide burrowed into the hole himself, to face a 20-foot, 200-pound serpent coiled around either her clutch of up to 100 eggs or the live hatchlings. Letting the snake bite onto his wrapped arm, he dragged her out of her den and killed her, taking the skin and drying the meat. While he let the salted hide cure, Davide lived off python eggs, raising the bar on the standard of what qualified as a real man.

Daniel was younger than Davide, small and neat and a fine dresser. He worked for "Mister Cam," an American outfitter, arranging licenses and permits with the wildlife department, meeting the planes of incoming hunters, checking them into their hotel in Yaoundé, booking the train, traveling back and forth with them, getting them to the camp, hunting with them, returning them to the airport, and looking after the trophies following the hunt. What Daniel was not was a professional hunter, officially only the unarmed head tracker on the hunt.

The morning after leaving Yaoundé we pulled into N'Gaoundéré, the terminus of the rail line. There, a hillock of baggage, and some (though hardly an oversupply of) provisions, were transferred to a white Hi-Lux mini-truck with a cramped crew cab. Crowding into the truck, we drove across the town, through zebu cattle being herded down a main street, past bare wooden tables standing at the intersections with plastic liter bottles of gasoline and loose change sitting on them, an honor-system self-serve gas station for the hundreds of motorcycles that made up most of the traffic; and after a short stop at Daniel's modern house, a work in progress, the five of us in the vehicle began the seven-hour drive to the camp at Rey Bouba.

In many of the former French colonies in western and central Africa exists the system of chasse libre, literally "free hunting," though sometimes translated as "rough hunt." Under this system a hunter can apply for permission to hunt without having to employ a licensed professional. The American outfitter handles, through Daniel, all the paperwork, hires the trackers, and has a cook and staff waiting in the camp of round, thatched-roofed boukarous set on the bank of the Mayo Rey, that in winter has fallen to green pools among the granite river rock erupting from the water like fiercely grinning occlusal surfaces.

If you ignore certain anachronisms such as a motorized vehicle and solar-powered lights, you can almost imagine the way Burchell or Stanley or Selous organized their safaris two centuries ago—at least as close as you will come to it in the 21st century. And you need only go back a century here to find the famed, or notorious, ivory hunter, Walter Dalrymple Maitland "Karamojo" Bell, come to the "mysterious city" of Rey Bouba, meeting with the lamido of the day and hundreds of his mounted "knights" and foot soldiers draped in leopard skins and carrying bows and arrow-filled quivers, Bell never having "seen so many hideous men together."

It was night when we drove the last miles on the sandy two-track into the camp, tired and sore from the dusty road, when out of the dark from the backseat behind me, Daniel began yelling, *"Allez, allez!"* Past the hood, what looked like a parachute ball of a giant dandelion waddled in the headlights. The Hi-Lux sped up, and from the passenger seat I could see it was the behind of a crested porcupine ahead of us, its quills barred in black and white, like dashes of written Morse code, their tips shaking like a sheaf of pointed straw. The truck overtook it, and it either rolled under the chassis or off the road because we couldn't feel the wheel going over it.

Now Daniel yelled at the driver, Joël, to stop; and he, Daniel, was out of the truck with a lighted flashlight, shouting, "Very good meat," and chasing after the vanished hystrix, with Lance following, the beams of their lights wigwagging farther and farther off into the bush and trees until they slowed and searchlighted among the branches and trunks, then lowered and moved back toward the truck, sweeping the dark ground ahead.

"No porcupine," said Daniel, hopping in the back door, repeating with regret, "Very good meat."

We had arrived.

Cam prevailed upon me to use one of his rifles in the camp, rather than spend over $600 on a Cameroon import permit, with no guarantee I would even obtain one, or that I would not lose my fee money in the process. So I handloaded TSX 270-grain bullets for my Model 700 375 H&H Magnum, and some of my precious few Speer 300-grain tungsten African Grand Slams; mounted a Zeiss Victory HT 1.5-6x42 scope on the rifle with QD rings; and sighted in at the snow-blanketed backyard range of my friend Leroy's in Story, Wyoming. Cam told me he had a Model 700 waiting in camp; so I unscrewed the mounts from my rifle, with the scope still in the rings, and carried it with me to Cameroon with solid-copper "softs" and a handful of solids.

Cam kept the rifles and a few rounds in a padlocked storage room in one of the boukarous, and Daniel brought them out for us the first morning. The Model 700 I was handed left something to be desired—apparently painted matte black at one point, the coating had worn off to bare steel; the battered synthetic stock had lost its original recoil pad and had a torn lace-on leather boot on the butt with a loose pad that slipped inside, and soon fell out on the trail and was gone, leaving me to stuff the space with wadded toilet paper and wrap silver duct tape around it, creating a recoil falsie, and a thoroughly stylish-looking firearm.

Sitting in the outside dining area under the thatched roof, I screwed the barreled action into the stock, then mounted the bases and the scope in its rings. It took entirely too many cartridges to sight in, but finally, using the rock wall around the patio as a bench and shooting at a target set out on the bank of the river behind camp, I got it hitting where I wanted.

There is no escaping the nervous anticipation of the first shot on a safari (and I was getting to that). And that shot so often dissolves into tsuris and chaos, at least for me. In Cameroon in the late morning on the second hunting day there was a fair-sized herd of Lelwel hartebeest, *kira wa poura* in Fula, shining like new-minted copper out on the open savannah under the towering sun. I got on the sticks and got a horse-faced antelope bull in the crosshairs and proceeded to flock shoot, sailing the bullet over one and all and sending them off at a gallop, not hitting anywhere near where I wanted, flashing me back to the initial shot I ever took in Africa, some 40 years before. At least it scrubbed the first miss out the barrel of the borrowed rifle.

The Black Meat of Interzone, Soylent Green, freeze-dried ice cream: the three courses of the Apocalypse. One existed on the bill of fare in Cameroon.

Daniel's betrothed, Hawa—in her twenties, with children from a previous marriage, very attractive with a sparkling laugh, set to be Daniel's second Muslim wife—cooked eggs for breakfast, invariably turning out wafer-thin and paper-dry omelets with tomatoes if there were any, or maybe sardines. No bread. Packets of instant coffee. Cold fresh fruit regularly. After several days on a diet of omelets, though, I strongly desired my eggs a different way before dawn and tried to explain to Hawa that I must have a runny yolk, or two.

As she listened, I mimicked breaking eggs, *œufs*, into hot oil in a skillet, making *p-ch-ch-ch-ch* frying sound effects with my mouth, *trois minutes*, then making my hand a spatula to demonstrate the turning of the eggs, one minute more and onto the plate.

Hawa nodded in eager comprehension of my demonstration.

"Ah oui," she said, beaming. "Omelet." And another yellow roundlet of eggs, no thicker than a sheet of vellum, appeared on the breakfast plate.

In the 25-page checklist cum dossier that Cam sent us before the chasse libre, he recommended including plates and forks, seasonings, and freeze-dried meals to supplement the food in camp. We three hunters consulted the website of a trail-food manufacturer and picked out assorted pouches for at least one meal a day. Boiled up at lunch, slid out onto a plate like molten magma, they proved entirely—edible. Pam went so far to as to bring desserts, which were generally, to my surprise, good. Then there was the freeze-dried Neapolitan ice cream that started out as sugary tricolor chalk and as it was chewed took on the mouthfeel of ice cream thoroughly melted and warmed before swallowing. It seemed hardly worth the candle.

All the real protein in camp was restricted to what we hunted or we caught from the Mayo Rey. Lance was relentlessly tracking roan, wading barefoot with two trackers across the cold river every dawn and walking up to six hours straight. On the days he came back in the noontime heat, he would fish religiously, providing us with wonderful Nile perch (esteemed as *le capitaine* in Central Africa) and good tigerfish to be fried up nicely for dinner by Hawa. I only fished a little at midday, managing to strike a substantial tiger that detonated out of the opaque green water like some thrashing ingot and tore the treble hook completely out of the lure. I did not provide any fish for the table.

★ ★ ★

There was a single-barreled shotgun in camp, and I had brought a box of no. 6s along with my rifle cartridges; and one day out in the noonday sun, Victor and I walked through the bush along the river, following a flock of helmeted guinea fowl. I might not have landed any fish, but I could try to supply some game bird. The guinea fowl stayed ahead of us on the ground as we were in pursuit. Finally, they flew into a tree and perched. And yes, creeping to the edge of a fringe of leaves, I sluiced one, the bird flapping from the limb. Let he who has ever been reduced to stark omelets and freeze-dried ice cream cast the first stone.

The amount of game we saw was hardly overwhelming, and for several days I concentrated my efforts in finding good heads. I didn't want to "waste" my trophy fees on camp meat. Then I thought that it wasn't just me who was missing out on protein but the trackers and camp staff, too, who regretted the loss of the very good meat of porcupine. It was time to shoot something.

At last light a few days into the safari, darkness rushing on, I spotted a young, adult kob ram—its name, *m'bada,* sounding better in Fula—moving from bush to bush about 150 yards away. The antelope was by now nearly undetectable to the naked eye, the air filling with the obscuring dim of twilight. None of the trackers could any longer see it, telling me it was gone. I got the jury-rigged 375 onto the sticks and put the Zeiss on the kob. Even with that, the animal was something through a glass darkly, though still visible. I could get the crosshairs on the kob and watch it move between cover. At the very last possible instant of daylight, the antelope stopped, standing broadside. I pushed off the safety and pressed the trigger. The kob vanished, but a boil of sooty dust rose where it had been standing. We had fresh meat for camp.

There's nothing to be explained about Africa. Either one has always known that he, or she, if finding the opportunity, would hunt there, or that it was a matter of no consequence, even if one were an enthusiastic hunter in other fields. Both stances make perfect sense without having to say why. Why, though, if one occupies the former camp, travel to Africa to hunt in the way I had chosen?

There were 40 years of Africa to answer that. Forty years of coming to Africa to hunt, from the Maasai Mara to the Matetsi, the Karoo, the

Waterbergs, Qasserine, across the Sudanian Savannah; with cities like Yaoundé, Nairobi, Mombasa, Arusha, Khartoum, Bangui, Dakar, Tunis, Harare, Lusaka, Jo'burg, and Cape Town, and the little towns like Beaufort West, Loitokitok, Ouadda, to walk in; along the Gambia, Limpopo, and Zambezi, and lesser lights like the Rombo and Komati; to west of Tsavo and perhaps east of Eden; all of the hunting done in the company of professional hunters. Fascinating people, the sort of competent, skilled, confident ones who do their jobs well, like those characters in Howard Hawks movies, before he ever considered making *Hatari!* Adept at organizing and managing hunting operations and camps. Boon companions to share campfires and snifters.

In time, though, and not necessarily 40 years, you wonder at least a little what the professionals are really there for. To make the executive decision of whether to turn right or left onto the trail each morning? As a backup on dangerous game, of course; though if you have killed enough buffalo you might be forgiven the notion that maybe you could do it yourself—and if you honestly didn't believe you could if you had to, you probably don't want to be trying to do it at all. Then if you look hard enough, you will notice that the ones doing the true hunting are the trackers, simply far better at it than anybody else in Africa, and possibly the world. Which makes the PH's task something like that of a tour guide-interpreter's, with just a touch of a sommelier's: If I might recommend the gemsbok. As a licensed professional he is obligated to stand between you and the game, but sometimes that can seem as if he is obscuring the view. And there can be in his job just a bit too much of a hand holder, leading to those most disheartening words from the lips of the returning safari hunter, "When I was in Africa, my PH told me..."

So just once in 40 years, perhaps for the final time in 40 years, I wanted to experience Africa free of anybody else's interpretation and with nobody else in front of me if the time came to shoot. And discovering new country in Cameroon seemed the way to go about doing that.

Cameroon's January weather was the best of the year. There were no bugs, except for the very last night when I wore shorts to dinner on the patio and wound up with milky pale legs erupting with strawberry welts. Under the nearly supererogatory mosquito net in bed I lay on top of an ultralight sleeping bag I'd brought, until it got too cool and I slept comfortably inside the thin bag.

At dawn it was cold riding in the back of the Hi-Lux as we drove out to where we would hunt. Through the gray light you sometimes caught the quicksilver line of a back or glint of horn among the scrub trees; and the brakes went on and the binocular came up, but it was usually a doe or cow or had already broken into a run. Or after we'd gotten out of the truck and made a stalk, Daniel or the trackers were saying, "Shoot! Shoot!"; but having no one to decide for me, I had to look it over and judge the head myself, and mostly held off.

In the afternoons as the day cooled we went out again. Eight days into the hunt we were traveling south on the two-track from camp. We'd seen *doumsa*, a waterbuck, from the road a few days earlier, but before we could go after it the bull vanished. Now there was another, a few hundred yards off the road.

When we crouch-walked forward and I got the rifle on the sticks, I saw the waterbuck's left shoulder through brush, the dense winter hide maple brown, lyre shaped ribbed horns rising like stacks of bangles of keratin. The buck spun at the shot and went off in a half circle, starting to wobble before lurching to a stop and toppling. We got to it; it lay on its side, a small spume of lung blood welling out of its fur, the trackers shouting.

We ate waterbuck that night. They always say that waterbuck is tough and awful, unfit for consumption. Nothing went to waste here in camp, or in the field, though; and because they are wrong, as "they" so often are, the meat was perfectly tender and good.

I contemplated whether these might be my last walks in Africa. As we went toward the rising sun along the intertwining game trails through the black fields cobbled in kiibi I wondered if I should number my steps, keeping a record to memorialize each possibly final pace on the continent. Stride 6,000: stepped over a whitened snail shell the size of a small pine cone; 8,000: passed the wooden frame of a meat-drying rack, abandoned by poachers; 9,053: caught by a wait-a-bit in my shirt.

Trails divided, and Daniel in his olive-drab military cap caucused with Victor and Theodore about which to follow. I looked up, drawn by an Abyssinian roller landing on the limb of a thorn tree, head alert, breast and coverts the incandescent blue of a gas flame. Daniel turned and it flew. We walked on.

We side-hilled, past a salt lick hollowed gray into the slope. We were moving through rocks when I looked down and saw the cloven buffalo track in the ash. It was big as a Southern buffalo's, with it the track of a smaller askari bull. We negotiated low rises now as we climbed higher from the flats, the wind favoring us, the rises able to conceal a buffalo on the other side. It was a quarter mile when we came to the elephant grass.

Seven-feet tall, as tight together as a shock so that Daniel pushing ahead of me would disappear within a step and it was impossible to see more than a few square inches of bare dirt under foot, this yellow grass is where the big bull and his askari had gone to ground, it seemed. If we pushed into it, we could not know if we were following the buffalo's track. Or if we happened by dumb luck on its trail, we would likely drive it out ahead of us at a gallop, never to see it. Or it was lying up after feeding out in the night, meaning it was probably facing its back trail, letting the wind from behind cover that direction; and until we stumbled onto it we wouldn't know it was there, giving us no chance of my getting a shot at a range of no more than feet.

The other matter is that if we went in, it would be Daniel in front with no rifle, not that he would have any way of getting off a meaningful shot even if he did, Daniel inexperienced with rifled weapons. Anyway you cut it, it would be a cluster.

The grass thicket covered half a football field. We circled it, hunting for tracks to see if the buffalo had come out; and the tracks were on the far side, moving uphill into the rocks.

We followed into a flat of rocks and gravel. It was clear that the buffalo, the Fula name *m'bana,* were some hours ahead of us; and now their tracks were lost on the hard ground. We broke off tracking and circled the hill, heading for the truck.

Step 11,201: this step around the skull of a doe bushbuck, *djama thirga,* lying bleached on the trail.

The tenth sunrise came, and already I was out from under the mosquito netting and washed at the sink. I had laced up my dusty boots and slipped the heavy worn-leather ammunition pouch onto my belt. Breakfast was another flat thin omelet and a packet of coffee in hot water. I filled the two Nalgene bottles from the purified-water cooler and zipped them into my fanny pack. The Hi-Lux idled in front of my boukarou where I picked up my borrowed rifle, checking that the chamber was empty, my binocular, walking staff, hat, and shemagh around my neck to keep the nape from burning. I climbed into the back of the truck, and we drove out of camp.

We traveled 30 minutes, spotting usual suspects, all does or young bucks, along the two-track dirt road. A flock of guineas ran for some distance ahead of us before they figured how to get out of the way. Coming to a halt, Daniel, Victor, Theodore, and I climbed down, leaving Joël with the truck.

The sky was the blue of a roller's wing, no smoke from burning fields drawn across it yet. In the slanting early-morning light the reddish felsite pebbles sparkled among blades of new green grass sprouting from the ashes. There was surprisingly little kiibi on the stony ground, making for easy walking in the cool morning air.

We saw the small band of hartebeest after an hour on the trails. They were about 400 yards away in thorn bushes; and we paid them little attention.

For a quarter hour we wound among different sets of tracks— roan, warthog, postage-stamp sized duiker's—the clean edges blown in, marking their age. The truth is that if this was my last walk in Africa, I was happy just to be walking it. I wasn't really thinking about taking another animal, content only to be feeling Africa, when we came onto the hartebeest again.

They had somehow worked back around and were moving in front of us, 200 yards away. Three cows went past, then the big bull stopped, broadside, looking at us. I still had no idea I was going after this animal until Daniel began the hissing chant of "Shoot. Shoot!"

I asked Daniel if it was good, and he said yes.

The bull was fair enough; and the meat would mean a great deal to all the people in camp, especially after we left the next day. I got the jury-rigged 375 onto the sticks and the crosshairs on the hartebeest. Working the bolt, I fed in a cartridge. Now I pulled the rifle into the rest so it felt dead steady and pressed the trigger. *Kira wa pura* dropped like a sack of oats.

"Good shoot!" Daniel shouted as he and the other trackers ran toward the hartebeest lying motionless. "You good shoot!"

The bull's horn formed a ribbed "S" growing out of the top of his head, then pointed straight back long and smooth and ebony. A perfect swirl of copper-yellow hair sat in the middle of his ludicrous equine face, and his winter hide gleamed in the morning sun.

"You good shoot," Daniel said once more, admiring the neat hole in the base of the hartebeest's neck, saving almost all the meat, not knowing that I'd been holding just above the elbow on the front leg. I said nothing.

My last hunt in Africa, perhaps for now, perhaps for always, ended like that, without my having to spoil it for Daniel.

We left the next morning at first light.

Back in Yaoundé as we were departing the lamido's residence after a two-hour visit—Daniel and the driver having sat on the floor beside the chair of the lamido, consciously keeping their heads lowered the whole time—I was thinking, as I'd spent so much of my life thinking, of ways to get back to Africa, when I noticed a large travel trailer backed into a car port, the tongue held up by a cinder block.

"Yes," said the lamido, "that is my caravan. Not good for over the roads between here and Rey Bouba." He sighed a bit for comic effect and added, "I have always really wanted an RV." His other dream was one day to visit Las Vegas. I dreamed something different.

The Trend of the Game

Afterword . . .

I T IS NOT the picture of the African safari that fills our dreams, but it may be the portrait of the safari's brave new future.

Whoever considered hanging red plastic identification tags from the ears of 50-inch Cape buffalo? As an emblem of the most wild, free, and dangerous elements of the African safari, a buffalo should deserve higher regard than a Hereford; but there it was, as inconspicuous as that tarantula on a slice of angel food, a breeding bull on the cover of a spring 2014 number of *The Wall Street Journal*'s magazine, *WSJ.Money*, red tag and all, apparently just another head of livestock in South Africa's burgeoning trade and industry in private game.

This buffalo was "Horizon," notable for fetching $2.6 million at a wildlife auction (which is not even the record for a lone animal, another buffalo with two-inch-wider horns going under the gavel for $1.4 million more). Overall, prices for top species, such as sable, roan, buffalo, and wildebeest—particularly genetically selected mutations such as the "golden" wildebeest—had, according to the *WSJ* article, "Into the Wild," by Patrick McGroarty, risen 50 percent in six years, while between 2009 and 2013 the

amount spent at auctions went from $18.3 million to over $100 million, inspired by what is widely regarded, and aggressively promoted, as the salvation of "African hunting." In all this, we are being asked to accept that what will save the safari is game breeding, husbandry, and enclosure; but if that is how it must be, it is clearly not how it was meant to be.

The African safari (and of course the word *safari*, meaning simply "journey," has been around as long as Swahili has been spoken; but the word now, and for a long time, means more) blossomed from a broken heart. According to author Bartle Bull in his excellent book, *Safari*, when botanist William John Burchell's fiancée, Miss Lucia Green, ended their engagement 200 years ago (she fell in love with the ship's captain bringing her to wed Burchell on the remote island of St. Helena where he was schoolmaster), Burchell set sail for Cape Town, where he struck off on a four-year expedition throughout Southern Africa, collecting 50,000 plant and animal specimens and firing the wanderlust of hunters with the accounts of his travels and descriptions of the inconceivable amount and variety of game he found and hunted.

For two centuries after that the safari was the ultimate hunting adventure, the tales of Henry Morton Stanley, Theodore Roosevelt, Ernest Hemingway, Robert Ruark, Robert F. Jones, and Peter Capstick catching the fancies of generation upon generation of hunters, offering visions of savage yellow savannah, incarnadine sunsets, and silhouettes of giraffe marching with rocking gaits through impressionable minds, my own included. What hunters could find in Africa were the golden joys of vast, unbroken bush with herds of animals scattered over its plains. Olive tents were clustered in fever-tree clearings, then were struck so the safari could "up sticks" and pilgrim on beyond the next line of green hills, with no knowing what might lie on the lee side. There would be meetings with warriors with ochred hair festooned with feathers, whose tall spears had been blooded, and the mesmerizing fascination of sitting by a red-coaled fire under the constellations of an unknown sky— and the ultimate experience of hunting wildlife untamed, unfenced, and native to an exotic land. It was the best dream that money could buy.

Even well after the end of colonialism, the classic African safari would not have been unrecognizable to Burchell, with the major alterations being Land Rovers and Bedford lorries supplanting his ox-wagons, and centerfire rifles replacing 10-bore "baboon butt" flintlocks prone to exploding. The wind of change, despite the repellant philippics of those nostalgic for the days of white rule, did not by itself alter the face of safari. Far greater agencies have been at work.

Wilderness has been vanishing in Africa since we hominids dropped from the trees, adopted an erect posture, and began modifying the landscape in even the most primitive ways; but while for a million years the pace was glacial, it has now reached the stage of tsunami. Just a quarter of Africa remains wilderness (some figures go as low as 10 percent), while almost 40 percent of North America is; and that African wilderness is increasingly fragmented, exploited, and exhausted. While the population of North America has multiplied four times since 1900, Africa's peoples have nearly decupled. The single African nation of Nigeria is expected to have a population larger than that of the United States by 2050. When I hunted Kenya in 1974, there were 13 million Kenyans. Today, there are more than 44 million.

A billion Africans understandably want jobs, material possessions, better health, and representative government, and are no longer satisfied with being the supporting cast of hunting anecdotes. As well, they have diminishing contact with wildlife, which in their lives was once a force of nature to be welcomed, or endured, like the rains, as the game's overall population contracts and the people migrate to the cities. (It is hardly reasonable to expect a street vendor in the Cameroon capital of Yaoundé to be concerned about, or even to record, the extinction, 500 miles away, of the Western black rhino—officially declared finished in 2013.)

❡ Disappearing wild lands, growing human populations, mounting urbanization, the traffic in bushmeat, the Asian demand for ivory, and other factors leading to fewer animals in their native habitats—and add an ever-more sophisticated global anti-hunting movement—are conditions not likely to slow or retreat for decades to come; and they now threaten to turn the face of the safari into a mask of anarchy as they give rise to more restrictions and closures like that disastrously imposed in Kenya nearly four decades ago, devastating its wildlife in the years since; the suspension of hunting in Botswana; the effective ban on lion hunting due to the United States Fish and Wildlife Service's listing of the two populations of African lion as threatened and endangered; and the rejection of trophy ivory from Zimbabwe and Tanzania for importation into the United States—all in effect at the time of this writing. Safaris are nonexistent because of continuing insurgency and chaos in two of the most massive nations, Angola and Congo, with over 75 million acres of nominal wild lands; and elsewhere the game is often restricted to obscure and limited species (one outfitter offers safaris on Zanzibar for rare duikers and giant shrews—no, seriously). And the solution that is to be found for all this is said to reside in South Africa, behind a 21-strand wire fence.

The argument made by many game breeders, ranch owners, professional outfitters, and booking agents, is that the Republic of South Africa may become the last place to hunt for the traditional game of Africa, because it has developed the perfect system to guarantee the preservation of the safari. Today, as this is written, the country has some 10,000 private preserves (14,000 if mixed livestock-wildlife properties are included) covering 17 percent of South Africa's territory (other figures suggest 25 percent), versus 6 percent within the boundaries of national and provincial protected areas. Animals on preserves reportedly number 16 to 17 million, estimated to be four times the wildlife population of South Africa's national parks. The claim of the preserve industry is that it is able to do more for the conservation of species and habitat than the public could ever do, because of the money those species and that habitat attracts from overseas hunters.

There is nothing inherently perverse about hunting on private preserves for raised game. It is in keeping with ancient tradition dating back as far as at least the Romans' vast *latifundia* that were maintained not only for agriculture but for game hunting, the wildlife considered the private property of the landlords. Hunting estates and royal forests are prominent features in the history of the Old World. Even Native Americans maintained what were in essence their own wildlife preserves by regularly torching the Great Plains and Eastern hardwoods (more timbered land is estimated to exist in North America today than in the time of Columbus). In Africa, the practice dates back at least half a century to game ranches in then-Rhodesia, and arguably as far back as pharaohs' raising hippos in ponds to hunt. Private wildlife on private land is not at issue. Something less tangible, yet even more vital, is—perhaps the very soul of the safari.

Preserve owners assure us, as quoted in the *WSJ.Money* article, that their calling represents an ideal of "breeding back the magnificent specimens that have been hunted out of existence." They claim that they treat their individual animals with utmost care, darting, inspecting, and ministering to them, and keep the bloodlines broadly diverse to ensure robust genetic wellbeing. From the website of one of the most prominent breeders, a South African brewery magnate: "[The owner] believes that just as brewing great beer requires high quality ingredients and impeccable attention to detail, breeding exceptional animals requires focus on superior bloodlines and genetics as well as nutritional health. That philosophy has been applied in carefully building herds of excellent conformation and horn length." In other words, this buff's for you.

"Magnificent specimens" are and always have been the exceptions, the freaks, and in no way emblematic of the health of a species overall; that's why so relatively very few of any species ever make the book. Average is what most animals are and should be, a gorgeous monster nature's way of saying that here's one who defied the odds, or more accurately fell through the cracks, not that this is the way all are meant to be. As well, the notion of "hunted out of existence" seems a rather curious tack to be taken by a breeder of game animals which are destined to be hunted, especially when there is nothing in regulated, scientifically managed hunting on open land that leads to degradation. In North America, that can be seen in Boone and Crockett's recognizing new world's records of nearly all species, all unfenced, on a regular basis (the club's latest whitetail book has 4,692 total new entries over the previous edition, for the planet's most democratic big-game animal, and yet one of the most difficult to qualify as a record).

It would seem that the breeder is talking about a different sort of hunting, the way society types refer to the wrong sorts of people. He seems to be saying that we can no longer depend on the wilds of Africa to produce big-game animals, at least not those we really ought to want, or deserve, to be hunting, or that no one truly wishes to be seen hunting out on open and, God forbid, publicly or tribally owned land. All of which does seem to lend further credence to the late novelist Jim Harrison's long-held opinion that, "By and large, the greater part of African hunting has been the rich sportsman's hoax on his gullible fraternity of hunters back home."

Another point of view of South African hunting preserves has to do with that stubborn word wildlife, defined as the "fauna of a region," by which is meant the natural or endemic animals. The word "natural" can be ragged over when so much fauna is managed even on public land. It is difficult to consider the notion soberly, though, when it is applied to the denizens of "wildlife ranches" that may be subjected, as noted in a paper, "The Challenge of Regulating Private Wildlife Ranches for Conservation in South Africa," in the journal *Ecology and Society*, to deliberate hybridization, breeding for recessive genes such as color variations, breeding for trophy size, unscientific intensive captive breeding of rare species that may lead to inbreeding, introducing wildlife species outside their native ranges, introducing invasive alien species (Himalayan tahr is one example in South Africa), burning and cutting native vegetation, and predator control to protect privately owned game, not to mention the disruptive impact of some 100,000 kilometers of game fencing on the movements of true wild animals outside the preserves. There is also the effect that conspicuous consumption has in fomenting public resentment toward hunters in South Africa, as when the deputy president of the ruling African National Congress admitted that his personal bid of $2 million for a buffalo cow was a "mistake" amid the runaway poverty of his nation.

The directory, called the "Threatened and Protected Species Regulations," or "TOPS," is tightening wildlife-ranching practices in South Africa. Verboten now, for example, is the abomination of "green" hunting to collect replica horns, in which large pachyderms would be darted, sedated, photographed, and plaster cast more times than Jimi Hendrix, turning rhino into potential junkies, waiting for the man on acacia-shaded street corners.

Bad practices and bad science, though, remain widespread; and there is the added caveat that a bubble is a bubble is a bubble. It's hard to calculate how a business model is supposed to function, based on approximately 9,000 foreign hunters spending $124 million (2012's number) within a herd of 16 million, placing the income potential from a single head of game at $7.75. What becomes of this wildlife when the bubble inevitably bursts? (In Spain's boom years in the late 1990s, an overheated market for pure-bred Andalusian horses sprang up among the newly rich with pretensions of being grandees. With the coming of less palmy days, those horses from foreclosed, and often abandoned, haciendas were being sent to slaughter or worse, left to starve and die.)

To the spirit of the safari, how real on the whole can the hunting be on some game ranches? In the article about the high cost of privately held buffalo, the fabulously wealthy landowners, described as roaming about on the earth in personal helicopters, were said to own properties of 3,700 to as much as 7,500 acres (some arithmetic shows an average size of 3,600 acres throughout the country). Arguably, the ranches described in the article are breeding, rather than hunting, facilities; but what is the true nature of an animal restricted to a life bound by five sections of land, when its normal home range can reach 25,000 acres, or 40 sections? Or in the case of some wildebeest and zebra, the quality of life in a fenced enclosure of conceivably any dimension when they evolved out of epic 1,800-mile clockwise migrations over open plains in search of new grass and the avoidance of crocodiles and lions?

The *Ecology and Society* paper seems to be stating the obvious when it says that "ranches are businesses first and foremost, competing to attract customers." So some hunters who can may turn to lavishly appointed lodges, Wi-Fi, swimming pools, airstrips, spa treatments, gourmet dining, perhaps a golf course off to the side, and quick jaunts in the Defender out to the north 40 for a spot of shooting. Or because of the marginal worth of much of the land in South Africa for farming and grazing, and the eliminating of agricultural subsidies to commercial landowners, the ranch might be a failed small-scale cattle operation where the owner is trying to stay above water with a few score head of fenced-in plains game, hunted on an overwhelmingly depressing put-and-take scheme.

Writer Thomas McGuane has given the Hunkpapa leader Sitting Bull the words "when the buffalo are gone, we will hunt mice, for we are hunters and we want our freedom." In what way that applies to Africa, I am not quite sure, except to express the dubious notion that any hunting is better than none. It is supremely unfair that not every hunter was born early enough or with enough wherewithal, or was able to earn the means, to safari, if he so wishes, in Africa as it once was and remains so in many places. It would be excellent if there existed scholarships or grants that allowed a regular hunter to spend a month in the best parts of the Selous or northern Mozambique or the valleys of Zambia. I can think of any number of skilled hunters with kids to raise and bills to pay, who would be far more appreciative and deserving of a true safari than many of the clients of game ranches. The question is whether any kind of hunting in Africa is sufficient to impart the experience of the African hunt. Or is it enough if it lets you say, "I hunted Africa," without mention of which Africa?

A safari is not about head counts or trophy size or species lists, and certainly not about convenience. A real safari should be inconvenient in time and effort. So, never hunt on any game ranch in South Africa? Of course not. There are certainly ranches on which the wildlife is naturally reproducing and free to wander within substantial areas in which they may not even realize there are boundaries to their movements, and on which a hunter can have a genuine hunt and find that dream that comes down from Burchell and those who followed after him. And if the Angolas and Congos, along with the Chads (recently reopened, in fact, to hunters) and South Sudans can ever stabilize, that opens almost 20 percent of the African landmass to new safari exploration.

Let's not pretend, though, that in the context of Africa, what is slouching toward Cape Town is not the mass industrialization of the safari and hunting. Many speak offhandedly of the "hunting industry" to defend it as a major economic force, and as such not to be trifled with. Personally, when I hear the word "industry" linked to "hunting," I thumb off the safety of my 375. And yet, I understand that industry may very well be the last-gasp for African wildlife. Traditional, hide-bound, command-and-control conservation has certainly proven that it is not.

That is not a reason, though, not to recognize that there is a tangible difference between a game ranch and the veldt. Or that hunting on one is the absolute equivalent of venturing out onto the other. Or that somehow the methods and motives of all game ranchers, even with the state-of-the-art in genetic science, represent progress or an actual hope for the future. Or that the fences are only there to keep poachers out and not to protect and warehouse an asset. Or that because of this "something new," we no longer have to worry about, or work for, keeping the real thing real.

The African safari as it always was, or at least as near as can be found in the 21st century, is worth every effort to preserve, and not simulate. Just because the safari began in a broken heart does not mean it must end in one.

There is the old African proverb, often quoted, that until the lions have their own historian, the history of the hunt will always glorify the hunter. One could also look, though, to Wittgenstein's belief that if a lion could speak, we could not understand him. Which means that it falls to the safari hunter not to glorify, but to attempt understanding, however inadequate.

Is it proper to judge the safari to be something of value, worth keeping even today? Yes, if only because when it is gone, there will never be anything else like it again. And that is an immutable fact.

Could there be another reason, some possible ulterior motive? Only that I am not yet finished with dreaming of another August in Africa, another walk from out of the sun and into the shade, another chance to see the buffalo, if only fleetingly.

Epilogue

Mapduzi anouira kusina hari
(Squashes fall where there are no pots)

THE HEADLIGHTS SWEPT across the empty orbits of the bare buffalo skull as we turned up the hill. Coupled curves of black horn dipped down on either side of a round stone carried up from the riverbed, the rock the almost-white of bone. Rory shifted down, the pitch of the lower gear rising as the Land Rover dug into the two-track road, disturbing the dust that reached my nostrils. Beyond the beams, the persistent flames of the leadwood stood in the fire ring, off to the side of the lighted main tent. The Land Rover accelerated a last time and came to a stop on the level place behind the tent. I opened the unloaded chamber of the 450 and climbed down from the left seat of the doorless vehicle, as Rory switched off the engine.

It was too late to shower, and nearly too late to eat. There was time, though, for a gin and tonic with a little ice in the camp chair by the fire, and a plate of small toast pieces with wafer slices of local cheddar. I stood the Nitro rifle in the rack in the main tent and walked to the fire ring with the drink I had mixed.

Rory came out later and stood at the edge of the firelight, smoking. It had been a good day, with game sighted, though nothing taken. We did not speak,

270

wanting a respite from the hours together in the Land Rover and on the trail. After a while, one of the African staff called softly that supper was ready.

At the long, red-varnished wooden table were serving dishes of sadza *and oxtail stew. Rory spooned portions for each of us and handed a plate to me. We ate in continuing silence, satisfied, sipping glasses of red wine that left a tannin feel in the mouth. When we were done, one of the staff, dressed in khaki, gathered the supper dishes and took them away. He returned from out of the darkness with the tray of pudding.*

Rory unapologetically served himself first so he could be certain to skim off the skin that formed on the top of the heated custard, taking him back to mealtimes in public school. I took some pudding for myself and swirled the skinless custard from the china pitcher, drawing a recumbent figure eight over the dessert.

Finishing, I lifted my pudding dish and scraped away the remnant crumbs and custard with the bowl of the spoon, the steel clanging against the ceramic. Rory lit a cigarette and leaned back in his chair, his naked scarred legs stretched out and his Courtney-shod feet crossed under the table. Saying good night, I stood, slung my rifle, gathered up my hat, and left the tent. Rory waved with the burning cigarette between two fingers.

The hat in my hand pulled up so I could hook the sling with my thumb, was cold and stiff with drying sweat. In my other hand my flashlight pointed at the earthen path. A few new orange leaves had fallen since the path had been raked during the day, the ground crosshatched with grooves from the tines of the rake. The light played over the path ahead, until it carried me to the large square tent pitched on a concrete pad.

I shifted the flashlight to my other hand and lifted the zipper on the mesh panels over the opening of the tent. Ducking in, I turned and zipped the panels closed and moved the flashlight back to the other hand. The day's heat could be smelled radiating through the waxed green canvas. I crossed to the small oilcloth-covered table with the lamp, beside the bed draped with mosquito netting. Placing the flashlight on the oilcloth cast a blue circle of light, its bottom flattened by the tabletop, onto the canvas wall.

I unclipped the lamp chimney and set it on the table, the flashlight shining through it. There was the odor of paraffin rising from the woven-tape wick folded in the glass fount half filled with clear liquid. From the box of Lion matches I shook one out and struck it on the side of the box. Lighting the flame, I extinguished the match with a flick, hearing it ring on the bottom of the aluminum ashtray as I dropped it in, a pale serpent of smoke coiling up from its head. I clipped the chimney back over the flame and adjusted it with the knurled brass knob on the side of the wick tube so soot would not blacken the inside of the glass. I switched off the flashlight.

Unslinging the 450, I leaned it against the table. I undid the buckle on my belt, and holding onto the heavy, worn-leather ammunition pouch containing the long straight-walled cartridges, slipped the belt through the loops. Laying the pouch on the table, I placed the rolled up belt beside it.

Kneeling on one knee, and then the other, I unlaced and removed my dusty boots and my socks, then pushed the boots under the table, out of the way. I took off my pants and shirt and folded them, laying them in a bundle on the concrete floor with the socks, unused to heaping them in a pile. The change of clothes for the morning sat on the wooden folding chair by the table, washed and dried and pressed with a smoothing iron heated by the fire, smelling of wood smoke and sunlight. I changed into a clean set of underwear from off the top of the stack on the seat. Folding the dirty ones, I placed them on top of the pants and shirt and socks on the floor, sliding bare feet into boiled-wool slippers.

The clean underwear felt fresh on my skin. Drawing aside the white mist of the mosquito netting, I pulled back the blankets and top sheet and sat on the edge of the metal bed on the cool bottom sheet, my slippered feet on the small oval rug on the floor. For a minute I was motionless, welcoming the fatigue relaxing my muscles. Attracted by the lamplight inside the tent, large flying insects landed on the outside of the zippered mesh doors, flying off again with a clicking noise as they opened out their wings.

Lifting my head when it lolled against my chest, I leaned out from the bed and cupped my hand above the top of the lamp chimney, feeling the rising heat. I blew sharply into my palm, and the flame guttered and died. Sliding the slippers off onto the rug, I drew up my legs and adjusted the mosquito netting around the metal bed, tucking the blanket under my arms.

I lay on my back, feeling the first cool breeze of the night passing through the mesh flaps and into the tent, the clicking noises diminishing as the insects flew away into the moonless August dark. After a time, I turned onto my left side with my arm under the pillow.

At the edge of the waterhole, the shining graphite-gray mud was tilled by the hooves of heavy antelope, black butterflies with yellow markings and azure *eyespots puddling in the wet, wings fluttering like petals blown by the wind. I was lying comfortably then, thinking, until the thinking stopped.*

In the shadowlight before daybreak, everything stood still and the colors of the thorn trees and pandanus fans were the same as the ground beneath them, motes stirring in shafts of light as the sun rose through the tall trunks in front of me.

I lay in the bed once more, knowing there was darkness beyond my closed eyelids. I changed my position a little and saw the gleam on the spines of a drove of dagga boys, flanks caked in cracked clay armoring them like chain mail, grazing amid a stand of mopane, scuffing cleft tracks as they made deep lowings, the lead bull with the broad flinty boss halting and lifting his head, muzzle forward, rumbling grunts that stopped the other bulls, who looked where he did, walleyed stares approaching glares. Then the buffalo went off, and I slept.

"Good morning," came the African voice.

I heard the hissing of the pressure lantern, and turning saw through the mosquito netting a bright, soft-edged globe of light entering the tent. In the light was a tray with a cup and plates and a small steel pot, balanced on the palm of a hand. The brightness kept me from seeing through the mesh flaps to measure how near to dawn it was, but I knew it was at least an hour away.

The African in the khaki uniform crossed to the small table and placed the tray and the light on it. Lifting the pot and cup, he started to pour.

"Tea?" he asked.

I pulled back the blanket and swung my feet onto the slippers on the rug.

Nodding to the African, I rubbed my face and hair, and said, "Yes."

*And then I said, "Thank you–*tatenda*," clapping together the flats of my hands.*

Author's Note

Thomas McIntyre has written hundreds of magazine articles and television scripts since 1975. He has published seven books about the outdoors, starting with *Days Afield* in 1984, and is the editor of, and contributor to, *Wild & Fair,* a collection of North American hunting stories, including works by Pulitzer Prize winners Philip Caputo and David Mamet. Tom's work has been included in a score of anthologies, was awarded Best Magazine Story in *The Sporting News*'s "Best Sports Stories 1982;" and he was named the 2013 Carl Zeiss Outdoor Writer of the Year. He is the author of the novella, *The Snow Leopard's Tale.* His son Bryan is a graduate of the University of Iowa; and Tom and his wife, Elaine, live in north-central Wyoming with their English field cocker, Mickey, a likely spawn of Satan.

Illustrator's Note

A native of northwest England, Andrew Warrington trained in fine arts and illustration, specializing in wildlife with pencil. His unique work with graphite and pastel has earned him an acclaimed international reputation. Having traveled extensively through Europe and North America, working in the outdoors and studying native game, he has had his art exhibited widely, and carried by publishers such as Wild Wings. Over the years, his illustrations have appeared on the covers, and with the content, of nearly all the magazines devoted to hunting, as well as with some of the finest books on the outdoors, hunting, and wildlife; and he has previously illustrated several of the author's books. The sales of his prints and original art have benefitted the efforts of major conservation organizations. He continues to exhibit in galleries around the world.

Acknowledgments

My thanks to the editors, past and present, of *Sports Afield, Gray's Sporting Journal, Sporting Classics, The Field, American Hunter* and the other publications in which some of these pieces first appeared. Especial thanks to Jay Cassell and Lindsey Breuer-Barnes for their invaluable editorial input in the production of this book.